PUBLISHED FOR

JUDAICA RESEARCH AT YALE UNIVERSITY

on the

LOUIS M. RABINOWITZ FOUNDATION

YALE JUDAICA SERIES

EDITOR

Julian Obermann

Volume IV

THE CODE OF MAIMONIDES

(*MISHNEH TORAH*)

BOOK NINE

The Code of Maimonides

BOOK NINE

THE BOOK OF OFFERINGS

TRANSLATED FROM THE HEBREW BY

HERBERT DANBY

Regius Professor of Hebrew
and Canon of Christ Church, Oxford

NEW HAVEN

YALE UNIVERSITY PRESS

LONDON · GEOFFREY CUMBERLEGE · OXFORD UNIVERSITY PRESS

1950

EDITOR'S NOTE

The present volume of the Yale Judaica Series appears on the editorial responsibility of the undersigned alone. Early in 1947, Professor Louis Ginzberg informed the Committee of Judaica Research at Yale University that, for reasons of health, he wished to be relieved of his duties as a member of the Board of Editors, while offering to help in the future to the extent of his ability. Since Professor Ginzberg had cooperated fully in the supervision of our first three volumes, the committee considered it a pleasant obligation, as well as a privilege, to associate his name with each of them. More recently, the Series suffered another loss. Having carried on his part of the editorial work until November, 1949, Professor Harry A. Wolfson felt obliged to resign from the board at that time. Preoccupied with a vast project of his own, he found himself unable to meet the increasing demands made on his time and attention when volumes under preparation for the Series began to reach us in close succession.

In a real sense, neither of the two scholars can be replaced. Nor will their contribution in preparing the groundwork of Judaica Research at Yale cease to make itself felt in future volumes of the Series. Even so, one would feel exceedingly overtaxed in assuming the sole accountability for the editorial management of the Series, except for the assurance of continued interest and assistance generously offered by both retiring editors—an assurance already tested and proven by deeds.

J. O.

New Haven, Connecticut
September, 1950

CONTENTS

CONTENTS

INTRODUCTION

Maimonides entitles the Ninth Book of his Code *Sefer Ḳorbanoṭ, The Book of Offerings*. The word *ḳorban,* "an offering," occurs some eighty times in the Hebrew Bible, rarely outside the books of Leviticus and Numbers,[1] and always in the sense of offerings brought to God, offerings which may be of animals, or of vegetable produce, such as wine, oil, flour, or incense, or of gold and silver, or even of wood for the altar fires.

The meaning of the root *ḳareḇ* is "to be near" or "to approach," and the noun ḳorban has the inherent sense of "a means of approach," the means whereby an inferior seeks to approach or propitiate his superior, i.e., "a gift" or "tribute." The noun is found in this sense in cognate Semitic languages; but in Hebrew the sense is almost entirely restricted to the gift which a worshiper presents to God, whether in token of loyalty, adoration, and gratitude, or from a need to propitiate God after some mischance, such as unintentional sin or ritual uncleanness, which had detracted from the worshiper's fitness to draw near to God. In the idiom of the sacrificial system a ḳorban was the symbol and the means of communion between the human and the divine.[2]

In rabbinical writings the word is used in the same way as in the Hebrew Bible, though there are indications (see Ned 2:5; B. Ḥul 8a; B. Zeb 116b) that the secular sense of ḳorban, "gift" or "tribute," was not forgotten.[3]

Both in biblical and rabbinical usage *ḳorbanoṭ* is a comprehensive term covering every type of offering, animal or nonanimal, communal or individual, regular or occasional, offerings for the

---

1. The exceptions are Ezek. 20:28; 40:43; Neh. 10:35; 13:31.

2. This symbolic meaning is preserved among certain oriental Christian communities who use *ḳurbana* as the name of the liturgical office of Holy Communion and also as the name of the consecrated bread and wine.

3. This secular sense is more evident in the contemporary Syriac usage. See, e.g., ḳurbana in the Syriac version of Gen. 33:10; 43:25; Dan. 2:46; and, especially, II Kings 16:8, where it is used of the silver and gold which Ahaz sent *for a present to the king of Assyria.*

altar or contributions toward the upkeep of the Temple and its ceremonies. It is thus in itself too wide and general a term to have been intended as a definition of the subject matter of the Ninth Book; it is equally applicable to more than half of the contents of the Eighth Book as well. Maimonides, however, in the very brief summary which he has prefixed to the Code, tells us, "In the Ninth Book I include the laws relating to the offerings of the individual (*korbanot yaḥid*), and I have entitled the Book *Korbanot*." It may, therefore, be assumed that korbanot is here a deliberate abbreviation of korbanot yaḥid, "offerings of the individual" or "private offerings." It is an abbreviation in keeping with Maimonides' practice: as with the rest of the titles of the fourteen Books (*Madda', 'Ahăbah, Zĕmannim*, etc.), a single-word title is used in preference to a more precise but more cumbersome phrase.

The Ninth Book is divided into six treatises bearing the titles
1) Laws Concerning the Passover Offering
2) Laws Concerning the Festal Offering
3) Laws Concerning Firstlings
4) Laws Concerning Offerings for Transgressions Committed through Error
5) Laws Concerning Those Whose Atonement Is Not Complete
6) Laws Concerning Substituted Offerings
Those offerings are first described which must be brought at specified times in the year: the Passover offering on the fourteenth of Nisan; the festal offerings at each of the three feasts; and tithe of cattle (discussed in the third treatise) also at the time of the three feasts. A further scheme in the sequence would seem to be that of giving precedence to what is of concern to the greater number. Thus every Israelite, male or female, was bound to keep the Passover, whereas no obligation to bring the various festal offerings rested on women and bondmen; and only the class which owned flocks and herds was affected by the laws of firstlings and tithe of cattle. The subject of the fourth treatise concerned only an

indefinite number of persons at uncertain times, while only four groups of persons formed the subject of the fifth treatise. The last treatise is of the nature of an appendix and applies only to those who would replace what they had already dedicated by something of, probably, less worth.

The first treatise defines the kind of beast which should be chosen for a Passover offering, the time, place, and manner of slaughtering it, those who may eat of it, circumstances in which some must delay their observance of Passover until a month later, the manner of roasting and eating the flesh of the offering, and the rules governing the optional "festal offering of the fourteenth."

The second treatise discusses the offerings which Israelites must bring at the three pilgrimage seasons—Passover, Pentecost, and Tabernacles—in fulfillment of the three commandments to *appear before the Lord* (Exod. 23:17), to *keep the feast* (Deut. 16:13), and to *rejoice* in the feast (Deut. 16:14). A concluding chapter describes the procedure on the Day of Assembly every seventh year at the close of the Feast of Tabernacles, in fulfillment of the law laid down in Deut. 31:10 ff.

The third treatise, Laws Concerning Firstlings, deals with the disposal of unblemished and blemished first-born of cattle: the age at which they must be given to the priests, those which must be slaughtered in the Temple, those which must be left to pasture, those which a priest may slaughter anywhere and dispose of as he pleases, precautions against fraudulent attribution of blemishes, and cases in which the status of a firstling is disputable. The last three chapters treat of the tithing of cattle: to what cattle this law applies, the manner in which the tithing should be carried out, and the seasons for tithing.

The fourth treatise, Laws Concerning Offerings for Transgressions Committed through Error, describes the several circumstances in which unintentional breaches of prohibitions render the transgressor liable, respectively, to a fixed sin offering, a suspensive guilt offering, an offering for undoubted guilt, or a rising and falling offering. The last four chapters treat of the offerings which must be brought when the Sanhedrin gives an erroneous ruling (Lev. 4: 13 ff.) and when the ruler or the anointed priest commits unintentional sin (Lev. 4: 3, 22).

The fifth treatise, Laws Concerning Those Whose Atonement Is Not Complete, treats of the woman after childbirth (Lev. 12: 6), the leper (Lev. 14: 10 ff.), and the classes of women and men described in Lev. 15: 13-15 and 15: 28-30. The distinctive feature common to these four groups is that, even though they immerse themselves after their uncleanness and duly await sunset, they still do not become fully clean until they bring their atonement offering.

The final treatise, Laws Concerning Substituted Offerings, works out the implications of the law of Lev. 27: 10, where it is laid down that once a beast has been dedicated its owner may not change his mind and offer another beast instead of it, and that if he does so, not only must he be scourged but the sanctity which attaches to a dedicated beast will then attach both to the first and to the second beast, so that both alike become subject to the restrictions which apply to Hallowed Things.

Of these six treatises only the third and the sixth cover approximately the same ground as corresponding tractates in the Mishnah. The subject matter of the treatise concerning firstlings is that of Tractate Bĕḳoroṭ (excluding chapters 6-9), while the treatise concerning substituted offerings deals with the same topic as the Tractate Tĕmurah in the Mishnah.

The first treatise covers only those chapters of Tractate Pĕsaḥim (5-9) which deal with the actual paschal lamb. It takes no account of the rules about leaven, unleavened bread, and the "Seder" meal: these details Maimonides has codified elsewhere (Laws Concerning Leaven and Unleavened Bread, III, v).

The treatise concerning the festal offering has the same subject matter as the first chapter of Tractate Ḥăḡiḡah but its concluding section on the Day of Assembly (Deut. 31: 10-13) is based in part on the Gemara to Ḥăḡiḡah (2a), but mainly on Tractate Soṭah 7: 8.

The treatise concerning transgressions committed through error is principally derived from Tractate *Kĕriṯoṯ;* the last three chapters, however, dealing with the offerings of the Sanhedrin, the ruler, and the anointed priest, correspond to the contents of Tractate *Horayoṯ.*

The remaining treatise on those whose atonement is not complete deals with four classes. For two of them, the *zaḇ* and the *zaḇah,* the Code draws on Tractate *Zaḇim;* for the woman after childbirth the chief source is Tractate *Kĕriṯoṯ;* while for the offerings of the leper the source is chapter 14 of Tractate *Nĕğa‘im.*

All of these mishnaic sources (except the Tractates *Nĕğa‘im* and *Zaḇim*) are supplied with Gemara, and all have their parallel Tosefta. Maimonides makes considerable use of such supplementary material as these provide. There is also occasional use of the Palestinian Gemara and of the tannaitic Midrašim *Mĕḵilta* and *Sifra.*

Throughout this Ninth Book there is no mention of post-Talmudic authorities, which is not unexpected in a treatment of subject matter which had little more than academic interest for the Jews in exile. Only rarely [4] do we meet the formula "In my opinion . . ." with which Maimonides is accustomed to introduce statements on his own authority.

Generally speaking, the Eighth and Ninth Books of the Code together cover the same ground as the Fifth Order of the Mishnah, *Ḳŏḏašim,* "Hallowed Things"; but in carrying out his scheme of bringing together in this Ninth Book the material bearing on private offerings, Maimonides draws also from the Second Order, *Mo‘eḏ,* (viz., from the Tractates *Pĕsaḥim* and *Ḥăğiğah*); the Fourth Order, *Nĕziḳin,* (viz., from the Tractate *Horayoṯ*); the Sixth Order, *Ṭŏharoṯ* (viz., from the Tractates *Nĕğa‘im* and *Zaḇim*); and even from the Third Order, *Našim,* (viz., from the Tractate *Soṭah*).

But even so the Ninth Book is not a complete survey of all those offerings which fall within the category of "private offerings." Twice elsewhere Maimonides gives us lists distinguishing between

4. III, i, 15; vi, 5; vii, 5; IV, vi, 9; vii, 6; ix, 3; v, iii, 6.

public and private offerings. In the Eighth Book of the Code (v, i, 5, 6) they are catalogued as follows:

Public offerings:

The two daily whole offerings; the additional offerings on Sabbaths, New Moons, and the three feasts; the offerings on the Day of Atonement; and those of the court which erred in its ruling.

Private offerings:

Firstlings; tithe of cattle; Passover offerings; festal peace offerings and the pilgrimage whole offering; the proselyte's offerings; vow offerings; freewill offerings; thank offerings; the nazirite's offerings; the leper's offerings, the offerings of women after childbirth and of men or women who suffer a flux; sin offerings for unintentional transgressions; suspensive guilt offerings and offerings for undoubted guilt; and the High Priest's own offerings on the Day of Atonement,

In the introduction to his Commentary on the Fifth Order of the Mishnah, Maimonides adopts a different classification under four heads:

1. *Public offerings:*

The two daily whole offerings; the additional offerings on Sabbaths, New Moons, and the three feasts; and the offerings on the Day of Atonement.

2. *Private offerings:*

a) incurred by the commission of some act or utterance (viz., by acts which transgress certain negative commandments or by false swearing);

b) incurred by some condition which happens to the body (viz., a woman after childbirth, men or women after suffering a flux, a leper, and a proselyte after circumcision);

c) incurred by some condition relating to a man's property (viz., in fulfillment of the law that the firstling of cattle and tithe of cattle be offered in the Temple);

d) incurred by the incidence of some season (viz., the Passover offering and the three offerings which worshipers must bring at each of the three feasts);[5]

e) incurred voluntarily (viz., vow offerings, freewill offerings, thank offerings, and the offerings of the nazirite).

3. *A public offering resembling a private offering:*

The offering of the Supreme Court which errs in its ruling (*the congregation shall offer it*, Lev. 4: 14); but like a private offering it does not override the Sabbath or the laws of uncleanness.

4. *Private offerings resembling public offerings:*

The Passover offering and the High Priest's own offerings on the Day of Atonement; but like public offerings they override the Sabbath in that an appointed time is prescribed for them.

The contents of the Ninth Book do not conform wholly with either of the two lists of private offerings. Thus the offerings of the court which, in the Eighth Book, are included among public offerings, and, in the Introduction to the Mishnah Commentary, are put in a third category, are in the Ninth Book included among private offerings. Of the two offerings which the Mishnah Commentary puts in a fourth category, the Passover offering is included among private offerings in both the Eighth and the Ninth Books; while the private offerings of the High Priest on the Day of Atonement are here omitted, since they are more conveniently treated in Book VIII, Treatise VII, with the other ceremonies proper to the Day of Atonement. The Ninth Book also omits the rules relating to vow offerings, freewill offerings, thank offerings, and nazirites' and proselytes' offerings. Although they all appear in both of Maimonides' lists of private offerings their treatment falls naturally in other contexts earlier in the Code. Thus vow offerings, freewill offerings, and thank offerings are all dealt with in the Eighth Book (v, ix and xiv–xvii); the nazirite's offerings fall naturally within

5. The Talmud (B. Pes 70b) speaks of the festal offering as a "public offering." Maimonides defends its inclusion among private offerings on the grounds that each person brings it for himself and that it does not override the Sabbath or the laws of uncleanness.

the scope of the general treatment of the nazirite's vow (VI, iii, ix), while the proselyte's offerings are dealt with (V, i, xiii, 5) in the course of the chapters concerning proselytes.

Nowhere in the Ninth Book does Maimonides stop to draw attention to any detail of personal or historical interest and rarely do philological points arise.[6] Only occasionally does he turn aside from his task of analyzing the material relating to private offerings to underline a moral application or interpretation of some usage of, apparently, mere ceremonial significance. There are, however, a few characteristic examples.

Chapter ii of the second treatise concludes with a short homily on hospitality, enlarging upon the verse Deut. 16:14, and emphasizing the point that no man fulfills the rule to *rejoice before the Lord thy God* (Deut. 27:7) by indulgence in feasting in the company of none but his wife and children, but that his own feasting should be an occasion for generosity toward the stranger, the fatherless, and the widow, and, particularly, toward the Levite. The homily appears again earlier in the Code (III, iv, vi, 18).

Toward the end of this same treatise the vivid picture of the reading of the Law by the king at the seventh-year assembly of all Israel is impressively finished off by Maimonides' grave words of advice to the listener (ii, iii, 6).

In the fourth treatise (iii, 10) a paragraph is devoted to the nature of the expiation afforded by the Day of Atonement. It is pointed out that the efficacy depends on the sinner's own penitence and faith and that it is not something *ex opere operato,* whereby wrongdoing is mechanically and automatically expiated.[7]

The Book ends with a characteristic ethical peroration, pointing out that the purpose of the law of the substituted offering is none other than to thwart man's innate avarice.

The present translation has been made from the text of the

6. See the definitions of *ḳoliṭ* (i, x, 10), *ṭinof* (iii, iv, 10), and *tĕnuḳ* (v, v, 1).

7. This is explicit in the Mishnah (Yoma 8:8): "Death and the Day of Atonement effect atonement if there is repentance."

Amsterdam edition dated 1702. Its many minor slips, often due to wrongly resolved abbreviations, have been checked on the basis of the Venice editions of 1524 and 1575. Major variants are few and not often of importance. With regard to them note has been taken of the readings preserved in the *editio princeps* of Rome, 1480 (?), the Constantinople edition of 1509, and the Bodleian MSS 568, 601, 602, and 603.[8]

8. For help in consulting these earlier editions and manuscripts I am much indebted to Mr. Otto H. M. Lehmann of the Department of Oriental Books in the Bodleian Library.

THE BOOK OF
OFFERINGS

COMPRISING SIX TREATISES IN
THE FOLLOWING ORDER

> I will offer to thee the sacrifice of thanks-
> giving,
> And will call upon the name of the Lord
> (Psalms 116:17).

TREATISE I

LAWS CONCERNING THE PASSOVER OFFERING

Involving Sixteen Commandments

Four Positive and Twelve Negative

To Wit

1. To slaughter the Passover offering at its appointed time;
2. Not to sacrifice it while there is anything leavened;
3. Not to suffer its sacrificial portions to remain overnight;
4. To slaughter a second Passover offering;
5. To eat the flesh of the Passover offering with unleavened bread and bitter herbs in the night of the fifteenth of Nisan;
6. To eat the Second Passover offering with unleavened bread and bitter herbs in the night of the fifteenth day of the second month;
7. Not to eat it raw or soddened;
8. Not to remove any of the flesh of the Passover offering outside of the company;
9. That no renegade eat thereof;
10. That no stranger or hireling eat thereof;
11. That no uncircumcised person eat thereof;
12. That no bone of it be broken;
13. That no bone of the Second Passover offering be broken;
14. That nothing of it be suffered to remain until morning;

THE BOOK OF OFFERINGS

15. That nothing of the Second Passover offering be suffered to remain until morning;
16. That nothing of the flesh of the festal offering of the fourteenth be suffered to remain until the third day.

An exposition of these commandments is contained in the following chapters.

NOTE

In the list of the 613 commandments prefixed to the Code, those which deal with the subject of this Treatise are cited in the following form.

Positive commandments:

[1] 55. To slaughter a lamb for the Passover, as it is said: *And the whole assembly of the congregation of Israel shall kill it at dusk* (Exod. 12:6);

[5] 56. To eat the flesh of the Passover offering, roast, in the night of the fifteenth day of Nisan, as it is said: *And they shall eat the flesh in that night, roast with fire, and unleavened bread; with bitter herbs they shall eat it* (Exod. 12:8);

[4] 57. To keep a Second Passover, as it is said: *In the second month on the fourteenth day at dusk they shall keep it* (Num. 9:11);

[6] 58. To eat the flesh of the Second Passover offering with unleavened bread and bitter herbs, as it is said: *They shall eat it with unleavened bread and bitter herbs* (Num. 9:11).

Negative commandments:

[2] 115. That the Passover offering be not slaughtered while any unleavened bread remains, as it is said: *Thou shalt not offer the blood of my sacrifice with aught leavened* (Exod. 34:25);

[3] 116. That the sacrificial portions of the Passover offer-

ing be not left until they become invalid by remaining throughout the night, as it is said: *Neither shall the fat of my feast remain all night* (Exod. 23: 18);

[14] 117. That nothing of the flesh of the Passover offering be left over, as it is said: *And ye shall let nothing of it remain until the morning* (Exod. 12: 10);

[16] 118. That nothing of the flesh of the festal offering of the fourteenth be left until the third day, as it is said: *And nothing of the flesh shall remain all night until the morning* (Deut. 16: 4). From tradition it is learned that this verse of Scripture speaks of the flesh of the festal offering of the fourteenth; and in that it is said *until the morning,* it signifies the morning of the second day from the day of the Passover, which is the third day from the time that it was slaughtered.

[15] 119. That nothing of the flesh of the Second Passover offering be left until the morning, as it is said: *They shall leave none of it unto the morning* (Num. 9: 12);

[12] 121. That no bone of the Passover offering be broken, as it is said: *Neither shall ye break a bone thereof* (Exod. 12: 46);

[13] 122. That no bone of the Second Passover offering be broken, as it is said: *Nor shall they break a bone thereof* (Num. 9: 12);

[8] 123. That nothing of the flesh of the Passover offering be taken out from the company, as it is said: *Thou shalt not carry forth aught of the flesh abroad out of the house* (Exod. 12: 46);

[7] 125. That the flesh of the Passover offering be not eaten raw or sodden, as it is said: *Eat not of it raw or sodden at all with water* (Exod. 12: 9);

[10] 126. That no sojourner be given to eat of the flesh of the Passover offering, as it is said: *A sojourner and a hired servant shall not eat thereof* (Exod. 12:45);

[11] 127. That none who is uncircumcised shall eat of the flesh of the Passover offering, as it is said: *But no uncircumcised person shall eat thereof* (Exod. 12:48);

[9] 128. That no Israelite who has apostatized be given to eat of the flesh of the Passover offering, as it is said: *There shall no alien eat thereof* (Exod. 12:43); that is to say, no Israelite who has joined himself to aliens and worshiped an idol like them shall eat thereof.

CHAPTER I

1. It is a positive commandment that the Passover offering is to be slaughtered on the fourteenth day of the month of Nisan, after midday; that it is to be slaughtered only from sheep or from goats; and that it be a male of the first year. This commandment is binding upon men and women alike.

2. If a man neglected this commandment wantonly and the fourteenth day passed by and he made no offering, he being neither *unclean* nor *on a journey afar off* (Num. 9:10), he is liable to extirpation; but if he neglected it through error, he is not liable.

3. The Passover offering may be slaughtered only in the Temple Court like other Hallowed Things. Even at a time when high places were permissible the Passover offering was not permitted to be offered at the high place of any private person; and whosoever offered the Passover offering at the high place of any private person was scourged, for it is said: *Thou mayest not sacrifice the passover offering within any of thy gates* (Deut. 16:5). From oral tradition it is learned that this was an express warning to him who would slaughter it at the high place of a private person, even at a time when high places were permissible.

4. The slaughtering of the Passover offering must be after midday, and if it was slaughtered before midday it is not valid. It should not be slaughtered until after the daily afternoon whole offering, after the burning of the afternoon incense. After the lamps have been trimmed the people begin slaughtering the Passover offerings and continue until the end of the day. But if it was slaughtered after midday before the daily afternoon whole offering, it is valid; and someone should keep on stirring the blood of the Passover offering until the blood of the daily whole offering has been tossed, and then the blood of the Passover offering should be tossed. Yet if the blood of the Passover offering was tossed before the blood of the daily whole offering, this is valid.

5. If a man slaughtered the Passover offering at its proper time but had in his possession an olive's bulk of anything leavened, he is to be scourged, for it is said: *Thou shalt not offer the blood of my sacrifices with aught leavened* (Exod. 34:25); that is, none should sacrifice the Passover offering while there remains anything that is leavened. No matter whether it was he who slaughtered or he who tossed the blood or he who burned the sacrificial portions; if, in the possession of any one of them or in the possession of any one of the company which was to eat of this Passover offering, there was as much as an olive's bulk of anything leavened at the time when it was offered, he must be scourged, but the Passover offering remains valid.

6. The blood of the Passover offering requires to be poured out against the altar base, and after its blood has been poured out it is flayed, its belly slit, and its sacrificial portions removed; and the fat pieces pertaining to each sacrifice are burned separately. Then the owner of the sacrifice may take up his Passover offering, together with its hide, and bring it to his home in Jerusalem and roast it and eat it at eventide.

7. If a man left the sacrificial portions unburned until they had remained all night and become invalid through remaining overnight, he transgresses a negative commandment, for it is said: *Neither shall the fat of my feast remain all night until the morning* (Exod. 23:18). But although he transgressed, he is not liable to scourging since no act was committed.

8. The fat pieces of the Passover offerings may be burned any time of the night until daybreak. This applies when the fourteenth falls on a Sabbath, since the fat pieces of the Sabbath can be offered on a festival day; but if the fourteenth falls on a weekday one may not burn the fat pieces of a weekday on a festival day.

9. The Passover offering should be slaughtered in three groups, for it is said: *And the whole assembly of the congregation of Israel shall slaughter it* (Exod. 12:6); to wit, an *assembly,* a *congrega-*

tion, and *Israel.* And the number of men in each group should not be fewer than thirty.

10. If there are fifty all told, thirty should first come in and ten should slaughter and go out, and ten others should come in, and again ten should go out and ten more come in.

11. If there are fewer than fifty they do not slaughter the passover offering to start with, but if they do, it is valid; and if they all slaughtered at the same time it is valid.

How is it slaughtered? The first group comes in until the Temple Court is filled. The gates of the Temple Court are then closed and the people begin to slaughter their Passover offerings, and all the time that they are slaughtering and offering them, the Levites sing the Hallel. If they have finished the Hallel and the group has not yet completed its offering, it is repeated; and if it is repeated and the group has still not completed its offering, it is sung a third time; but never was it, in fact, repeated a third time.

12. Each time the Hallel is sung three blasts are sounded on the trumpets—a sustained, a quavering, and a sustained blast. Inasmuch as the Passover offering requires no drink offerings when trumpets would be sounded during the libation, they are sounded during the slaughtering.

13. The priests stand in rows and in their hands are basins of silver and basins of gold: in one row all basins are of silver and in another all basins are of gold, and they are kept unconfused to maintain a comely display; nor have the basins bases lest the priests set them down and the blood congeal.

14. As soon as the offering is slaughtered, the priest catches the blood and gives it to his fellow and his fellow gives it to his fellow —so that many might play a part in the rite—until the blood reaches the priest nearest the altar. He pours it out in a single action against the altar base; he receives a full basin and then gives back an empty one. The entire carcass is hung up and flayed, and the slaughterer slits it and cleans out the entrails until dung and

excrements are removed; he takes out the sacrificial portions and puts them in a vessel; and the priest salts them and burns them on the altar.

How was the carcass hung up and flayed? Iron nails were fixed to the walls and the pillars, and on these the people hung and flayed the carcass; and if a man found no place to hang it, there were thin, smooth staves which he could put on his own and his fellow's shoulder, and thus would he hang and flay his offering.

15. When these had completed their offering the doors of the Temple Court were opened, and when the first group went out the second came in, and when the second went out the third came in; as was the procedure of the first group so was the procedure of the second and of the third. When the third group had finished and gone out, the Temple Court was swilled.

16. If the fourteenth fell on a Sabbath, as was the procedure on a weekday, so was the procedure on a Sabbath; even swilling of the Temple Court was permitted on a Sabbath, since the rules of šĕbut do not apply to the Temple. Even in a matter which is not needful for the Temple worship, the rules of šĕbut are relaxed in the Temple.

17. On the Sabbath none removes his Passover offering to his home; but the first group goes out with its Passover offerings and sits down in the Temple Mount; and the second group goes out with its Passover offerings and sits on the Temple Rampart; and the third remains where it is in the Temple Court. All wait until the Sabbath is over and then everyone goes with his Passover offering to his own home.

18. Slaughtering the Passover offering, tossing its blood, cleaning out its entrails, and burning its fat pieces override the Sabbath because they cannot be done before the Sabbath, since the time of the offering is fixed, for it is said: *At its appointed time* (Num. 9:2); but carrying it to the Temple or bringing it from outside to within the Sabbath limit or snipping off a wen with some implement—these do not override the Sabbath because they can be

done before the Sabbath. Yet if a man could snip off the wen with his hand he may snip it off on the Sabbath, and if it was withered dry he may snip it off even with some implement, since the rules of šĕbuṭ do not apply at all in the Temple. So, too, roasting it and rinsing its entrails do not override the Sabbath, since they can be done after the Sabbath.

19. If a man forgot to bring a knife to the Temple Court on the eve of Sabbath he may not bring it on the Sabbath; but he may put it between the sheep's horns or in its wool, and beat the beast until he drives it to the Temple Court, and there dedicate it as a Passover offering; for although he drives the beast on a Sabbath, it is an unusual way of driving, and because he thereby aims at fulfilling a command (to bring the Passover offering), such driving is permitted. This applies to one who had not yet dedicated his Passover offering and had not said, "This is a Passover offering." But if he had dedicated it he may not convey a knife on it, since he would then be using a consecrated beast to perform an act of work.

And why have the Sages made it permissible for a man to dedicate his Passover offering on the Sabbath? Inasmuch as the time of the offering is fixed, it is permissible to dedicate it even on the Sabbath.

So, too, a man may dedicate his festal offering on a festival day without scruple.

20. If a man slaughtered a Passover offering and it was found to be blemished or ṭĕrefah, he must slaughter another, whether it be on a weekday or on a Sabbath. Even if a hundred were found to be blemished or ṭĕrefah, one after the other, he must go on slaughtering until one is found valid or until it becomes dark, when he must be put off until the Second Passover, since he counts as one who was hindered through constraint.

CHAPTER II

1. The Passover offering may be slaughtered only for such as are enrolled for it, since it is said: *According to the number of the souls . . . ye shall make your count for the lamb* (Exod. 12:4)—teaching us that they who were to eat of it were to be enrolled while it was yet alive. And it is they who have been enrolled for a Passover offering who are called "members of a company."

2. If a single person slaughtered a Passover offering for himself alone this is valid, provided that he was capable of eating the whole of it, yet an effort should be made that it be not slaughtered at the outset for one person alone, since it is said: *They shall keep it* (Exod. 12:47; Num. 9:11, 12).

3. The Passover offering may be slaughtered only for such as are capable of eating it. If a member of the company is a child or sick or aged, yet could eat an olive's bulk, it may be slaughtered for him; but if he could not, it may not be slaughtered for him, since it is said: *According to every man's eating* (Exod. 12:4); it may not be slaughtered for him unless he is capable of eating. Even though there is a company of a hundred, yet not one of them could eat an olive's bulk, it may not be slaughtered for them.

4. A company may not be made up of women and bondmen or of children and bondmen, lest levity prevail among them; but a company may be made up wholly of women, even at the Second Passover, or wholly of bondmen. The Passover offering may be slaughtered for children so that they may be included within the company, but not so that the company shall be wholly of children, since they are not accountable. So, too, a company may not be made up wholly of such as are sick or aged or mourners. Even though they are capable of eating, yet inasmuch as what they eat is but little, they may perchance leave uneaten some of the Passover offering and cause it to become unfit; but if it is nevertheless slaughtered for such a company it is valid. So, too, a company may not be made up wholly of proselytes lest they be overborne by

scruples and cause the offering to become unfit; but if it is slaughtered for them it is valid.

5. If it is slaughtered for other than those enrolled for it or for persons not everyone of whom could eat as much as an olive's bulk, or if it is slaughtered for such as are uncircumcised or unclean, it is not valid. If it is slaughtered both for such as could and for such as could not eat an olive's bulk, or both for such as are and for such as are not enrolled for it, or both for such as are and for such as are not circumcised, or both for such as are clean and for such as are unclean, it is valid; for they who are eligible can eat of it lawfully, and as for the others it is as though they had not been taken into account.

6. If it is slaughtered for such as are circumcised but its blood is tossed for the sake both of circumcised and of uncircumcised, it is not valid; for the tossing of the blood is the decisive act, since it is the essence of the offering. If it is slaughtered for such as are circumcised, yet with a mind that such as are uncircumcised should thereby gain atonement, it is not valid, since there would then be intention on behalf of the uncircumcised in the act of tossing. If it is slaughtered for those who are to eat of it, yet with a mind that the blood should be tossed for such as are not to eat of it, the Passover offering is valid, but none can thereby fulfill his obligation, since in the act of tossing there would be no intention on behalf of those who are to eat of it.

7. If a man was hale at the time of slaughtering and sick at the time of tossing the blood, or if he was sick at the time of slaughtering and hale at the time of tossing the blood, it is not permitted to slaughter and toss the blood for him—but only if he was hale from the time of slaughtering to the time of tossing the blood.

8. A man may slaughter the Passover offering on behalf of his sons or his daughters who are minors or on behalf of his Canaanite bondmen or bondwomen, with or without their consent; but he may not slaughter on behalf of his sons or his daughters who are of

age or on behalf of his Hebrew bondmen or bondwomen or on behalf of his wife, except with their consent; and if they keep silence and do not protest, this signifies that the act is with their consent.

9. If he slaughters on behalf of his sons or his daughters who are minors or on behalf of his Canaanite bondmen or bondwomen, and they went and slaughtered for themselves, they fulfill their obligation only by eating of what was slaughtered by their master.

10. If he slaughters on behalf of his wife or on behalf of his sons or his daughters who are of age or on behalf of his Hebrew bondmen or bondwomen, and they slaughtered for themselves, there could be no protest greater than this; and they fulfill their obligation only by eating of what they themselves slaughtered.

11. If a woman was in her husband's house and her father slaughtered for her and her husband slaughtered for her, she should eat of what was slaughtered by her husband. If she was eager to go with her father's house on the first feast following her marriage, as is the way of all daughters, and her father slaughtered for her and her husband slaughtered for her, she should eat of what was slaughtered by her father. Thereafter she may eat from whichever she pleases, provided that she makes her choice at the time of slaughtering.

So, too, an orphan whose guardians have slaughtered for him may eat from whichever of their offerings he pleases. This applies if the orphan is a minor. But if he is of age he counts as one who was enrolled for two Passover offerings, and he who is enrolled for two Passover offerings may eat only from that which was first slaughtered.

12. A bondman belonging to two joint owners, such time as these are scrupulous with each other lest either steal some advantage, may eat of the Passover offering of neither of them; but if they are not thus scrupulous he may eat of whichever he pleases.

13. He who is half bondman and half free may eat neither from his master's offering nor from his own—unless he is made wholly free.

14. How long may the enrollment of fresh partakers of a Passover offering go on? So long as there is enough of it for each to have an olive's bulk. And members may go on enrolling themselves for it and withdrawing from it until such time as it is slaughtered; once it is slaughtered no one is able to withdraw since it was slaughtered on his behalf.

If some are enrolled for it and then still others are enrolled, the first for whom there is sufficient for an olive's bulk may eat thereof, and they are exempt from keeping the Second Passover; but the later ones who are so many that there is not enough for each to have an olive's bulk may not eat of it, and they must keep the Second Passover.

15. If a man enrolled others to share with him in his portion and the members of the company did not know of them, the members of the company have the right at the time of the meal to give him no more than his own portion after it is roasted; and the members of the company eat what belongs to them while he eats his portion with the others whom he had enrolled to share with him in a separate company.

So, too, if one of the members of a company is a glutton, they have the right to set him apart from themselves and give him his portion, to the end that he may eat it in his own company; but if he is not a glutton they have not the right to separate themselves.

CHAPTER III

1. If a man said to his servant, "Go and slaughter for me the Passover offering," and, although it was his master's habit each year to slaughter a lamb, the servant went and slaughtered him a kid, or, although it was his habit to slaughter a kid, the servant went and slaughtered him a lamb, the master may nevertheless

eat of it, since he had not told him expressly, "Slaughter me one of such a kind."

If the servant went and slaughtered a kid and a lamb, the master may eat of neither of them but both must go forth to the place of burning, since none may be enrolled for two Passover offerings. But if it was a king or a queen, and such a one had bidden his servant to slaughter for him, and he slaughtered a lamb and a kid, he may eat of the first that was slaughtered for the sake of the peace of the kingdom.

2. If a man said to his agent, "Go and slaughter for me the Passover offering," and he stipulated a kid or a lamb, and the agent forgot what his master had told him, he should slaughter both a kid and a lamb and say, "If he told me to slaughter a kid, let the kid be his and let the lamb be mine; and if he told me to slaughter a lamb, let the lamb be his and let the kid be mine." If then the man himself forgot what he had told him, both the lamb and the kid must be burned. If he forgot before the blood was tossed, master and agent must keep the Second Passover; if he forgot after the blood was tossed, they are exempt from keeping the Second Passover.

Such, also, is the rule if a man said to his servant, "Go and slaughter for me," stipulating which kind it should be, and the servant forgot what his master had told him. The master's shepherd should give the servant a kid and a lamb and say to him, "Slaughter them both that thou mayest slaughter as thy master bid thee; and one of them is thine, so that thy master has no right at all therein." If the shepherd acted thus, the servant may then lay down conditions in the manner we have stated.

3. If the members of a company said to one of their number, "Go and slaughter the Passover offering for us," and he said to them, "Do ye, rather, slaughter for me," and they slaughtered and he slaughtered, they must all eat of that which was first slaughtered, and the other offering must go to the place of burning.

4. If the members of a company lost their Passover offering and said to one of their number, "Go and seek it out and slaughter it

for us," and he went and found the Passover offering that was lost
and slaughtered it, and they took another Passover offering and
slaughtered it—if it was his that was first slaughtered, he should
eat of his and they should eat of it with him and the other must
be burned; but if it was theirs that was first slaughtered, they
should eat of theirs and he of his. If it was not known which of
them was first slaughtered or if they both were slaughtered at the
same time, he may eat of his but they may not eat with him, and
theirs must go to the place of burning. But they are exempt from
keeping the Second Passover.

5. If he whom they had sent to seek and slaughter the Passover
offering that was lost had said to them, "If I delay, do ye slaughter
for me," and he went and he found it and slaughtered it, and they
also took one and slaughtered it—if theirs was the first that was
slaughtered, they should eat of theirs and he should eat with them,
and the other must be burned. But if his was the first that was
slaughtered, he should eat of his and they should eat of theirs. If
it is not known which of them was first slaughtered or if both were
slaughtered at the same time, they should eat of theirs but he
should not eat with them, and his must go forth to the place of
burning; but he is exempt from keeping the Second Passover.

6. If they lost their Passover offering and he lost his, and he said
to them, "Go and seek one and slaughter it for me," and they said
to him, "Go and seek one and slaughter it for us," and he went
and found one and slaughtered it, and they too found one and
slaughtered it, they should all eat of the first one, and the other
must be burned. And if it was not known which of them was first
slaughtered or if both were slaughtered at the same time, they
must both be burned. But they are exempt from keeping the Second
Passover.

If he went to seek one and they went to seek one and they had
said nothing to each other, although it was in their hearts that each
should slaughter on behalf of the other or there had been hints
or grounds for supposing that whoever found one would slaughter
it for the other, since they had not thus spoken expressly nor said

anything one to the other, they are not responsible one to the other.

7. If the Passover offerings of two companies were confused before they were slaughtered, each company draws a lamb from the confused pair and a member of each company comes to the other company and each company says to him who comes to it, "If this Passover offering is ours, thy hands are withdrawn from thine and thou art enrolled for ours; and if this Passover offering is thine, our hands are withdrawn from ours and we are enrolled for thine." So, too, if there were five companies each made up of five members, or if there were ten companies each made up of ten members; they withdraw one from each company to the other company, and thus do they speak and lay down conditions; and afterward they may slaughter the Passover offerings.

8. If the Passover offering of A is confused with that of B, they each draw one offering from the confused pair and each enrolls for his Passover offering someone from the market place, so that there shall be two companies. Then one of the company of A is brought to that of B, and one of the company of B is brought to that of A, and each of these lays down conditions with his fellow who comes to him from the other company and says, "If this Passover offering is mine, thy hands are withdrawn from thine and thou art enrolled for mine; and if it is thine, my hand is withdrawn from my Passover offering and I am enrolled for thine." Thus they lose nothing at all.

9. If the hides of the Passover offerings of five persons were confused and a wen is found on the hide of one of them, all the Passover offerings must go forth to the place of burning, and if they were confused before the blood is tossed, their owners must keep the Second Passover. If they were confused after the blood is tossed, they are exempt from keeping the Second Passover, because if they brought a Second Passover offering then he who at the first had offered a valid offering would be bringing to the Temple Court what was unhallowed; and if they all were enrolled

for a single Passover offering it would thus be slaughtered for one on whom there rested no obligation and it would be as though it had been slaughtered for such as were not enrolled for it. Even if each of them had laid down conditions and said, "If it is not a Passover offering let it be a peace offering," this would not avail since the blood of Passover offerings requires pouring out and the blood of peace offerings requires tossing; and what ought to be applied to the altar base by tossing may not be applied at the outset by pouring out. Therefore they are exempt from keeping the Second Passover.

CHAPTER IV

1. It has been explained already in Laws Concerning Hallowed Things Which Become Invalid that the Passover offering must be slaughtered only for the sake of a Passover offering and for the sake of its owners, and that if it is slaughtered with any change of purpose in mind it becomes invalid.

If a man slaughtered the Passover offering on behalf of members of a company and, after some time, he said to them, "That Passover offering which I slaughtered on your behalf I slaughtered otherwise than for its proper purpose"—if he was trusted by them they may rely upon his words; but if he was not, in strict justice he should not be held trustworthy; yet he who would submit himself to a greater restriction is praiseworthy, and he should bring a Second Passover offering.

2. If the flesh of a Passover offering became unclean and this became known to him before the blood was tossed, even though the sacrificial portions remained clean, the priest may not toss the blood, because a Passover offering is brought only to the end that it shall be eaten. And if he tosses the blood it is not acceptable.

If it did not become known to him before the blood was tossed, it is acceptable, because the High Priest's Plate makes a sacrifice acceptable when its flesh has become unclean through error; but it does not effect its acceptance when anything is done wantonly.

If only some of the limbs became unclean, those which are unclean must be burned and those which are clean may be eaten.

If the sacrificial portions became unclean but the flesh remained clean, the blood may be tossed and the flesh may be eaten at eventide.

If its owner became unclean after it was slaughtered the blood may not be tossed, and if it is tossed it is not acceptable. Therefore he must keep the Second Passover, since the Plate effects acceptance when there is uncleanness of the person only if the uncleanness befell through uncleanness from the deep, as we have explained in Laws Concerning Entering into the Temple.

3. If a Passover offering was taken outside Jerusalem or if it became unclean on the fourteenth, it must be burned at once. If its owner became unclean or died or withdrew, even if he became unclean or died before its blood was tossed, it must be left until its appearance is spoiled, when it must be burned. This is the general rule: wherever the invalidity lies in the offering itself it must be burned at once; if in the blood or in the owner, its appearance should be allowed to spoil and then it must be burned. Therefore if it was slaughtered after it became known that the owner had withdrawn or had died or had become unclean and was compelled to await the Second Passover, it must be burned at once.

This applies—namely, that it must be burned if the owner became unclean—when all other members of the company became unclean. But if only some of them became unclean, they who remain clean gain a right to the portions of the unclean. Even if some of them became unclean after they had begun to eat, the clean who had not yet begun to eat gain the right; but if all had begun and some of them became unclean, the clean do not gain a right to the portions of the unclean, but the clean eat their own portions and the portions of the unclean must be burned. This also is the rule if some of them die.

If the whole or the greater part of the Passover offering became unclean, it must be burned before the *birah* in the presence of all, to shame them into paying greater heed to it; and it is burned with wood from the altar pile so that none suspect them and say that they had stolen wood from the altar pile. Therefore if they would burn it with straw or with reed, wishing to burn it with their own fuel, they may do so.

If the lesser part of it became unclean—so, too, with what is left over—they may burn it in their own courtyards with their own wood, but not with wood of the altar pile lest any of this remain over and therewith they commit sacrilege.

4. If for his Passover offering a man set apart a female beast or a male two years old, it must be left to pasture until it suffers a blemish when it must be sold and a valid Passover offering be bought with the price thereof; and if no blemish had befallen it before he brought his Passover offering, he should bring a peace offering with the price thereof.

5. If he set apart his Passover offering and then died, his son after him may not offer it as a Passover offering but only as a peace offering; yet he may offer it as a Passover offering if he had been enrolled for it together with his father. This applies if his father died after midday on the fourteenth; but if it was before midday on the fourteenth, he must be put off until the Second Passover since he counts as "a mourner"—as will be explained—and he must bring this offering of his at the Second Passover.

6. If a man's Passover offering was lost and he found it after he had set apart another Passover offering, so that now he has two of them, he may offer which of them he pleases as a Passover offering, and the other should be brought as a peace offering.

If he found it after he had slaughtered his Passover offering, it should be brought as a peace offering. So, too, if he had substituted another beast in place of that which was found after he had slaughtered the Passover offering: this substituted beast should be brought as a peace offering.

But if he found it before slaughtering that which he had set apart, inasmuch as this one which was found was such that could be brought either as a Passover offering or as a peace offering—as we have explained—if he had substituted another beast for this which was found, whether before slaughtering the one set apart in place of it or after slaughtering it, its substitute may not be offered, but it must be left to pasture until it suffers a blemish, and a peace offering should be brought with the price thereof.

7. A beast which had been dedicated as a Passover offering but was more than one year old, also any peace offering brought by reason of a Passover offering, counts as peace offerings in every respect: they require laying on of hands, drink offerings, waving of breast and shoulder—acts which do not apply to a Passover offering.

8. If a Passover offering is confused with peace offerings, all must be offered as peace offerings. If a Passover offering is confused with other animal offerings, all must be left to pasture until they suffer a blemish [and be sold]; for the price of the best of them, an animal offering must be brought of the same kind as those that had been confused; and for the price of the best of them, a peace offering must be brought; and the owner of the Passover offering must bear the added cost from his own property, as we have stated in Laws Concerning Hallowed Things Which Become Invalid.

If it is confused with firstlings they must all be left to pasture until they suffer a blemish and then be eaten as though they are all blemished firstlings; and the owner should offer a beast which is as good as the best among the confused beasts; and let him say, "Wherever the Passover offering may be, let its sanctity fall upon this beast"; and if his Passover offering has already been offered, he should offer this as a peace offering.

9. If one set apart his Passover offering before he became a proselyte and he then became a proselyte, or before he was set free and he then was set free, or before he had grown two hairs and he then grew them, he may still offer it as a Passover offering, since dedicated animals are not for ever to be discarded, as we have explained in Laws Concerning Hallowed Things Which Become Invalid.

10. If a man set apart money for his Passover offering and he set apart too much, let him bring a peace offering with the surplus.

If a man enrolls others for his Passover offering or for his festal offering, the money which he takes from them for their portion does not count as hallowed. Even though one man set apart a lamb as his Passover offering and another set apart money for his Passover offering and the one took the other's money and enrolled him for his Passover offering, the money does not count as hallowed, since it is to this end that Israelites dedicate their Passover offerings and festal offerings and money for their Passover offerings and festal offerings.

11. Wood used in roasting the Passover offering is subject to the above rule of the Passover offering; so, too, the unleavened cakes and the bitter herbs. Inasmuch as they are accessory to the Passover offering they are counted as the Passover offering. Therefore if a man takes any of the Passover money from those whom he has enrolled with him, so that they might share in the unleavened cakes and the bitter herbs or share in the wood used for roasting, such money does not count as hallowed.

CHAPTER V

1. If a man was unclean when the Passover offering was slaughtered so that it could not be slaughtered on his behalf, or if he was *on a journey afar off* (Num. 9: 10), or hindered by other manner of constraint, or if he erred and failed to make his offering at the First Passover, then he must bring his Passover offering on the fourteenth of the second month in the afternoon. The slaughtering of this Passover offering is a positive commandment in its own right and overrides the Sabbath, since the Second Passover is not a supplement to the First but a feast in its own right. Therefore by reason of it a man can become liable to extirpation.

2. Thus, if through error or constraint a man failed to make his offering at the First Passover and wantonly failed to make his offering at the Second, he is liable to extirpation; but if it was

through error or constraint that he failed to make his offering also at the Second, he is not liable.

If he wantonly failed to make his offering at the First Passover, he must offer it at the Second. And if he failed to offer it at the Second, even though this was through error, he is liable to extirpation, since acting wantonly, he had not made the Lord's offering *at its appointed time* (Num. 9: 3).

But if a man was unclean or *on a journey afar off* and did not keep the First, even though he wantonly failed to keep the Second, he is not liable to extirpation, since he became exempt from extirpation at the First Passover.

3. If a man was *on a journey afar off* and Passover offering was slaughtered and the blood tossed on his behalf, even if he came back at eventide, it is not accepted and he must keep the Second Passover.

4. If an unclean person could have become clean at the First Passover but did not immerse himself and remained in his uncleanness until the time for the offering passed by, or, if an uncircumcised person was not circumcised until the time for the offering passed by, such a one behaves wantonly toward the First Passover; therefore if he failed to keep the Second, even through error, he is liable to extirpation.

5. Just as lack of circumcision in a man himself hinders him from keeping the Passover, so lack of circumcision in any of his sons who are minors and the lack of circumcision in any of his bondmen, whether of age or minors, hinders him, for it is said: *Let all his males be circumcised and then let him come near and keep it* (Exod. 12: 48); and if he slaughtered before he circumcised them, the Passover offering is not valid.

So, too, lack of immersion by his handmaids in respect of their bondage hinders him. And this comes from tradition—that for bondwomen immersion is equal to circumcision for bondmen.

6. As for him who is yet a minor, neither lack of circumcision in his bondmen nor lack of immersion by his bondwomen hinders

him from being enrolled for a Passover offering, for it is said: *But every man's servant* (Exod. 12: 44), thus excluding him who is still a minor.

7. If a man became a proselyte between the First Passover and the Second Passover, or if a minor became of age between the two Passovers, each of them is bound to keep the Second Passover. But if some company had slaughtered on behalf of such a minor at the First, he is exempt.

8. If women had been put off until the Second Passover, whether through constraint or through error, whether through uncleanness or because they were *on a journey afar off,* for them the Second Passover is optional. If they please they may slaughter; if they do not please they need not slaughter. Therefore a Passover offering may not be slaughtered only on their behalf on the Sabbath at a Second Passover; but if a woman is among members of a company, it is permissible.

And what is accounted *a journey afar off* (Num. 9: 10)? Fifteen miles outside the walls of Jerusalem.

9. If at sunrise on the fourteenth there lay fifteen miles or more between a man and Jerusalem, this is deemed *a journey afar off*. If less than this lay between him and the city, it is not deemed *a journey afar off,* since he can reach Jerusalem after midday with ease, traveling on foot. If he was on his way thither but could not reach it because cattle hindered him by their crowding, or if he was in Jerusalem but was infirm in the feet and could not reach the Temple Court until the time for the offering was passed, such a one is deemed to suffer constraint and not to be *on a journey afar off*.

If a man is imprisoned outside the wall of Jerusalem and it has been promised him that he should go out at eventide, the Passover offering may be slaughtered on his behalf, and when he comes out at eventide he may eat of it. This applies if he was imprisoned by Israelites; but if he was imprisoned by Gentiles, the Passover offering may not be slaughtered on his behalf until he is come out. But if it had been slaughtered on his behalf and he came out, he may eat of it. If he did not come out, he is still exempt from keeping the Second Passover, since an offering had already been slaughtered on his behalf.

So, too, with a mourner or one who was sick or aged, yet was capable of eating, and for whom the offering had been slaughtered —if, after the blood had been tossed, he was rendered unclean by a corpse and so was not able to eat, he is exempt from keeping the Second Passover.

CHAPTER VI

1. Who is accounted *unclean* (Num. 9: 10) and is put off until the Second Passover? Any who cannot eat the Passover offering during the night of the fifteenth of Nisan by reason of his uncleanness: for example, men or women with flux, menstruants, women after childbirth, or such as had intercourse with menstruants. But any who had touched carrion or a creeping thing or the like on the fourteenth may immerse himself, and the Passover offering may be slaughtered on his behalf after he has immersed himself; and at eventide, after awaiting sunset, he may eat of the Passover offering.

2. If a man suffered corpse uncleanness and his seventh day fell on the fourteenth, even though he had immersed himself and was sprinkled and is thus capable of eating Hallowed Things at eventide, the offering may not be slaughtered on his behalf, but he is put off until the Second Passover, for it is said: *But there were certain men who were unclean by the dead body of a man so that they could not keep the Passover that day* (Num. 9: 6). From oral tradition it is learned that this was their seventh day, and so they inquired whether the Passover offering could be slaughtered for them that they might eat of it at eventide, and it was explained to them that it could not be slaughtered for them. This applies if a man had incurred some uncleanness from a corpse for which a nazirite must needs cut off his hair; but if he incurred other uncleanness from a corpse for which a nazirite need not cut off his

hair, the Passover offering may be slaughtered for him on his seventh day after he has immersed himself and has been sprinkled; and after awaiting sunset he may eat of his Passover offering.

3. If a man suffered two issues of flux and counted seven days and immersed himself on the seventh, the Passover offering may be slaughtered on his behalf and he may eat of it at eventide. If he suffered an issue after the blood had been tossed, he is not compelled to keep the Second Passover.

So, too, she who awaits day against day may immerse herself on the day of awaiting, as we have explained in Laws Concerning Forbidden Intercourse, and the offering may be slaughtered on her behalf and she may eat of it at eventide. If she suffered a flow after the blood of the Passover offering had been tossed, she is not compelled to keep the Second Passover.

The Passover offering may not be slaughtered on behalf of a menstruant on her seventh day, since she may not immerse herself until the night of the eighth day, and she is not capable of eating Hallowed Things until the night of the ninth day.

4. As for those whose atonement is not complete—if the day for bringing their offerings falls on the fourteenth, the Passover offering may be slaughtered on their behalf and they may bring their offerings on the fourteenth of Nisan either before or after the slaughtering of the Passover offering and they may eat their Passover offering at eventide. But it may not be slaughtered on their behalf unless they have delivered their offerings into the hands of the court, lest they should transgress and forbear to offer them.

5. If a leper's eighth day falls on the fourteenth and he suffers an emission the same day, he may immerse himself and enter the Court of the Women and bring his offerings, although one who was immersed that day is otherwise forbidden to enter the Court of the Women. Inasmuch as the rule against his entering therein rests only on the authority of the Scribes—as we have explained in Laws Concerning Entering into the Temple—whereas this day is the day for offering the Passover offering *at its appointed time*

(Num. 9:3), the positive commandment involving extirpation comes and overrides a prohibition resting only on the authority of the Scribes.

6. If the seventh day of one who suffered corpse uncleanness falls on a Sabbath he may not be sprinkled until the morrow, and although his seventh day falls on the thirteenth of Nisan which was a Sabbath, he must be put off until the fourteenth, when he is sprinkled; and the offering may not be slaughtered on his behalf —as we have explained—and he is put off until the Second Passover.

But does not the rule against sprinkling on the Sabbath depend only on the rules of šĕbuṯ whereas breach of the Passover law involves extirpation? How, then, can the rulings of the Scribes be maintained where extirpation is involved? It is because the day when sprinkling is forbidden by virtue of the rules of šĕbuṯ is not the time of the offering for which there is liability to extirpation; therefore the ruling of the Scribes is maintained even though it bears thereafter on a matter involving extirpation.

7. If an uncircumcised Israelite is circumcised on the eve of Passover, the offering may be slaughtered on his behalf after he has been circumcised; but if a Gentile who became a proselyte on the fourteenth is circumcised and immerses himself, it may not be slaughtered on his behalf, because he may not eat it at eventide since he counts as one who severs himself from the grave and needs to await seven days, and only then does he become clean—a precautionary rule lest this proselyte should incur corpse uncleanness in the coming year on the fourteenth and immerse himself and eat at eventide and say, "Thus did the Israelites with me last year: after I was circumcised I immersed myself and ate at eventide!"

But does not this precautionary rule rest only on the authority of the Scribes, whereas breach of the Passover law involves extirpation? How then, can the rulings of the Scribes be maintained where extirpation is involved concerning the day of the offering, namely, the fourteenth? It is because the proselyte is bound by the commandments only after he has been circumcised and has immersed himself; and he cannot immerse himself until he is healed of the circumcision, as we have explained on the subject of conversion. Therefore the ruling of the Scribes is maintained: since one who is circumcised need immerse himself only when he is healed, till then he incurs no obligation at all.

8. If a man enters a grave area he should sift the soil as he goes along, and if he does not find any bone and become unclean he may slaughter his Passover offering and eat it even though he had walked in a grave area, since the uncleanness of a grave area rests only on the authority of the Scribes—as we have explained in Laws Concerning Corpse Uncleanness—and their rulings are not maintained where extirpation is involved. So, too, a grave area which is trampled down is deemed clean for him who would keep the Passover.

9. A mourner becomes capable of eating the Passover offering at eventide, since the extension to nighttime of the law concerning the mourner rests only on the authority of the Scribes, and their rulings are not maintained in this case where extirpation is involved; therefore the Passover offering may be slaughtered on his behalf and he may immerse himself and then eat, so that he may separate himself from his state of mourning and be undistracted in mind.

This applies if his kindred died after midday, because he had then already become liable for the Passover offering; but if his kindred died before midday, it may not be slaughtered on his behalf but he must be put off until the Second Passover. Yet if it was slaughtered on his behalf and the blood tossed, he may immerse himself and eat of it at eventide.

If his kindred died on the thirteenth and was buried on the fourteenth, on the authority of the Scribes he counts as a mourner also on the day of burial, but he does not include also that night, on their authority. Therefore the Passover offering may be slaughtered on his behalf and he may immerse himself and eat of it at eventide, also of other Hallowed Things.

Moreover the day of hearing of the death and the day of col-

lecting the bones are deemed like to the day of burial. Therefore if
a man collected the bones of his kindred on the fourteenth, or
first heard on that day that his kindred had died, the Passover
offering may be slaughtered on his behalf and he may immerse
himself and eat of Hallowed Things at eventide.

10. If a man was digging in the heap of a fallen house in search
of a corpse, the Passover offering may not be slaughtered on his
behalf lest he find the corpse in the heap and so be unclean at the
time of slaughtering. If it was slaughtered on his behalf and no
corpse was found there, he may eat of the Passover offering at eventide. If the corpse was found there after the blood had been tossed
and it was known to him of a certainty that he was unclean when
the blood was tossed—if, for example, it was a round heap—he
must keep the Second Passover.

If it was in doubt and, perchance, he was not standing over
the uncleanness when the blood was tossed, and he became unclean only after it was tossed, he need not keep the Second Passover.

11. If a man passing along a path found a corpse lying across the
width of the path, and the corpse was "uncleanness from the deep,"
although he is deemed unclean for heave offering, he is clean for
the Passover offering and he may slaughter and eat his Passover
offering. And although it is possible that he touched the corpse,
yet inasmuch as it was uncleanness from the deep, he is deemed
clean for the Passover offering. And even if it was a complete
corpse and stretched from one edge of the path to the other, he
may nevertheless keep the Passover—unless he knew of a certainty
that he had become unclean.

This applies if he was traveling on foot, since then it is possible
that he may not have touched it; but if he was riding or bearing
a burden he becomes unclean even though it was uncleanness from
the deep, since it is impossible that he should not then have touched,
shifted, or overshadowed it. And we have already explained this
uncleanness from the deep in Laws Concerning the Nazirite's
Vow.

12. If a man kept the Passover on the presumption that he was clean and it became afterward known to him that he was unclean by uncleanness from the deep, he is not bound to keep the Second Passover. This is a rule learned from tradition. But if it was known to him that he had become unclean from some known uncleanness, he is bound to keep the Second Passover.

13. If a man incurred corpse uncleanness and was sprinkled because of it on the third day and on the seventh, and on his seventh day he incurred uncleanness from some grave "in the deep," and he did not know it, and he kept the Passover on the presumption that he was clean, and it became afterward known to him that he had been unclean by uncleanness from the deep, he is not bound to keep the Second Passover; for so soon as he immersed himself on the seventh day the first uncleanness was severed from him. But if he incurred uncleanness by uncleanness from the deep on the sixth day of his uncleanness, and he did not know it until he had kept the Passover, he is bound to keep the Second Passover, because he who is unclean is presumed still to be unclean until he is clean of a certainty, since there are grounds for so presuming.

CHAPTER VII

1. If there were many who suffered corpse uncleanness at the First Passover, yet they formed the lesser part of the congregation, they must be put off until the Second Passover, like other unclean persons; but if the greater part of the congregation suffered corpse uncleanness, or if the priests or the vessels of ministry were unclean with corpse uncleanness, they are not to be put off, but all bring their Passover offerings in uncleanness, the unclean together with the clean, for it is said: *But there were certain men who were unclean by the dead body of a man* (Num. 9:6): particular persons are to be put off, but the congregation is not to be put off. This applies only in the case of corpse uncleanness, as we have explained in Laws Concerning Entering into the Temple.

2. If half of the congregation were clean and the other half suffered corpse uncleanness, all keep the First Passover, the clean keeping it by themselves in cleanness and the unclean keeping it by themselves in uncleanness and eating it in uncleanness. If they who suffered corpse uncleanness exceeded even by one those who were clean, all keep it in uncleanness.

3. If half of the menfolk suffered corpse uncleanness and the other half were clean, and if, by including the women among the menfolk, the greater number would then be clean, the clean keep the First Passover and the unclean keep neither the First Passover nor the Second: they may not keep the First since they were a minority; and they may not keep the Second since, the Second not being obligatory upon womenfolk, the unclean would constitute a half, and a half does not keep the Second Passover.

4. If the greater part of the congregation were men who suffered a flux or were leprous or had intercourse with menstruants, and the lesser part suffered corpse uncleanness, they who suffered corpse uncleanness do not keep the First Passover since they are a minority; and they do not keep the Second, since particular persons do not keep the Second except when the greater part of the congregation keeps the First. And here, since the greater part of the congregation did not keep the First, these, the minority, who suffered corpse uncleanness do not keep the Second.

5. If the greater part of the congregation suffered corpse uncleanness and the lesser part were men who suffered a flux or a like uncleanness, they who suffered corpse uncleanness keep the First Passover and they who suffered a flux or a like uncleanness keep neither the First nor the Second; they do not keep the First, since no uncleanness in the community is cause for deferment except corpse uncleanness; and they do not keep the Second, since the Second Passover is kept only when the First has been kept in cleanness; but if the first was kept in uncleanness there can be no Second Passover.

6. If a third part of the congregation were clean and a third part were men who suffered a flux or a like uncleanness and a third part suffered corpse uncleanness, they who suffered corpse uncleanness keep neither the First Passover nor the Second: they do not keep the First, since they are a minority compared with the clean and those suffering a flux; and the Second they do not keep, since a minority will have kept the First, as we have stated.

How are the numbers at Passover estimated to know whether the greater part of the congregation is unclean or clean? They are estimated not from those who eat, since perhaps twenty may have enrolled themselves for a single Passover offering and made one man their agent to slaughter it for them, but they are estimated from all who enter into the Temple Court; and while they are yet outside, before the first group comes in, their numbers are estimated.

7. If a single person is accounted unclean by reason of a condition of doubt affecting private domain—as will be explained in its proper place—he must be put off until the Second Passover, like others who suffer corpse uncleanness. And if a community is accounted unclean by reason of a condition of doubt affecting private domain, they all keep the First Passover in uncleanness.

8. If a Passover offering is brought in uncleanness it may be eaten in uncleanness, since from the outset it is brought only to the end that it should be eaten. It may not be eaten by all who are unclean, but only by those who suffer corpse uncleanness, since it was this uncleanness that was cause for deferment for them and for their like who were become unclean by contact with (corpse) uncleanness. But unclean persons whose uncleanness comes upon them from their own body, such as men or women with flux, menstruants, women after childbirth, and the leprous may not eat of it; yet if they do eat, they are not culpable.

From oral tradition it is learned that, because of what may be eaten only by those who are clean, penalty is incurred on account of uncleanness; but because of what may be eaten by those who are unclean, no penalty is incurred on account of uncleanness:

even if they who suffer corpse uncleanness eat of the sacrificial portions, they are not culpable.

This applies, namely, that the Passover offering is to be eaten in uncleanness, only when the community had become unclean before the blood was tossed; but if they became unclean after the blood was tossed, it may not be eaten in uncleanness.

9. If it was slaughtered in cleanness but the greater part of the community became unclean before the tossing of the blood, the blood is to be tossed; but the offering may not be eaten—a precautionary rule lest, some other year, they become unclean after the blood is tossed and eat the offering in uncleanness.

If the vessels of ministry were rendered unclean by a creeping thing or a like uncleanness, inasmuch as the vessels do not render men unclean—as will be explained in its proper place—although they render the flesh of the offering unclean, none may prepare it except those who are clean; but it may be eaten even though it was unclean: it is better that it be eaten with its flesh unclean, thereby transgressing a negative commandment, than that those unclean in their persons should eat it, thereby becoming liable to extirpation, as we have explained in Laws Concerning Hallowed Things Which Become Invalid.

CHAPTER VIII

1. To eat of the flesh of the Passover offering during the night of the fifteenth (of Nisan) is a positive commandment, for it is said: *And they shall eat the flesh in that night, roast with fire, and unleavened bread; with bitter herbs shall they eat it* (Exod. 12:8).

2. Lack of unleavened bread and bitter herbs is no hindrance: if no unleavened bread and bitter herbs are to be found, the obligation can be fulfilled by eating the flesh of the Passover offering by itself. But to eat bitter herbs without the Passover offering is no fulfilling of a commandment, for it is said: *With unleavened bread and bitter herbs shall they eat it* (Num. 9:11).

3. It is especially commendable to eat the flesh of the Passover offering to repletion. Therefore if a man brings a festal peace offering on the fourteenth, let him first eat of that and then eat of the flesh of the Passover offering so that thereby he may reach repletion; but if he eats only an olive's bulk, he will have fulfilled his obligation.

Similarly, eating the flesh of the offering at the Second Passover, during the night of the fifteenth of the month Iyyar is a positive commandment, for it is said thereof: *With unleavened bread and bitter herbs shall they eat it* (Num. 9:11).

4. Neither of them may be eaten unless the flesh be roasted with fire, and if any eats as much as an olive's bulk of it raw or sodden during the two nights of Passover, he incurs punishment by scourging, for it is said: *Eat not of it raw or sodden at all with water* (Exod. 12:9). If a man ate of it both raw and sodden at the same time, he is to be scourged but once, since the two are included within a single prohibition. If he ate of it raw or sodden before sunset, he is not to be scourged at all, for it is said: *But roast with fire* (Exod. 12:9). Only when it becomes a duty to eat of it roasted does a man become culpable by eating it raw or sodden; but before sunset he is not culpable.

5. If he eats an olive's bulk of it roasted before sunset, he transgresses a positive commandment, for it is said: *And they shall eat the flesh in that night* (Exod. 12:8), namely, in the night and not in the day; and a negative command which is implied in a positive command counts as a positive command.

6. The *raw* flesh which the Law has prohibited is flesh on which fire has begun its work and which is somewhat roasted yet is still not fit for human food. But if he ate its flesh wholly uncooked, he is not liable to scourging; yet he disregards a positive commandment, for it is said: *roast with fire;* hence, what is not roasted is forbidden. If he roasted it sufficiently for it to be scorched and so ate it, he is exempt from penalty.

7. The *sodden* flesh which the Law has prohibited is flesh sodden with water or sodden with any other liquid or fruit juice, for it is said, *or sodden at all,* to include all of these.

8. If a man roasted it and then boiled it, or boiled it and then roasted it, or if he prepared it roasted in a pot and so ate it, he is culpable. But it is permissible to baste it with wine, oil, honey, or other liquid or fruit juice, except water. And it is permissible to immerse the flesh after it is roasted in liquid or fruit juice.

9. The Passover offering may not be roasted over any utensil of stone or metal, for it is said: *roast with fire,* not roast with anything else. Therefore if a utensil was so perforated that the fire prevailed therein, it may be roasted over this. It may not be roasted on a metal skewer since the whole skewer becomes heated and roasts the flesh at the place where it touches.

10. If a man heated an oven and raked out all the fire and hung the Passover offering in the oven and so roasted it, such is forbidden since it was not *roast with fire*. If he cut into it and hung it over burning embers, this counts as *roast with fire*. If he roasted it upon heated lime or clay or the hot springs of Tiberias, such is forbidden since it was not *roast with fire*.

How should it be roasted? It should be pierced through from its mouth to its buttocks with a wooden skewer and hung inside an oven with the fire beneath it. Its legs and its entrails should be hung apart in the oven: they should not be put inside the carcass since this would be in the nature of soddening. It was customary to choose a skewer of pomegranate wood with which to roast it so that it should not spirt forth any sap and so sodden the flesh.

11. If the flesh touched the earthenware of the oven, that part must be pared away since this would be roasted not with fire but by earthenware.

12. If some of its juice dripped on to the earthenware and splashed back again on the carcass, that part must be removed, since

all juice and moisture which is severed from it while roasting is forbidden, because it is not roasted flesh.

13. If some of its juice dripped on to the flour, that part must be pared off and thrown away.

14. If it was basted with heave-offering oil and the company was a company of priests, they may eat it; but if they were (lay) Israelites and it was yet uncooked, it must be rinsed and dried; and if it had been roasted, the surface must be pared off. If it was basted with second-tithe oil its value may not be charged to the members of the company, since second tithe may not be redeemed in Jerusalem, as we have explained in its proper place.

Two Passover offerings may not be roasted together for fear of confusion, even though they were a kid and a lamb.

We have already stated in several places that the Passover offering may be eaten only until midnight, to keep far from transgression; on the authority of Scripture it may be eaten throughout the whole night until daybreak.

We have already explained in Laws Concerning Leaven and Unleavened Bread that the Hallel must be recited at the time when it is eaten, and that members of the company should not eat again after they had fallen asleep, even though this was but at the beginning of the night.

CHAPTER IX

1. He who eats of the Passover offering may eat of it only in one company. Nothing of it may be carried forth from the company in which he eats, and he who carries forth an olive's bulk of its flesh from one company to another during the night of the fifteenth incurs punishment by scourging, for it is said: *Thou shalt not carry forth aught of the flesh abroad out of the house* (Exod. 12:46). This applies provided that he lays it down outside; for the expression *carry forth* is written here as it is written also of the Sabbath; therefore as in the forbidden act of carrying things on the

Sabbath, so here, the expression *carry forth* includes both taking up and laying down.

And there can be none who transgresses by carrying forth anything of the Passover offering which has already been carried forth, for so soon as the first person has carried it forth it is rendered invalid.

From the doorjamb inward counts as inside, from the doorjamb outward counts as outside, and the jamb itself, which is of the thickness of the door, counts as outside. The window spaces and the thickness of the walls count as inside. The roofs and upper rooms are not included in the term "house."

2. If flesh of a Passover offering was carried forth outside the company, whether willfully or through error, it is forbidden to eat of it: it corresponds to flesh of Most Hallowed Things which is carried forth from the Temple Court, or flesh of Lesser Hallowed Things which is carried forth outside the walls of Jerusalem, both of which are accounted ṭĕrefah. And punishment by scourging is incurred for eating thereof, as we have explained in Laws Concerning the Manner of Making Offerings.

If part of a limb protruded outside its appointed place, the flesh must be cut until the bone is reached and the flesh pared off. All that is inside may be eaten and all that is outside must be burned. And when the bone is reached, it is chopped off with a hatchet if it was one of the other Hallowed Things, and if it was a Passover offering—a bone of which may not be broken—the flesh must be pared off as far as the joint, and the limb, of which a part protrudes, must be broken off at the joint and thrown away outside.

3. If two companies eat in a single room each company must form itself into a separate band, for it is said: *Thou shalt not carry forth aught of the flesh outside* (Exod. 12: 46). From oral tradition it is learned that an *outside* must be provided for the place where the Passover offering is eaten. And they of the one company eat with their faces turned in one direction and the others eat with their faces turned in the other direction, so that they shall not seem to be mixed up together.

4. If the water with which they mix their wine is in the middle of the room between the two companies, whenever the attendant gets up to mix it he should keep his mouth tight shut and his face turned away until he reaches again his own company and there he may eat what is in his mouth; for to him who eats it is forbidden to eat in two companies. But it is permissible for a bride to eat with her face turned away from her company, since she feels diffident at eating in their presence.

5. If the partition between two companies was broken through, they may not go on eating; so, too, if there was one company and a partition was made between them they may not go on eating until it is removed, since the Passover offering may not be eaten in two companies, and none may be drawn away from one company and become one of another.

6. If three or more of the members of a company came in to eat of their Passover offering and the other members of the company did not come, and they had come in at a time when people usually eat the Passover offerings and he who summoned them all went again to the others and yet they did not come, then they who had come in may eat until they are replete without waiting for the others. And even if the dilatory ones came afterward and found that the three had eaten everything, these need not reimburse the others for their share. But if only two had come in, they must wait. This applies to the time when they come in to eat; but when they go away none need wait for his fellow: even if only one had finished eating, he may go out and he has no need to wait.

7. If a man gives as much as an olive's bulk from either the First or the Second Passover offering to be eaten by a convert to idolatry or a resident alien or a hireling, he transgresses a negative commandment: he is not to be scourged but beaten with the beating of contumacy. The *alien* spoken of in the Law (Exod. 12:43) is one who worships *an alien god* (Deut. 32:12).

Nor may any of it be given as food to a Gentile, even a resident alien or a hireling, for it is said: *A sojourner and a hired servant shall not eat thereof* (Exod. 12:46).

8. If one who was uncircumcised ate as much as an olive's bulk of the Passover offering, he incurs punishment by scourging, for it is said: *But no uncircumcised person shall eat of it* (Exod. 12: 48); it is *of it* that he shall not eat, but he may eat of the unleavened bread or the bitter herbs. So, too, it is permissible to allow a resident alien or a hireling to eat of the unleavened bread and the bitter herbs.

9. Just as lack of circumcision in his sons and in his bondmen hinders a man from slaughtering the Passover offering, so it hinders him from eating of it, for it is said: *When thou hast circumcised him then shall he eat of it* (Exod. 12: 44). Thus if he acquired a bondman after the Passover offering was slaughtered or if he had a son whose time for circumcision did not come until after the Passover offering was slaughtered, he is forbidden to eat of it until after he has circumcised them. And how can the son be fit for circumcision after the Passover offering is slaughtered and not be fit before it is slaughtered? It is so if, for example, his fever subsided and a space of seven days exactly was needful from the day of his healing, or if, for example, his eye suffered hurt but was healed after the offering was slaughtered, or if he was of doubtful sex and the impediment was torn away after the Passover offering was slaughtered and he was found to be a male.

CHAPTER X

1. If a man broke a bone in a Passover offering which was clean, he incurs punishment by scourging, for it is said: *Neither shall ye break a bone thereof* (Exod. 12: 46). So, too, it is said of the Second Passover offering: *Neither shall ye break a bone thereof* (Num. 9: 12). But a Passover offering which was brought in uncleanness—if a man broke a bone thereof, he is not to be scourged. From oral tradition it is learned that *Neither shall ye break a bone thereof* refers to an offering which was clean and not to one which was unclean.

No matter whether he broke a bone during the night of the

fifteenth or whether he broke a bone thereof before nightfall or whether he broke it many days afterward, he is to be scourged.

2. Therefore the bones of a Passover offering must be burned together with what is left over of its flesh, that they do not become a stumbling block.

3. None becomes culpable save by breaking a bone on which there was at least an olive's bulk of flesh or in which there was marrow; but a bone in which there was no marrow or on which there was less than an olive's bulk of flesh, none becomes culpable by breaking it.

If there was an olive's bulk of flesh on it and he broke the bone at a place where there was no flesh, he is culpable, even though the place where he broke it was bereft of its flesh.

4. If one man broke it after another had broken it, he is to be scourged.

5. If a man burned the bones or if he cut the sinews, he does not become culpable because of breaking a bone.

6. If a Passover offering was *raw or sodden* and a man broke a bone thereof, he is to be scourged. Even if it had become invalid through uncleanness or through being carried outside or the like, it still comes under the rule against breaking a bone. This applies if there had been a time when it was valid and it then became invalid; but if there never had been a time when it was valid—if, for example, it had become "refuse" or if it was sacrificed with some other intention as to season or with some other intention as to purpose—it does not come under the rule against breaking a bone.

7. If he broke the bone in the fat tail he is not to be scourged, since this is not suitable for food.

8. The gristly parts which are like soft bones—these it is permissible to eat.

9. If it was a small and tender kid having soft bones, a man may not eat these since he would be breaking a bone; and if he ate them

he is to be scourged since it is all one whether he breaks a hard bone or a soft bone. This is the general rule: whatever can be eaten of a full-grown ox after it is seethed, the corresponding parts may be eaten in a tender kid after it is roasted, such as the ends of the shoulder blades and the gristly parts.

10. As for the tender sinews which will later harden, although they are now fit for eating and can be eaten in the Passover offering, no one may be enrolled for them. One may be enrolled for the brain since this can be extracted without breaking a bone; but none may be enrolled for the marrow in a *kolit*—which is a bone blocked up at either end—since it can only be extracted by breaking the bone.

11. When a man eats of the Passover offering he should cut away the flesh and eat it and cut away the bones at the joint and, if he wishes, sever them. When he reaches the sinew of the hip he should extract it and lay it with the other sinews and bones and hard bits of skin which are discarded at the time of eating. For it is not cleansed like other flesh, nor is it cut up, but roasted whole. Yet if it was all cut up into pieces (before it was roasted) it is valid, provided that no member of the carcass was missing.

Moreover a man should endeavor to leave nothing of the flesh of the Passover offering by the morning, for it is said: *And ye shall let nothing of it remain until the morning* (Exod. 12:10); and the same applies to the Second Passover offering, for it is said: *They shall leave none of it unto the morning* (Num. 9:12). And if a man left some of it remaining, whether at the First Passover or at the Second, he transgresses a negative commandment, but he is not to be scourged on account of this prohibition, since this is a prohibition transformed into a positive commandment, for it is said: *But that which remaineth of it ye shall burn with fire* (Exod. 12:10).

12. When the Passover offering is offered at the First Passover on the fourteenth day there may be offered with it other offerings taken from the oxen or from the sheep, large cattle or small, male or female, as are any other animals offered as a peace offering.

This is what is called "the festal offering of the fourteenth," and of this it is said in the Law: *And thou shalt sacrifice the passover offering unto the Lord thy God of the flock and of the herd* (Deut. 16:2).

When is this festal offering brought with it? When the Passover offering is brought on a weekday and in cleanness and is insufficient; but if the fourteenth fell on a Sabbath or if the Passover was kept in uncleanness or if the Passover offerings were ample, no additional festal offering is brought, but only the Passover offerings are sacrificed.

13. The festal offering of the fourteenth is optional and not obligatory, and it can be eaten during two days and one night, like any other peace offering. And it is forbidden to leave anything of the flesh of the festal offering of the fourteenth until the third day, for it is said: *Neither shall any of the flesh which thou sacrificest the first day at even remain all night until the morning* (Deut. 16:4). From oral tradition it is learned that this is a rule against leaving any flesh of the festal offering of the fourteenth until the sixteenth day, for it is said: *Until the morning;* namely, until the morning of the second day. And he who leaves anything remaining is not to be scourged; but what remains of it is to be burned, like any other remnants of offerings.

14. The flesh of a festal offering which is served on the table together with the Passover offering and any bakemeats which are served together with it on the table must be consumed together with it, and they may be eaten only until midnight, like the Passover offering itself—a precautionary rule to avoid confusion.

15. Wherein does the First Passover offering differ from the Second? At the First Passover, whatever is leavened is forbidden by the rules *It shall not be seen* (Exod. 13:7) and *It shall not be found* (Exod. 12:19); it may not be slaughtered if anything that is leavened is present; nothing of the Passover offering may be removed outside the company; the Hallel must be recited when it is eaten; a festal offering may be brought with it; and

it is possible to offer it in uncleanness if the greater part of the congregation becomes unclean with corpse uncleanness, as we have stated.

But at the Second Passover there may be leavened and unleavened bread in the same room with the Passover offering; the Hallel need not be recited when the offering is eaten; it may be removed outside its company; no festal offering is brought with it; and the Second Passover may not be kept in uncleanness.

Both Passovers override the Sabbath; at both the Hallel must be recited while the offering is sacrificed; at both Passovers the offering must be eaten roasted with unleavened bread and bitter herbs in the same room; nothing of it may be left over; and a bone of it may not be broken.

And why is not the Second made equal to the First in every respect since it is said: *According to all the statute of the Passover they shall keep it* (Num. 9:12)? It is because but a part of the statute of Passover is prescribed for it, to teach us that it is equal to the First only in the things expressly laid down for it, namely, those commandments pertaining to itself which constitute *the statute of the Passover*. For (similarly) the general injunction which was ordained in Egypt—that the Passover offering be taken on the tenth day (of Nisan) and that the lintel and the two doorposts be touched with blood on a bunch of hyssop and that it be eaten in haste—these things do not require permanent observance but were carried out only at the Passover of Egypt.

TREATISE II

LAWS CONCERNING
THE FESTAL OFFERING

Involving Six Commandments
Four Positive and Two Negative

To Wit

1. To appear before the presence of the Lord;
2. To keep the feast at the three pilgrimage seasons;
3. To rejoice at the pilgrimage seasons;
4. Not to appear empty;
5. Not to forsake the Levite by not suffering him to rejoice and not giving him his dues at the feasts;
6. To assemble the people together at the Feast of Tabernacles at the close of the year of release.

An exposition of these commandments
is contained in the following chapters.

NOTE

In the list of the 613 commandments prefixed to the Code, those which deal with the subject of this Treatise are cited in the following form.

Positive commandments:

[6] 16. To assemble the people together to hear the Law at the close of the seventh year, as it is said: *Assemble the people . . . that they may hear . . . and observe to do all the words of this law* (Deut. 31: 12);

[2] 52. To keep the feast at the three pilgrimage seasons, as it is said: *Three times shalt thou keep a feast unto me in the year* (Exod. 23: 14);

[1] 53. To appear at the pilgrimage seasons, as it is said: *Three times in a year shall thy males appear before the Lord thy God* (Deut. 16: 16);

[3] 54. To rejoice at the pilgrimage seasons, as it is said: *And thou shalt rejoice in thy feast* (Deut. 16: 14).

Negative commandments:

[4] 156. That none go up to the feast without an offering, as it is said: *And none shall appear before me empty* (Exod. 23: 15);

[5] 229. That the Levites be not left without support, as it is said, *Take heed to thyself that thou forsake not the Levite* (Deut. 12: 19); but the Levites should be given their dues whereby they may have cause to rejoice at every pilgrimage season.

CHAPTER I

1. Three positive commandments were laid upon the Israelites at each of the three pilgrimage seasons, namely, the duty to appear, as it is said: *All thy males shall appear* (Exod. 23:17); the duty to keep the feast, as it is said: *Thou shalt keep a feast unto the Lord thy God* (Deut. 16:15); and the duty to rejoice, as it is said: *And thou shalt rejoice in thy feast* (Deut. 16:14).

The duty to appear, spoken of in the Law, means that the Israelite be seen in the Temple Court on the first festival day of the feast and that he bring with him a whole offering either of birds or of cattle; and if a man should come to the Temple Court on the first day and bring no offering, not only does he fail to fulfill a positive commandment but he transgresses a negative commandment also, for it is said: *And none shall appear before me empty* (Exod. 23:15); but he is not to be scourged by reason of the prohibition, since he performed no act.

The duty to keep the feast, spoken of in the Law, means that he offer a peace offering on the first festival day of the feast when he comes to make his appearance; and it is well known that peace offerings are brought only from cattle.

These two commandments, the duty to appear and the duty to keep the feast, are not incumbent upon women.

And the duty to rejoice, spoken of with regard to the pilgrimage seasons, means that he bring a peace offering in addition to the festal peace offering. And this is what is called "the peace offering of rejoicing in the feast," as it is said: *And thou shalt sacrifice peace offerings, and shalt eat there; and thou shalt rejoice before the Lord thy God* (Deut. 27:7). This commandment is incumbent upon women as well.

2. For the pilgrimage offering and the festal offering the Law enjoins no prescribed measure, for it is said: *Every man shall give as he is able* (Deut. 16:17); but on the authority of the Scribes a pilgrimage whole offering should be worth at least one *ma'ah* of silver and the festal peace offering at least two pieces of silver. And

it is a man's duty to offer in proportion to his wealth, as it is said: *Every man shall give as he is able.*

3. For the peace offering of rejoicing the Sages have not given any prescribed measure.

If at the time when he would go up to Jerusalem to keep the feast a man had in his possession offerings suitable for the pilgrimage offering, he may bring them or he may take up with him money wherewith to buy the offering. If he had no money in his possession, he may not bring anything of money's worth; even if he had in his possession the worth of many gold pieces he is forbidden to go up *empty* (Deut. 16: 16), namely, without money or an offering.

And why have the Sages forbidden him to take up with him money's worth in place of money? It is a precautionary rule lest he fail to sell it or lest the money he receives for it be found base metal.

4. If a man does not bring his pilgrimage whole offering and his festal peace offering on the first festival day, he may bring them during the other days of the feast, for it is said: *Seven days shalt thou keep a feast unto the Lord thy God* (Deut. 16: 15), thus teaching us that they are all suitable days on which to keep the feast and are all supplementary to the first day.

5. It is commendable to hasten and bring the offerings on the first day. If a man does not bring them on the first day, whether through error or wantonness, let him bring them on the second. He who is dilatory is blameworthy, and of him it is said: *I will gather them that are far from the appointed season* (Zeph. 3: 18).

6. If the feast went by and he had brought no offering, it is not incumbent upon him to make it good; and of such a one and his like it is said: *That which is crooked cannot be made straight* (Eccles. 1: 15).

7. If he had brought no offering on the first festival day of the Feast of Tabernacles, he may bring one any time during the feast,

even on the last festival day, which is the eighth; for the eighth day also is supplementary to the first day.

So, too, if a man had brought no offering on the day of the Feast of Pentecost, he may bring one any time during seven days, for all six days after the Feast of Pentecost are supplementary to it. And this is known from oral tradition: that the Feast of Pentecost is like the Feast of Unleavened Bread as regards supplementary days.

8. The pilgrimage whole offering and the festal peace offering override neither the Sabbath nor the laws of uncleanness, since they have no fixed time as have the public offerings, in that if a man brings no festal offering one day he may do so on the morrow, as we have explained. But they override the laws of a festival day; for although vow offerings or freewill offerings may not be brought on a festival day, the pilgrimage whole offering and the festal peace offering and the peace offering of rejoicing may be brought, since these are obligatory and not vow offerings or freewill offerings.

9. When a man brings his pilgrimage whole offering and his festal peace offering and his peace offering of rejoicing on a festival day, he should lay his hand upon them with all his might, as he would do on other days. Although lack of laying on of hands is no hindrance—as we have explained in Laws Concerning the Manner of Making Offerings—it is not prohibited in virtue of the rules respecting šĕbut.

10. If a man set apart his pilgrimage whole offering and then died, it is incumbent upon his heirs to offer it.

It is permissible to offer vow offerings and freewill offerings on mid-festival days, for it is said: *These shall ye offer unto the Lord in your appointed seasons beside your vow offerings and your freewill offerings;* implying that they may be offered at the pilgrimage season—*whether they be your whole offerings,* such as the leper's whole offering and the offering of a woman after childbirth, *or your meal offerings,* such as the sinner's meal offering and the meal offering of jealousy, *or your peace-offerings,* including the nazirite's peace offering (Num. 29: 39). All these may be brought during the mid-festival days but they may not be brought on the festival day proper.

11. If a man had many who ate with him but few possessions, he should bring many festal peace offerings and few pilgrimage whole offerings. If he had few who ate with him but many possessions, he should bring many pilgrimage whole offerings and few festal peace offerings. If he had few of either, of such a one the Sages have said: He must give at least one ma'ah for a whole offering and two pieces of silver for a peace offering. He who has many of both, of him it is said: *According to the blessing of the Lord thy God which he hath given thee* (Deut. 16: 17).

CHAPTER II

1. Women and bondmen are exempt from the law to *appear before the Lord,* but it is incumbent upon all men excepting him who is deaf, dumb, or imbecile, or a minor, or blind or lame, or unclean or uncircumcised. So, too, the aged and the sick and the tender and the very delicate, who cannot go up to the Temple on their own feet—all of these eleven are exempt. But the command to *appear before the Lord* is incumbent upon all other men.

The deaf, even though he can speak or even though he is deaf in but one ear, is exempt. So, too, he who is blind in but one eye or lame in but one leg is exempt. The dumb, even though he can hear, is exempt. They who are of doubtful sex or of double sex are exempt, since there is a doubt that they may be women. He who is half bondman and half freedman is exempt because of the element of bondage in him.

And whence do we know that all these are exempt from the law to *appear before the Lord?* It is said: *All thy males shall appear* (Exod. 23: 17), thus excluding women. And a positive commandment not binding on women is not binding on bondmen. Again it is said: *When all Israel is come to appear before the Lord thy God in the place which he shall choose* (Deut. 31: 11), thus excluding bondmen. And it is said: *When all Israel is come to*

appear; as they come to be seen before the Lord, so do they come
to see the splendor of His sanctuary and the place of His Shekinah,
thus excluding the blind who does not see, even though but
one eye be blind, since his seeing would not be complete. And it is
said there, *That they may hear* (Deut. 31: 12), thus excluding him
whose hearing is not complete; *and that they may learn,* thus excluding him who cannot speak, for everyone commanded to learn
is also commanded to teach. And it is said: *When thou goest up to
appear before the face of the Lord* (Exod. 24: 34); he must be one
who is able to go up on his own feet, thus excluding the lame and
the sick and the aged and the delicate. And we have already explained, in Laws Concerning Entering into the Temple, that the
unclean is unfit to enter. So, too, the uncircumcised is repellent,
like one who is unclean.

2. A scavenger, namely, one whose work it is to collect the dung
of dogs or the like to tan hides or as a medicine, or one who smelts
copper in his quarry, and tanners—although these are repellent by
reason of their labor, they may make clean their person and their
raiment and go up with the general company of Israelites *to appear
before the Lord.*

3. If a child can hold his father's hand and go up from Jerusalem
to the Temple Mount, it is incumbent upon his father to take him
up and *to appear before the Lord* with him to initiate him in the
commandments, for it is said: *All thy males shall appear* (Exod.
23: 17). And if the child was lame or blind or deaf, even in but one
of his legs or eyes or ears, it is not incumbent upon his father to
initiate him even though he was likely to be cured, since if he had
been of age and in like case he would have been exempt, as we have
stated.

4. All who are obliged to bring the pilgrimage offering are
obliged also to bring the festal offering, and all who are exempt
from bringing the pilgrimage offering are exempt also from bringing the festal offering. And all are obliged to bring the peace offering of rejoicing, except the deaf, the imbecile, those under age, the

uncircumcised, and the unclean: the deaf, the imbecile, and those under age, because they are not duty bound they are exempt from all the commandments laid down in the Law; and the uncircumcised and the unclean are exempt because they cannot eat of Hallowed Things and are unfit to enter into the Temple, as we have explained in Laws Concerning Entering into the Temple and in Laws Concerning the Manner of Making Offerings.

5. If any man was lame or blind on the first day and was healed on the second, he is exempt from bringing the pilgrimage offering and the festal offering because on the day when the obligation fell upon him he was exempt, since all other days of the feast are but supplementary to the first, as we have stated. So, too, if a man became unclean in the night of the first festival day, although he became clean on the morrow, he is exempt. But if he became unclean on the first day, he is still obliged to bring his festal offering and his pilgrimage offering during the other days of the feast when he is become clean.

6. If a man came to the Temple Court during the days of the feast, he is not obliged to bring with him a whole offering each time he enters, for though it is said: *They shall not appear before my face empty* (Exod. 23:17), this applies only to the essential time of the feast, which is the first day, or to a time supplementary to the first. But if he did bring yet another offering, it is accepted of him each time he brings one and offered under the name of a pilgrimage whole offering, since the pilgrimage offering has no prescribed limits.

7. If a man set apart ten cattle as his festal offering and on the first day offered only some of them and then interrupted his offering, he may not come again and offer the rest, since he had left them over as a remainder; but if he had not himself interrupted his offering but the time of day pressed upon him and he was not able to offer them on that day, he may offer the rest on the morrow.

8. The pilgrimage whole offering may be brought only from cattle bought with money which was not yet hallowed, as is the

rule for other obligatory offerings. But the festal peace offering may be brought from what was bought out of second-tithe money which was mingled with money which was not hallowed. From the money so mingled he may buy a beast and offer it as a festal peace offering, provided that the prescribed measure for the first meal be from money which was not hallowed, since the festal peace offering is an obligatory offering, and no obligatory offering may be brought from what was already hallowed.

9. A man may fulfill his obligation respecting the festal peace offering with tithe of cattle; but he may not offer it on a festival day—a precautionary rule lest he take tithe of cattle on a festival day.

10. (Lay) Israelites may fulfill their obligation as regards the peace offering of rejoicing with vow offerings and freewill offerings or with tithe of cattle; and priests may fulfill them with a sin offering or a guilt offering or a firstling or with breast and shoulder; for this commandment requires that they rejoice by eating flesh before the Lord; and thus, indeed, they eat flesh.

But they may not fulfill their obligation with bird offerings or meal offerings, which are not flesh which promotes rejoicing.

We have already stated in Laws Concerning Passover Offerings that the festal offering of the fourteenth is not an obligatory offering; therefore none can fulfill therewith his obligation as regards the obligatory festal offering, but he can fulfill therewith his obligation as regards the peace offering of rejoicing.

11. If a man had a vow offering or a freewill peace offering and he slaughtered it on the eve of a festival day, although he ate it on the festival day, he does not therewith fulfill his obligation as regards the festal offering, which can be offered only from beasts which were not already hallowed; but he may fulfill therewith his obligation as regards the peace offering of rejoicing.

12. Although he slaughtered it before the feast, yet inasmuch as he ate it during the feast he has fulfilled his obligation, because

he need not slaughter the peace offering of rejoicing at the very hour of his rejoicing.

13. A thank offering may not be brought on the fourteenth day owing to the leaven therein, since Hallowed Things may not be so treated as to render them invalid. But if a man brought it he fulfills therewith his obligation as regards the peace offering of rejoicing, as we have explained.

14. If a man said, "I pledge myself to a thank offering wherewith I shall fulfill my obligation as regards the festal offering," he is obliged to bring a thank offering, but he does not therewith fulfill his obligation as regards the festal offering, since the festal offering may be brought only from what was not already hallowed.

When a man sacrifices a festal peace offering or a peace offering of rejoicing he should not eat of it with his children and his wife alone and think that he thus fulfills his entire duty; but it is incumbent upon him to give joy to the poor and the unfortunate, for it is said: *And the Levite, and the stranger, and the fatherless, and the widow* (Deut. 16:14). In proportion to his riches he should suffer them all to eat and to drink.

And if a man ate his sacrifices and did not suffer these also to rejoice with him, of him it is said: *Their sacrifices shall be unto them as the bread of mourners, all that eat thereof shall become unclean, for their bread shall be for their appetite* (Hos. 9:4).

The duty toward the Levite surpasses all, since he has neither portion nor possession, nor has he any dues from the flesh of the offerings. Therefore a man must needs invite Levites to his table and give them cause to rejoice. Or he should give them gifts of flesh, together with their tithes, that they may find therein enough for their needs. But he who forsakes the Levite and gives him no cause to rejoice or is dilatory in paying him his tithes at the feast transgresses a negative commandment, for it is said: *Take heed to thyself that thou forsake not the Levite* (Deut. 12:19).

CHAPTER III

1. It is a positive commandment to assemble all Israelites, men, women, and children, after the close of every year of release when they go up to make the pilgrimage, and in their hearing to read chapters from the Law which shall keep them diligent in the commandments and strengthen them in the true religion, for it is said: *At the end of every seven years, in the set time of the year of release, in the feast of Tabernacles, when all Israel is come to appear . . . assemble the people, the men and the women and the little ones, and thy stranger that is within thy gates . . .* (Deut. 31: 10 ff.).

2. Whosoever is exempt from the law to *appear before the Lord* is exempt from the law *Assemble the people,* except women and children and the uncircumcised. But he who is unclean is exempt from the law *Assemble the people,* for it is said: *When all Israel is come to appear,* and such a one is unfit to *come to appear.* And it is obvious that it is incumbent upon those of doubtful or double sex, since it is incumbent upon women.

3. When do they read? At the close of the first festival day of the Feast of Tabernacles, which is the beginning of the mid-festival days of the feast in the eighth year.

It is the king who reads in their hearing; and the reading used to be in the Court of the Women. He may read sitting, but if he reads standing this is deemed praiseworthy.

Where does he read? From the beginning of the Book of Deuteronomy, *These are the words* . . . to the end of the section *Hear, O Israel* . . . (Deut. 6: 4); and he resumes at *And it shall come to pass if ye shall hearken* . . . (Deut. 11: 13), and thence begins again at *Thou shalt surely tithe* . . . (Deut. 14: 22 ff.), reading from *And thou shalt surely tithe* in due order until the end of the Blessings and the Cursings (Deut. 27: 15–28: 69) as far as *beside the covenant which he made with them in Horeb.* And there he breaks off.

4. How does he read? Trumpets are blown throughout all Jerusalem to assemble the people and a high pulpit which was made of wood is brought and set up in the midst of the Court of the Women. The king goes up and sits thereon so that they may hear his reading and all Israel who go up to keep the feast gather round him. The minister of the synagogue takes a scroll of the Law and gives it to the chief of the synagogue, and the chief of the synagogue gives it to the prefect, and the prefect to the High Priest and the High Priest to the king, to do him honor through the service of many men. The king receives it standing, but if he pleases he may sit. He opens it and looks in it and recites a benediction in the way which all do who read the Law in the synagogue. He reads the chapters which we have cited until he comes to the end, when he rolls up the scroll and recites a benediction after it in the way it is recited in synagogues.

He adds seven benedictions, and these are they:

"Look favorably, O Lord our God, upon thy people Israel . . ."; "We give thanks to thee . . ."; "Thou hast chosen us from among all nations . . ." as far as "who sanctifiest Israel and the appointed seasons"; and he recites them in the way the benedictions are recited in the *tĕfillah*. These three benedictions are in accordance with their established form.

In the fourth he prays for the Temple that it may endure, concluding it with "Blessed art thou, O Lord, who dwellest in Zion."

In the fifth he prays for Israel that its kingdom may endure, concluding it with "Blessed art thou, O Lord, who hast made choice of Israel."

In the sixth he prays for the priests, that God may accept their ministration, concluding it with "Blessed art thou, O Lord, who sanctifiest the priests."

In the seventh he offers supplication and prayer, according as he is able, concluding it with "O Lord, save thy people Israel, for thy people are in need of salvation: blessed art thou, O Lord, who hearest prayer."

5. The reading of the Law and the benedictions must be in the Holy Language, as it is said: *Thou shalt read this law* (Deut.

31:11)—in its very language, even though foreign tongues are spoken there.

6. As for proselytes who do not know the Law, they must make ready their heart and give ear with their ears to hearken in awe and reverence and trembling joy, as on the day when the Law was given on Sinai. Even great scholars who know the entire Law must listen with utmost attention. Even if there is any who cannot hear, he should keep his heart intent on this reading, for Scripture has ordained it solely for the strengthening of true religion; and a man should so regard himself as though the Law was now laid upon him for the first time and as though he now heard it from the mouth of the Lord, for the king is an ambassador to proclaim the words of God.

7. If the day of assembly fell on the Sabbath, it is put off until after the Sabbath because of the trumpet blowing and the supplications which do not override the Sabbath.

TREATISE III

LAWS CONCERNING FIRSTLINGS

Involving Five Commandments

Two Positive and Three Negative

To Wit

1. To set apart firstlings;
2. That no unblemished firstling be consumed outside of Jerusalem;
3. That a firstling may not be redeemed;
4. To set apart tithe of cattle;
5. That tithe of cattle may not be redeemed.

And I have included tithe of cattle with firstlings since the procedure for them both is the same, and Scripture has included them both together, for it is said: *And their blood shalt thou toss* (Num. 18: 17). From oral tradition it is learned that this refers to the blood of the tithe and the blood of the firstling.

An exposition of these commandments
is contained in the following chapters.

NOTE

In the list of the 613 commandments prefixed to the Code, those which deal with the subject of this Treatise are cited in the following form.

Positive commandments:

[4] 78. To give tithe of the cattle, as it is said: *And all the tithe of the herd or the flock, whatsoever passeth under the rod, the tenth shall be holy unto the Lord* (Lev. 27: 32);

[1] 79. To sanctify the first-born of clean cattle and bring it as an offering, as it is said: *All the firstling males that are born of thy herd and of thy flock thou shalt sanctify unto the Lord thy God* (Deut. 15: 19).

Negative commandments:

[3] 108. That the first-born of clean cattle may not be redeemed, as it is said: *But the firstling of an ox, or the firstling of a sheep, or the firstling of a goat, thou shalt not redeem* (Num. 18: 17);

[5] 109. That the tithe of cattle may not be redeemed, as it is said: *It shall not be redeemed* (Lev. 27: 33);

[2] 144. That an unblemished firstling may not be consumed outside of Jerusalem, as it is said: *Thou mayest not eat within thy gates . . . the firstlings of thy herd or of thy flock . . . but thou shalt eat them before the Lord thy God* (Deut. 12: 17-18).

CHAPTER I

1. It is a positive commandment to set apart all males which open the womb, whether among men or among clean cattle or among any kind of ass, whether they are unblemished or whether they are ṭĕrefah, for it is said: *Sanctify unto me all the first-born, whatsoever openeth the womb among the children of Israel, both of man and of beast* (Exod. 13:2). And these must all be given to the priests.

2. The first-born of man and the first-born of an ass must be redeemed, and their redemption price falls to the priests. The first-born of clean cattle must be slaughtered in the Temple Court, like other Lesser Hallowed Things, its blood tossed, and its sacrificial portions burned—as we have explained in Laws Concerning the Manner of Making Offerings—and the rest of the flesh is to be consumed by the priests, for it is said: *Howbeit the first-born of man shalt thou surely redeem . . . But the firstling of an ox thou shalt not redeem; they are holy . . . and the flesh of them shall be thine* (Num. 18:15-18).

3. If the firstling of a clean beast was blemished, whether it was born blemished or whether a blemish befell it after it had been unblemished, it must be given to the priest; if he pleases he may eat it anywhere or sell it or give it as food to whom he will, even to a Gentile, since it is profane, for it is said: *And if there be any blemish therein, lameness or blindness . . . the unclean and the clean may eat it alike, as the gazelle and as the hart* (Deut. 15:21-22). It is the property of the priest.

4. It is a man's duty to sanctify the firstling of a clean beast and for him to say, "This is holy!" for it is said: *Thou shalt sanctify it unto the Lord thy God* (Deut. 14:10). Even if he does not sanctify it, it is sanctified of itself, and its sanctity is from the womb.

5. The commandment respecting the firstling of a clean beast is binding both within the Land (of Israel) and outside the Land;

but firstlings may not be brought into the Land from outside the Land, for it is said: *And thou shalt eat before the Lord thy God . . . the tithe of thy corn, of thy wine and of thine oil, and the firstling of thy herd and of thy flock* (Deut. 14:23), implying that from any place whence tithe of corn may be brought, firstling of herd and of flock may be brought; and from any place whence no tithe of corn may be brought, no firstling of herd or of flock may be brought, for such counts as profane and may be eaten after it incurs a blemish. If a man brings it, it may not be accepted from him or treated as an offering, but he may eat it after it incurs a blemish.

6. This commandment is binding whether the Temple is in existence or whether the Temple is not in existence, as is also the law respecting tithe of corn; but it is not binding upon dedicated beasts so long as they continue in their sanctity, being yet unredeemed, whether they were dedicated to the altar or dedicated to the Temple treasury.

7. Priests, Levites, and (lay) Israelites are all bound by the law of the firstling of a clean beast. Although a firstling belongs to the priest, if a firstling was born to him from his own beast, he must offer its blood and its sacrificial portions, as we have explained, and eat the rest of its flesh after the manner of a firstling, for it is said: *All the firstling males that are born of thy herd and of thy flock* (Deut. 15:19). But priests and Levites are exempt from the laws of the first-born of man and the firstling of an unclean beast, as we have stated in Laws Concerning Priestly Dues.

8. A firstling must be eaten during its first year whether it be unblemished or blemished, for it is said: *Thou shalt eat it before the Lord thy God year by year . . . and if there be any blemish therein . . . thou shalt eat it within thy gates* (Deut. 15:20-22).
From what time is its year reckoned? If it was unblemished, its year is reckoned from the eighth day, when it became suitable for offering; and if it was born blemished, its year is reckoned from the day when it was born, provided that all its months of gestation

were complete, for it was suitable for eating from the day when it was born. But if it was not known of a certainty that its months were complete, its year is reckoned from the eighth day.

9. If a blemish arose in it during its first year, it may be kept alive the whole twelve months. If a blemish arose in it toward the end of its first year, it is permissible to keep it alive for thirty days from the time when the blemish arose, even though it is withheld until after its first year. Thus, for example, if a blemish arose in it on the fifteenth day before the end of its first year, it is allowed to complete the remaining fifteen days after its first year. If the blemish arose in it after its first year, it is permissible to keep it alive only for thirty days, when it must be eaten.

10. In these days a firstling is left until a blemish befalls it, and then it must be eaten.

11. So long as there has not seemed due cause to show it to a sage, it may be kept alive for two years or three; but after there has seemed cause to show it to a sage, if the blemish arose in it during its first year, it may be kept alive the whole twelve months; if it arose after its first year, it may be kept alive only another thirty days.

12. The year of the firstling is a complete lunar year, twelve months from day to day; but if the year was intercalated the firstling has the benefit of the intercalated month and thirteen months are assigned to it. If two lambs were born, one on the fifteenth day of First Adar and one on the first day of Second Adar, as for the one born on the first day of Second Adar, so soon as the first of Adar arrives the following year, its year expires and as for the one born in the middle of First Adar, its year does not expire until the middle of Adar in the following year: inasmuch as it was born when a month was intercalated, this month also is assigned to it.

13. If a man transgressed and withheld the firstling until after its first year, although he transgresses a negative commandment,

the firstling does not become invalid if it was unblemished but it may still be offered. If it was blemished it may be slaughtered anywhere. For it is said: *the tithe of thy corn, of thy wine and of thine oil, and the firstling of thy herd and of thy flock* (Deut. 14:23), making a firstling comparable with tithe: as tithe does not become invalid from one year to another, so a firstling does not become invalid from one year to another.

14. A firstling should not be given to the priest so soon as it is born, for this would be no honor to the priest; but its owner should tend it until it is partly grown and then give it to the priest. For how long is an Israelite bound to tend it? Thirty days if it was from small cattle, and fifty days if it was from large cattle. If the priest said to him, "Give it to me within such a time: I will tend it for myself," he has not the right to give it to him, since the priest would count as one who gave help for the sake of his priestly dues; and we have already explained in Laws Concerning Heave Offerings that priests who give help at the threshing floors or in the slaughterhouses or among the shepherds may not be given their priestly dues as their hire.

15. If the firstling was blemished and the priest said to him within this period, "Give it to me that I may eat it now," or if it was unblemished and he said to him within this period, "Give it to me that I may offer it now," then he may give it to him. And it seems to me that a man may give the firstling to any priest he pleases.

16. If a priest ate an olive's bulk of an unblemished firstling outside Jerusalem he incurs punishment by scourging, on the authority of Scripture, for it is said: *Thou mayest not eat within thy gates the tithe of thy corn, or of thy wine, or of thy oil, or of the firstlings of thy herd or of thy flock* (Deut. 12:17). So, too, if a nonpriest ate an olive's bulk of a firstling, whether before its blood was tossed or after it was tossed, he is to be scourged. It is learned from oral tradition that this prohibition applies also to a nonpriest

who ate of a firstling, whether before its blood was tossed or after its blood was tossed.

17. A firstling may not be redeemed, for it is said: *But the firstling of an ox, or the firstling of a sheep, or the firstling of a goat, thou shalt not redeem* (Num. 18: 17). So, too, it may not be sold if it was unblemished, for so soon as it stands in readiness to be offered the priest has no right over it to sell it. But in these days when there is no Temple, inasmuch as it stands in readiness only to be eaten, it is permissible to sell it either to a priest or to a (lay) Israelite even though it was unblemished.

18. If a firstling is blemished the priest may sell it at all times, whether the Temple is in existence or whether the Temple is not in existence, whether the firstling is alive or whether it is slaughtered. And when he sells the flesh of a firstling which is blemished he should sell it at home and not in the market, as we have explained in Laws Concerning Things Forbidden for the Altar. But flesh of an unblemished firstling may not be sold, since it is consecrated flesh.

And priests who are enrolled as sharers in a firstling may weigh out portion for portion.

19. When a man flays a blemished firstling it is permissible to flay it in any manner he pleases: if he would begin at the feet he may begin at the feet. So, too, with other Hallowed Things which become disqualified: if he would flay them from the feet, he may do so.

CHAPTER II

1. If any of the abiding blemishes which render Hallowed Things invalid and for which they must be redeemed befell a firstling, it may be slaughtered anywhere on account of them. And we have already explained in Laws Concerning Things Forbidden for the Altar that, of these blemishes, those which are such as may arise in a male are sixty-seven.

2. And as for any of those things which we have there enumerated which detract from an offering's fitness, and because of which Hallowed Things may not be offered, yet neither may they be redeemed, a firstling, likewise, may not be slaughtered on account of them, nor may it be offered, but it must remain until an abiding blemish arises in it. So, too, if a passing blemish arose in a firstling, it may not be slaughtered in any place, nor may it be offered, but it must be left to pasture until an abiding blemish befalls it for which it may be slaughtered.

3. So, too, if it had suffered unnatural crime, or if it had killed a man according to the evidence of a single witness or according to its owner's word, or if it had been set apart for idolatry or had been worshiped, it must be left to pasture until some blemish befalls it, as we have explained in Laws Concerning Things Forbidden for the Altar.

4. If a firstling came forth from the side and another was born after it, neither of them is deemed a firstling: the first because it was not one which *openeth the womb,* and the second because another came before it. Even though it was a female which came from the side and a male by way of the womb, this is not deemed a firstling.

5. If a firstling was of double sex no sanctity at all attaches to it; it counts as a female to which the priest has not any claim. It may be used for labor and it may be shorn like other beasts which are not hallowed.

If what was born was of doubtful sex, it counts as a firstling which is in doubt and it may be eaten by its owner when it has incurred a blemish, whether it stales by way of the male organ or by way of the female organ.

6. If a sheep bore young the like of a goat or if a goat bore young the like of a sheep, it is exempt from the law of the firstling, for it is said: *But the firstling of an ox* (Num. 18:17): it counts as a valid firstling only if the dam was an ox and its firstling an ox. If it had only few of the marks of its dam it still counts as a firstling,

yet as one which suffers an abiding blemish, for there is no blemish greater than a change of its natural form. Even if a heifer bore the like of an ass, yet it had some of the marks of a heifer, it counts as a firstling which belongs to the priest, since the law of the firstling applies to the like of the ass. But if it bore young the like of a horse or a camel, even if it had some of the marks of a heifer, it counts as a firstling which is in doubt. Hence it may be eaten by its owner. But if a priest seized it none may take it out of his hand.

7. If a man inflicted a blemish upon a firstling, inasmuch as he has committed a transgression he must suffer penalty; and it may not be slaughtered on account of the blemish, but only after some other blemish has befallen it by natural means. But if this sinner died, his son may slaughter it on account of the blemish which his father imparted, for no penalty is imposed upon his son after him.

8. If a man brought it to pass that a blemish befell a firstling—if, for example, he applied a cake of dates to its ear so that a dog came and took it and bit off its ear; or if he drove it among pieces of iron or masses of glass so that its foot might be severed, and it was severed; or if he bid a Gentile inflict some blemish on it—for such a blemish it may not be slaughtered. This is the general rule: if any blemish happened with his consent, it is forbidden for him to slaughter it because of that blemish; but if it happened without his consent, because of that blemish it may be slaughtered.

9. If he said, "Should any blemish befall this firstling I will slaughter it," and a Gentile heard and inflicted a blemish on it, he may slaughter it because of that blemish, since it did not come about with his consent.

10. If we saw a man do something which would bring it to pass that a blemish would be inflicted on a firstling, and a blemish befell it, yet we do not know whether or not he intended this blemish, he may not slaughter it because of that blemish. Thus, for example, if he gave it barley in a narrow place hedged about with thorns and when it ate its lip was slit, even if he was an "associate"

he may not slaughter it because of that blemish. And the same applies in every like case.

11. If a firstling ran after a man and he kicked it to repel it, or even if he kicked it because it had run after him before, and through this kick a blemish happened to it, it may be slaughtered because of that blemish.

12. If children in play inflicted a blemish on a firstling or if a Gentile did so wittingly, it may be slaughtered because of that blemish; but if they did so to make it permissible for slaughtering, it may not be slaughtered because of that blemish.

13. If a firstling suffered from a congestion of blood, it may be bled provided that there was no intention thereby to impart a blemish to it; and if a blemish was made in it by this bloodletting, it may be slaughtered because of that blemish.

14. It is permissible to inflict a blemish on a firstling before it comes forth into the world, and it may be slaughtered because of that blemish. This applies to these days when the Temple is not in existence, because it is the end in view that the firstling shall be eaten after it incurs a blemish; but at a time when the Temple is in existence it is forbidden.

15. If a witness testified from the mouth of another witness that a certain blemish happened by accident he may be believed. Even a woman may be believed if she says, "In my presence such a blemish happened of itself"; and it may be slaughtered because of that blemish.

16. As for any blemishes which are likely to have come about at man's hand, the shepherd may be believed if he says, "They happened of themselves and were not done of set purpose"; and it may be slaughtered because of such a blemish. This applies if the shepherd was a (lay) Israelite and the firstling was in the possession of a priest; but if the shepherd was a priest and the firstling was still in the possession of its owner, a (lay) Israelite, he may not

be believed, and he is under suspicion lest he inflicted a blemish on it so that it could be given to him.

17. If a priest testified for another priest that such a blemish befell of itself, he may be believed; and it need not be supposed that they were acting to their mutual advantage. For all priests are under suspicion of inflicting a blemish on firstlings so that they may eat them outside; therefore they may not be believed on their own word. But his fellow may testify for him, since one man does not commit sin for another's sake. Even a priest's sons or the members of his household may testify for him concerning a firstling; but not his wife, since she counts as his own self.

18. If a firstling was in a priest's possession and a blemish befell it, and a witness testified that this blemish befell of itself, and we do not know whether or not this was a blemish for which the firstling may be slaughtered, and the priest in whose possession it was came and said, "I have shown this blemish to one who is skilled and he permits it for slaughtering," he may be believed; and there need be no scruple lest he had not shown it or lest it was an unblemished firstling. For the priests are not under suspicion of slaughtering Hallowed Things outside the Temple since that is an offense punishable by extirpation, as we have explained.

19. So, too, a priest may be believed if he says of a blemished firstling, "This firstling was given to me by a (lay) Israelite when it was already blemished, and the blemish did not befall it while in my possession"; and there need be [no] scruple about him that, perchance, he himself inflicted it, since the matter is prone to come to light and he is in fear lest its owner be asked and he say, "It was unblemished when we gave it to him."

CHAPTER III

1. A firstling may be slaughtered only at the bidding of one who is skilled to whom the Patriarch in the Land of Israel has

granted authority and said, "Do thou give permission for the slaughtering of firstlings when they are blemished." Even if there was a great blemish and manifest to all, none save one who is skilled and who has received authority may declare the firstling permissible for slaughtering. (Such) a person may inspect any firstlings except his own firstlings.

2. If there was none who was skilled and the blemish was among the more manifest and conspicuous blemishes—if, for example, its eye was blind or its paw severed or its leg broken—it may be slaughtered on the authority of three members of the community. So, too, if a firstling went outside the Land and a conspicuous blemish befell it, it is permissible to slaughter it on the authority of three members of the community.

3. None may inspect the firstling of a (lay) Israelite unless a priest be with him, lest he who was skilled should say, "It is a blemish and it is permissible to slaughter it on that account," and the Israelite should go and slaughter it for himself and not give it to a priest. For although he is not under suspicion of eating Hallowed Things outside Jerusalem, he is under suspicion of robbing priests of their dues. Therefore if the man was a scholar and known to be strict with himself, one who was skilled may inspect his firstling. If the blemish was manifest to all—if, for example, its paw was severed, or its leg—inasmuch as he had brought it to one who was learned and skilled he is presumed to be strict with himself; therefore one who was skilled may inspect his firstling even though there was no priest with him.

4. If a man slaughtered a firstling and then revealed its blemish, even though it was a manifest blemish which would not be changed by the slaughtering—if, for example, its paw was severed, or its leg —inasmuch as it was not slaughtered on the authority of one who was skilled, it is forbidden; and it should be buried, like a firstling which has died.

5. If a firstling had one testicle but two pouches and a skilled person examined it and set it on its buttocks and squeezed, and

the second testicle did not come forth, and the skilled person declared it permitted, but when it was slaughtered the second testicle was found cleaving to the groin, it remains permitted, since it had been squeezed. But if it had not been squeezed, even though it was slaughtered on the authority of one who was skilled, it must be buried.

6. If a man was not skilled and he inspected a firstling and it was slaughtered on his authority, it must be buried and he must make restitution from his own property. And how much does he pay? A quarter of the value for small cattle, and a half for large cattle. And why does he not pay the whole of its value? A penalty is imposed on the owner of the beast so that thereafter he will not hold it back or rear small cattle in the Land of Israel.

7. If a man takes payment for inspecting firstlings no beast may be slaughtered on his authority, unless he was one who was most highly skilled, and the Sages, knowing him to be without equal, had stipulated that a fee be given him for the inspection and the examination, whether a blemish was found or whether no blemish was found. But he may take a fee for any beast only once and must go on inspecting it as often as it is brought to him, so that he shall not fall under suspicion.

8. If a man was under suspicion respecting firstlings, namely, of selling them as beasts which were profane, none may buy from him even flesh of gazelles, since this is like calf's flesh; and none may buy from him untanned hides, even of a female beast, lest he cut away the male organ and say, "It is female"; and none may buy wool from him, even such as is bleached and, needless to say, such as is still dirtied. But what is spun or felted stuff or tanned hides may be bought of him, for he would not tan the hide of an unblemished firstling, since he would fear to keep it in his possession lest the judges hear and punish him according to his wickedness.

9. If a man slaughtered a firstling and sold it, and it became known that he had not shown it to one who was skilled, what has been eaten has been eaten, but he must give them back its

price; and what is not eaten must be buried and he must give them back its price. Such also is the rule if a man gives ṭĕrefah for food, as will be explained in Laws Concerning Buying and Selling.

10. Concerning a firstling found to be ṭĕrefah: if it was un-blemished and found to be ṭĕrefah after its hide was flayed, the hide must be burned—as we have explained in Laws Concerning Hallowed Things Which Become Invalid—and the flesh must be buried; but if it had been slaughtered after it had become blemished, the flesh must be buried but the priests may make gainful use of its hide, provided that it was slaughtered on the authority of one who was skilled.

11. If a firstling's flesh was eaten in lawful manner, whether it was unblemished or blemished, just as gainful use may be made of its hide, so gainful use may be made of its fleece; but any wool shorn from it while it was alive, even if it fell off of itself, may not be put to gainful use—even if it fell off after a blemish befell it, or even after it was slaughtered, or, needless to say, after its death—since that wool which fell from it during life continues to be a thing forbidden. And the same applies to tithe of cattle.

We have already explained in Laws Concerning Sacrilege that this decree has been ordained only respecting firstlings and tithe because these are not offered as an atoning sacrifice, and it may be that a man will let them remain with him in order to take the wool which falls from them. And we have already stated that it is a duty to eat the firstling within its first year, whether it is un-blemished or blemished.

12. If some of a firstling's wool dangled loose and it was slaughtered, such wool as is manifestly part of the fleece is per-mitted for gainful use; and such as is not manifestly part of the fleece, namely, wool whose root is upturned, is forbidden, since it counts as wool which fell off while the firstling was alive.

13. If the fleece of a firstling—even if the firstling was blemished —was confused with the fleeces of beasts which were profane, though it be one in many thousands, all are forbidden. For this

is a thing of import and conveys its sanctity however small its quantity. If a man wove a half-span of firstling's wool into a garment, the garment must be burned. If anything from the wool of Hallowed Things be woven into a garment, it conveys its sanctity however small its quantity.

CHAPTER IV

1. A beast belonging to joint owners is subject to the law of the firstling. The words *of thy herd and of thy flock* (Deut. 15: 19) exclude only what is owned jointly with a Gentile, so that if he was the joint owner of a heifer or of unborn young, even though the Gentile had but a thousandth share in the dam or in the offspring, it is exempt from the law of the firstling. If the Gentile owned a single member in either of them—for example, a foreleg or a hindleg—inspection is made of it: if it was something which, if cut off, would cause a blemish, it is exempt, and if the member owned by the Gentile could be cut off without the beast becoming invalid, it is subject to the law of the firstling.

2. If a man bought the unborn young of a heifer owned by a Gentile, or sold the unborn young of his heifer to a Gentile, even though he had not the right, it is exempt from the law of the firstling, nor does he incur any penalty for this.

3. If a man received a beast from a Gentile to the end that he should tend it and that the offspring should be shared between them, or if a Gentile received a beast from an Israelite on like terms—in either case the beast is exempt from the law of the firstling, for it is said: *Whatsoever openeth the womb among the children of Israel* (Exod. 13: 2): the law applies only if the Israelite is the sole owner.

4. If a man received a flock from a Gentile for a fixed sum and stipulated with him that any gain should be shared between them but that if loss was incurred the loss should fall on the Israelite, even though the beasts are in the Israelite's control and they count

as his possession, yet inasmuch as the Gentile, if he found with the Israelite no other money from which to collect his dues, could collect them from these beasts and their offspring, he is become as one who has a lien upon them and their offspring. Thus the hand of the Gentile still rests upon them and they and their offspring are exempt from the law of the firstling. But their offspring's offspring are not exempt since they belong to the Israelite and the Gentile has no control over them.

5. If an Israelite paid money to a Gentile and thereby acquired a beast from the Gentile according to Gentile laws of purchase, even though he did not draw it to himself, he has effectively acquired it and it is subject to the law of the firstling. So, too, if a Gentile acquired it from an Israelite according to Gentile laws of purchase and paid him money, even though he did not draw it to himself, he has effectively acquired it and it is exempt from the law of the firstling.

6. If a man became a proselyte and it was not known whether his heifer gave birth before he became a proselyte or after he became a proselyte, the offspring counts as a firstling because of the doubt.

7. If a man bought a beast from a Gentile and it was not known whether it had borne a firstling or not, and it gave birth while in his possession, this counts as a doubtful firstling and it may be eaten by its owner after it incurs a blemish: the priest has no claim to it, since on him who would exact aught from his fellow lies the burden of proof.

8. If he bought from a Gentile a beast which was giving suck, he need not scruple lest it be suckling the young of another beast, but the presumption is that it had itself borne it; and even if its suckling was like some other species, even like a species of pig, it is exempt from the law of the firstling. So, too, the offspring of a beast which was in milk is exempt from the law of the firstling, since the greater number of beasts are not in milk unless they have already given birth.

9. If a man bought a beast from an Israelite it can be presumed to have borne a firstling unless the seller informed him that it had not yet given birth, for an Israelite would not keep silence and cause him to eat Hallowed Things outside Jerusalem: it is doubtless that it had already borne a firstling and therefore he sold it without comment.

10. If a sheep or a goat cast an embryo whose form was not yet fully manifest or recognizable by all—and this is what is called *ṭinof,* "womb discharge"—and the shepherds said, "It is an embryo but its shape is spoiled," it becomes exempt from the law of the firstling; but the embryo must needs be shown to a shepherd who is a scholar. Therefore if a man bought a beast from a Gentile, even if it was still young, and it gave birth while in his possession during its first year, this counts as a doubtful firstling, from fear lest it had cast a womb discharge while in the control of the Gentile.

So, too, with large cattle which cast an afterbirth; for this is a token of offspring, since there can be no afterbirth without offspring, and it is exempt from the law of the firstling. It is permissible to throw that afterbirth to the dogs, for only a recognizable male can be deemed hallowed by virtue of the law of the firstling. And the presumption is that half of whatever beasts are born are males and half females; and we have already explained that if a male does not bear some of the marks of its dam, it is not deemed hallowed by virtue of the law of the firstling. Thus only the lesser part among what are born are to be deemed hallowed by virtue of the law of the firstling; and none need have scruples respecting the lesser part.

11. But if a beast which was hallowed cast an afterbirth, this must be buried, since male and female offspring alike are hallowed.

12. If large cattle cast a clot of blood they are thereafter exempt from the law of the firstling, since the presumption is that there was offspring therein and that the blood exceeded it in quantity and destroyed it and made it of no account. And this must be buried as the abortion of a beast bearing its first young, even though this clot is not deemed to be hallowed. And why should it be buried?

To proclaim the fact that it was exempt from the law of the first-ling.

We have already explained in treating of the menstruant that in human kind offspring is full-fashioned after forty days, and an abortion of less than forty days' growth is not accounted "off-spring." But for offspring of cattle the Sages have not specified the number of days in which it is fashioned; yet they have said that if a beast casts a womb discharge it does not thereafter grow pregnant or receive other offspring in less than thirty days.

13. If a beast went out "full" and came back "empty" what is born afterward counts as a firstling because of the doubt, from fear lest the beast may have cast something which did not exempt it from the law of the firstling. The term "to open the womb" does not apply to abortions of beasts unless the head was already rounded like a coil of woof thread.

14. If a beast which had not before borne young was in hard travail, a limb of the unborn offspring may be cut off and this may be thrown to the dogs, and what comes afterward counts as a first-ling. If the greater part emerged, this should be buried, and the beast is exempt from the law of the firstling. If one limb was cut off and laid down and then another cut off and laid down, until these made up the greater part of it, all the members must be buried, and the beast is exempt from the law of the firstling. So soon as the greater part is come forth, whether whole or cut up, and lies before us, it acquires sanctity retroactively.

15. If a third part emerged and it was sold to a Gentile, and again another third emerged, it acquires sanctity retroactively, and the dam is exempt from the law of the firstling.

If a third part emerged from the side and two thirds by the womb, it is not accounted hallowed, since the greater part which first emerged was not by way of the womb; but it acquires sanctity retroactively.

16. If the lesser part of a greater limb emerged, and what emerged was the greater part of the unborn young, the dam is

exempt from the law of the firstling, and what has emerged must be buried. If half of the unborn young emerged and it was the greater part of a limb which emerged, it remains in doubt whether or not the dam is exempt from the law of the firstling. Therefore what emerges after it is a doubtful firstling.

17. If a firstling was brought forth wrapped around in bast and did not touch the womb, or if it was wrapped around in the after-birth of another beast, or if it emerged wrapped around by its sister, inasmuch as no part of it touched the womb, it counts as a doubtful firstling.

18. If there were two wombs stuck together and a firstling emerged from the one and entered into the other, it is in doubt whether that beast into whose womb the firstling entered is exempt from the law of the firstling in that this had opened the womb, or whether it is not exempt until its own offspring opens the womb.

19. If the sides of the womb mouth were extended and the first-ling emerged, it remains in doubt whether it is contact with the womb that bestows sanctity or its contained space.

20. If the sides of the womb mouth were severed and hung about the firstling's neck, it remains in doubt whether the womb bestows sanctity only when in its proper place or whether it bestows sanctity outside its proper place.

21. If the sides of the womb mouth were razed, it is not holy. If part of it was rent but what remained was more than what was rent, and the firstling emerged by way of the rent, or if what was rent was more than what remained, and it emerged by way of what remained, it counts as a doubtful firstling.

CHAPTER V

1. If a ewe which had not before borne young bore two males, even if their two heads emerged together, it is not possible but that one must have preceded the other. Inasmuch as it is not known

which of them emerged first, the priest takes the leaner one and the second counts as a doubtful firstling. If one of them died, the priest cannot claim anything, for the sanctity of that which is alive is in doubt, and on him who would exact aught from his fellow lies the burden of proof.

So, too, if it bore a male and a female, the sanctity of the male is in doubt: perchance the female emerged first. Therefore the priest cannot claim anything, for on him who would exact aught from his fellow lies the burden of proof.

2. If two ewes which had not before borne young bore two males, these both fall to the priest; if they bore a male and a female, the male falls to the priest; if they bore two males and a female, the priest may take the leaner of the males and the other counts as a doubtful firstling; and if one of them died, the priest cannot claim anything, since this living male is a doubtful firstling, and on him who would exact aught from his fellow lies the burden of proof.

If they bore two females and a male, or two males and two females, then the males count as doubtful firstlings, for we might say, "Perchance the female was born first and afterward the male." Therefore in such case the priest cannot claim anything, since on him who would exact aught from his fellow lies the burden of proof.

If the one had before borne young and the other had not, and they bore two males, one will fall to the owner and the other to the priest, but each of them counts as a doubtful firstling, and the priest takes the leaner. If one of them died, the priest in this case cannot claim anything, for the sanctity of that which is alive is in doubt. So, too, if they bore a male and a female: in this case the priest cannot claim anything, since the male counts as a doubtful firstling.

3. The rule for any doubtful firstling is that it shall pasture until a blemish befalls it, when it may be eaten by its owner; but if a priest seized it, none may take it out of his hand. He may eat it after it incurs a blemish; but it may not be brought as an offering,

since none but what is an undoubted firstling may be brought as an offering, lest what was unhallowed be slaughtered in the Temple Court.

4. If among his flock a man had beasts which had borne young and beasts which had not, and they gave birth when no man was there, and he came and found those which had borne young giving suck to females and those which had not borne young giving suck to males, he need feel no scruple lest the offspring of one dam had come to another dam; but the presumption stands that each dam was suckling her own offspring.

5. If two men put two male beasts into a shepherd's charge, the one a firstling and the other an ordinary beast, and one of them died, the shepherd may lay the other one between them and go his way. Such a one will count as a doubtful firstling and the two of them share it between them, since neither of them recognizes which is his.

6. If a man put a firstling in a householder's charge and the householder left it with an ordinary beast of his own, and one of them died and it is not known which of them, on him who would exact aught from his fellow lies the burden of proof. Such a one will count as a doubtful firstling. Even if a shepherd who was a priest left his firstling in the courtyard of a householder together with an ordinary beast belonging to the householder, and one of them died, on him who would exact aught from his fellow lies the burden of proof; and the other beast may not be removed from the court-yard of the householder except on production of proof, since it was with the consent of the firstling's owner that the householder's ordinary beast was left with it.

7. (Lay) Israelites are not under suspicion respecting firstlings; therefore a (lay) Israelite may be believed when he says, "This is a doubtful firstling," and he may have its blemish inspected and eat it if it is blemished.

8. All dedicated beasts which before they were dedicated suffered a lasting blemish and which have been redeemed are subject to the

law of the firstling; and if before they were dedicated they suffered a passing blemish, or if they were dedicated while unblemished and there afterward arose in them an abiding blemish and they were redeemed, they are exempt from the law of the firstling, for they have not in all respects become profane beasts, since they are forbidden to be shorn or used for labor, as we have explained in Laws Concerning Sacrilege.

9. If a man bought a beast in Jerusalem with second-tithe money, it is subject to the law of the firstling; but if he bought a beast with seventh-year produce, it is not subject to the law of the firstling, for he has not the right to traffic in seventh-year produce, since there is said of it: *For food* (Lev. 25:6); it must be used for food and not for trafficking. And if it were subject to the law of the firstling, he could derive advantage by means of the firstling, since it would cease to come under the law of seventh-year produce.

We have already explained in Laws Concerning Forbidden Foods that it is forbidden to traffic in things forbidden to be eaten. So, too, we have explained about heave offerings—that it is forbidden to traffic in heave offerings. So, too, it is forbidden to traffic in firstlings, although it is permissible to sell them in the manner which we have described.

10. If a man took a firstling for his son's wedding feast or for a pilgrimage offering, and there was no need for it, it is permissible to sell it.

11. No assessment may be made of the value of unblemished firstlings belonging to (lay) Israelites, but assessment may be made of the value of their blemished firstlings. And in these days assessment may even be made of the value of unblemished firstlings belonging to priests, since they stand in readiness to be eaten when they become blemished; and, needless to say, assessment may be made of the value of their blemished firstlings.

CHAPTER VI

1. It is a positive commandment to set apart one out of ten from all clean cattle which are born unto men year by year; but this commandment applies only to herds and to flocks, for it is said: *And all the tithe of the herd or the flock . . . the tenth shall be holy unto the Lord* (Lev. 27: 32).

2. The tithing of cattle is binding upon beasts which have not been dedicated but not upon those which have been dedicated, and it is binding both within the Land and outside the Land, both while the Temple is in existence and while it is not in existence; but the Sages have forbidden the tithing of cattle in these days and enacted that cattle be tithed only while the Temple is in existence— a precautionary rule lest men eat tithe of cattle which is un-blemished and so offend against a prohibition entailing extirpation, namely, by the slaughtering of Hallowed Things outside the Temple. But if a man transgressed and tithed his cattle it would count as valid tithe and could not be eaten until it had incurred a blemish.

3. All are bound to give tithe of cattle: priests, Levites, and (lay) Israelites.

4. The rule for tithe of cattle is that it be slaughtered in the Temple Court, its blood tossed in a single tossing against the altar base, its sacrificial portions burned, and the rest of its flesh eaten by the owner in Jerusalem, as it is with other Lesser Hallowed Things; nothing of it falls to the priests, but all belongs to the owner, as it is with the Passover offering. If it was blemished, whether the blemish befell later or whether it was set apart blemished at the outset, it may be eaten anywhere.

5. It is forbidden to sell tithe of cattle such time as it is unblem-ished, for there is said of it: *It shall not be redeemed* (Lev. 27: 33). It is learned from oral tradition that whereas Scripture says *It shall not be redeemed,* it also implies a prohibition against selling it, meaning that it is not redeemable or saleable at all. And it seems

to me that he who sells tithe does so to no avail, and he who buys it does not acquire anything; therefore he is not to be scourged as neither is he who sells what is dedicated as priestly property, because the buyer does not acquire anything; and he is like him who sells *a beautiful woman* (Deut. 21:11), as will be explained in its proper place.

6. On the authority of the Scribes it is forbidden to sell it even when it is blemished, or even when it is slaughtered—a precautionary rule lest anyone sell it alive. Therefore flesh from tithe of cattle may not be weighed out portion against portion in the way that flesh of a firstling may be weighed out, since a person would thus seem to be selling it.

7. If tithe of cattle belonging to orphans was slaughtered when it was blemished, it is permissible to sell it in ordinary fashion: because of the duty to guard the orphan against loss the Sages have made no decree against it.

8. If tithe of cattle was slaughtered when it was blemished, it is permissible to sell its fat, sinews, hide, and bones, for its flesh alone is forbidden to be sold; but if the value of the flesh was included in a single bargain together with the value of the hide, fat, and sinews, and all were sold in one inclusive bargain, this is permissible. And if the value of the bones was high and the value of the flesh was included in a single bargain together with the value of the bones, this is permissible.

9. Anyone may be trusted concerning blemishes in tithe of cattle if he says, "This blemish happened of itself and was not done wittingly." Even they who cannot be trusted concerning a firstling may still be trusted concerning tithe; and if a man was skilled he could inspect the blemishes of his own tithe and declare it permissible for slaughtering; for if a man wished, he could impart blemishes to all his flock and then give tithe for them, and the tithe would thus be blemished from the outset.

10. If a man bought lambs born during the current year, or if they were given him as a gift, they are not liable to tithe: they are

liable only if they were born while in his control. Therefore if joint owners entered into a partnership as cattle owners, each of them bringing in a hundred lambs, and they mingled them to-gether and possessed them jointly, then the two hundred are not subject to tithe, since each lamb among them counts as something "sold." So, too, if brothers inherited lambs from their father, these are exempt from tithe. But what were thenceforward born to them from the same beasts during the partnership, whether those of the joint owners or those of the brothers, are liable to tithe.

So, too, if they held money jointly and bought beasts out of the jointly held money, or if the brothers bought beasts with the money of the inheritance, what were thenceforward born from them are subject to tithe, since they were born while in their control, and the two of them count as a single person.

If the brothers or the joint owners parted after the beasts were born in their control, and then once again they became joint own-ers, their beasts are exempt from tithe, since at the time when they parted all counted as beasts which were "bought," and what is bought is exempt. And when they again became partners they became joint owners of the beasts and as yet none were born to them in their control after this second partnership. And although they had divided equally among them kid for kid, lamb for lamb, ten for ten, all are exempt from tithe, since they counted as beasts which were "bought."

11. If each of the brothers or joint owners took his share in the money but not in the beasts, these remain subject to tithe, since they do not yet count as beasts which were "bought"; but if each took his share in the beasts although they had not yet taken their share of the money, the beasts are exempt.

12. If a man bought ten unborn beasts in their mothers' womb, they must all enter the fold and be tithed, since they were born in his possession.

13. If ten beasts fell to a priest as restitution for robbery commit-ted against a proselyte, they are exempt from tithe, since the priestly

dues count as gifts, and we have already stated that what is given as a gift is exempt from tithe.

14. All cattle must enter the fold to be tithed whether they are unblemished or whether they are blemished, also all such as are forbidden for the altar, excepting beasts which are crossbred or ṭĕrefah or born from the dam's side or too young, since all these are exempt from tithe. So, too, an orphan—namely, a beast whose dam had died or been slaughtered at its birth—is not to be tithed. And these are things learned from oral tradition.

15. A beast which was bought is not exempt unless it was bought after the time when it was fit for tithing. Therefore if a man bought lambs within seven days of birth, he is bound to give tithe from them when their season comes round: since beasts too young are not suitable for tithing, he counts as one who had bought unborn young which were born while they were in his possession.

16. If it was in doubt whether or not a beast was subject to tithe, it is exempt from tithe. Therefore if an orphan beast or a beast which was bought or the like was confused with other lambs, all are exempt from tithe, since each of them is in doubt.

CHAPTER VII

1. If a man had ten lambs and he set apart one of the ten, or if he had a hundred and he set ten apart as tithe, they do not count as valid tithe. But how ought he to tithe them? He must bring all the lambs and all the calves into the fold and make an opening so small that no two can get out at the same time. Their dams are left outside and bleat so that the lambs hear their voice and leave the fold to meet them; for it is said: *whatsoever* passeth *under the rod* (Lev. 27: 32), meaning that each must pass under of itself and not that it be pulled out by its foreleg. And when they go out of the fold, one after the other, their owner begins to count them with the rod: one, two, three, four, five, six, seven, eight, nine—and that which goes out tenth, whether male or female, unblemished or

blemished, he marks with a red mark and says, "This is tithe." If he does not mark it with a red mark, or if he does not count them with the rod, or if he counts them while they are lying down or standing, they still count as tithe: inasmuch as he counted them ten by ten and dedicated the tenth, it is valid tithe.

2. He need not bring together into a single fold every beast born in his possession, but he may bring each flock together by itself. If he had five lambs in Jerusalem and five in Acco they are not reckoned together as one flock, and neither flock is subject to tithe. How near to each other must they be to be reckoned as one flock? Within sixteen miles.

3. If there were three flocks with sixteen miles between each of them, the three must be included together. Thus, if there were nine here and nine there and one in between them, the three groups must enter into the fold together to be tithed.

4. Tithe may not be given from the flock for the herd or from the herd for the flock; but tithe may be given from sheep for goats or from goats for sheep, for it is said: *And all the tithe of the herd or the flock* (Lev. 27:32): all which come within the term *flock* are accounted alike, for the young both of sheep and of goats are called *śeh* and count as a single species.

5. Tithe may not be given from beasts born this year for beasts born some other year, just as tithe from the seed of the earth may not be given from new crops for old or from old crops for new, for it is said: *That which cometh forth from the field, year by year* (Deut. 14:22). But it seems to me that if a man gave tithe from beasts of one year for those of another year it counts as valid tithe, because of the stringency pertaining to Hallowed Things, since the Law has not been so precise about tithe of cattle as to say expressly that it shall be *year by year*.

6. All beasts born from the first day of Tishri to the twenty-ninth day of Elul can be included together, and tithe can be given from one flock among them for another. If five lambs were born on the

twenty-ninth day of Elul and five on the following first day of Tishri, they may not be included together. If two generations were born within the same year both the dam and her daughter must enter the fold to be tithed.

7. Young lambs are not like untithed field produce from which it is forbidden to eat until it is tithed, as we have explained in its proper place; but a man may sell or slaughter what he pleases until he tithes them, when what is designated tithe becomes consecrated and must be eaten in the manner prescribed by rule, as we have explained.

8. Three seasons in the year have the Sages appointed for giving tithe of cattle, and when one of these seasons arrives a man is forbidden to sell or to slaughter until he has given tithe. But if he does slaughter, it is permissible. And these are the three seasons: the fifteenth day before Passover, the fifteenth day before Pentecost, and the fifteenth day before the Feast of Tabernacles. Each of these seasons is called "the harvesting season" of tithe of cattle. Thus thou mayest say that the harvesting seasons of tithe of cattle fall on the last day of Adar, on the thirty-fifth day of the counting of the 'omer, and on the last day of Elul.

And why have the Sages appointed harvesting seasons on these days? In order that the beasts shall be in readiness for those who go up to keep the feasts. For although it is permissible for a man to sell them before he gives tithe—as we have stated—the people used to abstain from selling them until they had given tithe and so fulfilled the commandment.

9. If a man brought all the flock or the herd into the fold and began to count and to dedicate the tenth and, at the last, there remained fewer than ten within the fold, he must leave them until another harvesting season. They are to be included together with those yet to be born, and all tithed at a single harvesting season. Even if he knows that some will be left over in the counting, he is bound to bring them all into the fold, and what remains over remains over.

CHAPTER VIII

1. If a man brought a flock into the fold and they began to go out one by one while he counted them in the manner which we have described, and he erred in his counting and called the eighth —or some lower number—the tenth, or the twelfth—or some higher number—the tenth, they are not validly dedicated. But if the ninth or the eleventh he called the tenth, it is validly dedicated. And this is a rule which has come down by tradition: that a beast wrongly designated "tenth" is validly dedicated as tithe if its order was immediately above or below the tenth; but this is not so with beasts which come before the ninth or after the eleventh. Although he called the ninth "tenth" or the tenth "ninth" or the eleventh "tenth," whether through error or intentionally, all three are validly dedicated.

2. What is the law concerning them? The ninth may not be brought as an offering but may be eaten when it becomes blemished; the tenth is normal tithe; and the eleventh must be offered as a peace offering, and it requires drink offerings as do peace offerings, and it may not be replaced by a substitute, since it is itself, as it were, a substitute.

This applies if he who counted was the owner of the beasts; but if a man appointed an agent to tithe for him who erred respecting either the ninth or the eleventh, that alone which is certainly the tenth is deemed dedicated, since he did not appoint him as an agent to err and to cause loss but to tithe in proper fashion.

3. Insofar as we have said that if he called the eleventh "tenth" it is validly dedicated this holds only if he called the tenth "ninth"; but if he called the tenth "tenth" and then called the eleventh "tenth," the eleventh is not validly dedicated, since the name "tenth" has not been eradicated from what was of a certainty the tenth. And even if the tenth beast came out and he called it neither "tenth" nor "eleventh" but kept silence, and afterward the eleventh came out and he called it "tenth," this is not validly dedicated, since the tenth had automatically become dedicated; and

although he had not called it "tenth," yet inasmuch as the name "tenth" was not eradicated from it, the eleventh does not become dedicated.

4. If the ninth and the tenth came out together, whether he called them both "tenth" or called them both "ninth," both are validly dedicated: they may be eaten only when they incur a blemish, but they may not be brought as an offering. So, too, if the tenth and the eleventh came out together. If he called them "tenth" then the tenth and the eleventh are confused together and they are, as it were, tithe confused with peace offerings, which may be eaten only when they have incurred a blemish, as we have explained in Laws Concerning Hallowed Things Which Become Invalid. And if he called them "eleventh" then they are tithe confused with profane beasts, which may be eaten only when they have incurred a blemish.

5. If he began to count and at the beginning two came out together, which were the first and the second, he must count them all pair by pair and dedicate the tenth pair. So, too, if he counted them three by three each time, or five by five, he must dedicate the tenth group.

6. If at the beginning two came out together and he counted them as "one" and the third which came out after them he called "second," and then counted in usual fashion, one by one, then both the ninth and the tenth are validly dedicated and may be eaten only after they have incurred a blemish: the ninth, because it was of a certainty the tenth, since two came out at the beginning; and that which he called "tenth," that is, the eleventh; and if a man calls the eleventh "tenth" it is validly dedicated, as we have stated.

7. If he counted them in reverse order, namely, if the first came out and he said "ten" and the second came out and he said "nine," and so on, until the tenth came out and he counted it as "one," then this is dedicated, since the tenth is automatically dedicated.

8. If he called the ninth "tenth," and the tenth was left in the fold, the ninth may be eaten only after it has incurred a blemish,

and that which is left in the fold is normal tithe, even though it did not come forth and he did not single it out, for the tenth is automatically dedicated.

If the tenth died in the fold, the ninth may be eaten only after it has incurred a blemish, and all eight of those which had come out and had been numbered are exempt, even though the tenth among them had not been dedicated in such wise that it could be brought as an offering but had died before it came out; since the proper numbering (of the eight) renders them exempt.

9. If a man brought ten lambs into the fold and, as he went on counting them, one of those died which had been numbered, he must finish counting in his usual way and declare the tenth dedicated, even though there were now only nine live beasts.

10. If one died among those which were still inside the fold, those which had been numbered are exempt, since the proper numbering for tithe exempts those already numbered even though a tenth had not been set apart on their account, as we have explained. Those which are still inside the fold are left for another harvesting season until they can be included together with others.

So, too, if a man had fourteen lambs and he brought them into the fold, if four came out and were counted at one opening and six came out and were counted at another opening and four remained inside the fold—if these remaining four came out by the opening from which the six had come out, one of them may be taken as tithe and the rest are all exempt, since those four which went out first by the first opening are rendered exempt in that they had been of the numbering proper for providing tithe.

And if those four which remained had gone out by the opening from which the four had first gone out, then those four which went out first and those six which went out after them by the second opening are exempt; for each of them was counted among a number which was appropriate for providing tithe, since there remained in the fold others to complete the prescribed number and provide tithe.

But those four which remained, even though they came out and were numbered at the first opening, would not make up the appropriate number; therefore they must be included within another harvesting season.

If four went out by one opening and four by another opening and six remained, if the six went out by one of the two openings, one should be taken as tithe and all the others are exempt. If the six went out by two openings, the six must be included within another harvesting season; but the eight which went out first, whether by this opening or by that, are exempt, since each four was counted from among a number which was appropriate for making up the ten and for providing tithe, inasmuch as there still remained six within the fold.

11. If a man had nineteen lambs inside the fold and nine came out by one opening and nine by another opening, the last one must be taken as tithe and all the rest are exempt, since the other nine were numbered by "proper numbering."

12. If while he counted, a lamb thrust its head and the greater part of itself outside the fold and then came back, it is deemed to have been counted in all respects.

13. If while he counted, he broke off his counting because of his fellow who spoke with him or because the nightfall of Sabbath drew near, he must return and complete his counting afterward.

14. If, while he counted them that went out one by one and dedicated every tenth beast, one of them that had been counted jumped back inside the fold among those that had not been counted or tithed, all are rendered exempt, since there is a doubt about every one whether it was the one which had been counted and which had jumped back or whether it was another. And we have already stated that all which have been counted are exempt.

15. If one of them which had been counted as "tenth" jumped back inside the fold, all must be left to pasture until they incur a blemish and they may be eaten when they are blemished.

TREATISE IV

LAWS CONCERNING OFFERINGS FOR TRANSGRESSIONS COMMITTED THROUGH ERROR

Involving Five Positive Commandments

To Wit

1. That a single person shall bring a fixed sin offering because of his error;
2. That if it is not known to a man whether he had sinned or had not sinned, he shall bring a guilt offering until the matter become known to him when he must bring his sin offering: and this it is which is called a suspensive guilt offering;
3. That he who sins shall bring a guilt offering for known transgressions, and this is what is called an offering for undoubted guilt;
4. That he who sins shall bring an offering for known transgressions—a beast if he was rich, and birds or the tenth part of an ephah if he was poor; and this is what is called a rising and falling offering;
5. That the Sanhedrin shall bring an offering if they erred and gave a ruling contrary to traditional law concerning any matter of gravity.

An exposition of these commandments
is contained in the following chapters.

NOTE

In the list of the 613 commandments prefixed to the Code, those which deal with the subject of this Treatise are cited in the following form.

Positive commandments:

[5] 68. That the court must bring an offering if they erred in their ruling, as it is said: *And if the whole congregation of Israel shall err . . . then the assembly shall offer a young bullock* (Lev. 4: 13–14);

[1] 69. That a single person must bring a sin offering if he transgressed through error against a negative commandment involving extirpation, as it is said: *And if any one of the common people sin through error . . . he shall bring for his offering a goat, a female without blemish, for his sin which he hath sinned* (Lev. 4: 27–28);

[2] 70. That a single person, if he was in doubt whether or not he had committed a sin involving a sin offering, must bring an offering, as it is said: *And if anyone sin . . . though he know it not . . . he shall bring a ram without blemish . . . for a guilt offering* (Lev. 5: 17, 18): and this is what is called a suspensive guilt offering;

[3] 71. That he who transgresses through error in a matter of sacrilege or anything wrongly gotten or a betrothed handmaid or in denying a deposit or in swearing falsely must bring a guilt offering, as it is said: *And his guilt offering shall he bring unto the Lord, a ram without blemish* (Lev. 5: 15); and this is what is called an offering for undoubted guilt;

[4] 72. That a man bring a rising and falling offering, as it is said: *And if his means suffice not for a lamb, then he shall bring . . . two turtledoves or two young pigeons . . . but if his means suffice not for two turtledoves or two young pigeons then he shall bring . . . the tenth part of an ephah of fine flour* (Lev. 5: 7–11).

CHAPTER I

1. If through error a man transgressed any negative commandment involving an act whereby he is liable to extirpation, he must bring a sin offering. And it is a positive commandment that he shall bring a sin offering for his error.

2. For any transgression whereby men are liable to extirpation if they trangress wantonly, if they transgress through error they are liable to a sin offering, excepting those who are guilty of (one of) three transgressions, namely, he who blasphemes and he who neglects circumcision or the Passover offering. He who neglects the Passover offering or circumcision is excepted because these are positive commandments, and a sin offering is brought only for an act committed through error against a negative commandment, for it is said: *in doing any of the things which the Lord hath commanded not to be done* (Lev. 4:27). And he who blasphemes is excepted in that no act is thereby involved, for it is said: *For him that doeth aught in error* (Num. 15:29): he who blasphemes is thus excluded in that no act is thereby involved. Therefore if a man accepted an idol as a god—although he is liable to extirpation—he is to be stoned if he transgressed wantonly, but if he accepted it through error he is exempt from the offering, since he committed no act, for it is said: *In doing any of the things . . .*

3. For all transgressions set forth in the Law which entail extirpation—excepting the three which we have stated—if a single person transgressed any of them through error he must bring a fixed sin offering, unless he was an unclean person who ate what was hallowed or an unclean person who entered into the Temple, neither of whom brings a fixed sin offering but a rising and falling offering, as will be explained.

4. A fixed sin offering is one which is brought from cattle only. A rising and falling offering is an offering which is not fixed; but if a man is rich he brings a sin offering from cattle, and if he is

poor he brings bird offerings or the tenth of an ephah, as will be explained.

Thus we learn that the transgressions for which a single person must bring a fixed sin offering if he committed them through error are forty-three all told. And these are they: he who has intercourse with (1) his mother, (2) his wife's mother, (3) her mother's mother, (4) her father's mother, (5) his daughter, (6) his daughter's daughter, (7) his son's daughter, (8) his wife's daughter, (9) his wife's daughter's daughter, (10) her son's daughter, (11) his sister, (12) his sister that is the daughter of his father's wife, (13) his father's sister, (14) his mother's sister, (15) his wife's sister, (16) his father's wife, (17) his father's brother's wife, (18) his son's wife, (19) his brother's wife, (20) another man's wife, (21) a menstruant, (22) a male, (23) his father, (24) his father's brother, (25) a beast, and (26) a woman who brings a beast upon herself.

Thus forbidden acts of intercourse punishable by extirpation are twenty-six all told. Of other transgressions punishable in like manner there are seventeen, and these are they: (1) he who worships an idol, committing some act; (2) he who offers any of his seed to Moloch; (3) he who divines by a ghost; (4) he who divines by a familiar spirit, committing some act; (5) he who profanes the Sabbath; (6) he who does an act of work on the Day of Atonement; (7) he who eats or drinks on the Day of Atonement; (8) he who eats remnant of Hallowed Things; (9) he who eats leaven during Passover; (10) he who eats forbidden fat; (11) he who eats blood; (12) he who eats refuse of Hallowed Things; (13) he who slaughters Hallowed Things outside the Temple Court; (14) he who offers up any offering outside the Temple Court; (15) he who compounds oil of unction; (16) he who compounds incense; (17) he who anoints himself with the oil of unction.

These are the forty-three transgressions for which a man must bring a fixed sin offering if he committed any of them through error.

And what is the offering which he must bring who commits

through error one of these transgressions? If he erred in a matter
of idolatry he must bring a year-old goat as a sin offering; and
this it is which is spoken of in the chapter of the Book of Numbers (13:22 ff.). Whether he who sins is an ordinary person or a
king or a High Priest or he who is anointed for battle, they are
all equal in the offering which they must bring for idolatry
committed through error.

But if a man erred in committing any of the other forty-two
transgressions, and he was an ordinary person, he must bring a
female of the goats or a female of the sheep; and this is the sin
offering of *one of the common people* spoken of in the chapter
of the Book of Leviticus (4:27). If he was a king who erred in
committing any of them, he must bring a female of the goats as a
sin offering; and if he was the anointed priest he must bring a
bullock from the herd as a sin offering. And it must be burned in
the manner there described.

5. It is all one whether it was a single person or many persons
who erred in committing any of these transgressions, for it is
said: *Ye shall have one law for him that doeth aught in error*
(Num. 15:29). Thus if the men of some region erred and thought
that the day was a common day, and it was the Day of Atonement,
and they all ate and performed acts of work, every one of them
must bring two sin offerings, female sheep or female goats. So,
too, if they all erred and burned incense to an idol, every one of
those who worshiped must bring a year-old goat as a sin offering.

CHAPTER II

1. A man becomes liable to a sin offering for an act committed
through error only if he erred from the beginning to the end; but
if at the beginning he acted through error but at the end he
acted wantonly, or if at the beginning he acted wantonly but at
the end he acted through error, he is exempt from a sin offering.
Thus, if he removed an object on the Sabbath from one domain
into another domain and took it up wantonly but laid it down

through error, or if he took it up through error but laid it down wantonly, he is exempt: he is liable only if he both takes it up through error and lays it down through error. And the same applies in every like case.

2. If a man committed a transgression knowing that it was contrary to a negative commandment but not knowing that extirpation was thereby incurred, this counts as an act committed through error and he must bring a sin offering; but if he knew that it was punishable by extirpation and erred respecting the offering, not knowing whether or not liability to an offering was thereby incurred, he is deemed to have acted wantonly, for error respecting the offering does not count as error respecting those transgressions which are punishable by extirpation.

3. If the very sin itself which he had sinned was not known to a man, even though he knew of a certainty that he had transgressed a negative commandment involving extirpation, he is exempt from a sin offering, for it is said: *his sin, wherein he hath sinned* (Lev. 4:23): he is liable only if he knows what was the sin wherein he had sinned.

Thus if forbidden fat and remnant lay before him and he ate one of them and it is not known which of them he ate, or if his menstruant wife and his sister were in the room and he had intercourse with one of them and it is not known with which of them he had intercourse, or if there came a Sabbath and a Day of Atonement and he performed an act of work on one of them and it is not known on which of them he did so, he is exempt from a sin offering.

4. If a man sinned and his sin became known to him, but he again forgot what it was, he must bring a sin offering for whatever the sin was, and it must be eaten in the manner of other sin offerings which are to be eaten.

5. If he transgressed through error in a single class of transgression involving two possible objects, he is liable to a sin offering. Thus, if there were two menstruants and he transgressed through

error with one of them and he does not know which it was, or if there were two sisters of his and he transgressed through error with one of them and he does not know which it was, he is liable to a sin offering, since he knew what was the sin itself. To what is this like? To two burning lamps, one of which he extinguished and it is not known which lamp it was, or to two dishes of forbidden fat from one of which he ate and it not known from which dish he ate; in which case he is liable to a sin offering. And the same applies in every like case.

6. Whosoever is liable to a fixed sin offering for a transgression committed through error, if he transgressed through error and it became known to him later that he had sinned, although at the outset he had no knowledge that this was a sin, he is liable to a sin offering. Thus, if a child was held captive among the Gentiles and grew up not knowing what the Israelites were or what was their religion, and he committed an act of work on the Sabbath or ate fat and blood or the like, when it becomes known to him that he is an Israelite and that commandments are laid upon him concerning all these things, he is under obligation to bring a sin offering for every single transgression. And the same applies in every like case.

7. If through error and without intent a man transgressed the laws of forbidden intercourse or forbidden foods, he is liable to a sin offering; but if it concerned the laws of the Sabbath, he is not liable to a sin offering. Thus, if a man was busied with a woman and he had intercourse with her without intention of intercourse and she was a woman forbidden to him, or if he thought that what was in his mouth was spittle and he swallowed it without any intention whatever of eating, and it was fat, he is liable to a sin offering.

If his intention was to lift up (on the Sabbath) what was already plucked but he severed what was still attached to the ground without any intention of severing it, he is not liable. It is a deliberate act of work which the Law has forbidden, as we have stated in its proper place.

9205

8. If a man was fulfilling any of the commandments and in so doing there was committed through error a transgression punishable by extirpation, he is exempt from a sin offering since what he did was done permissively.

Thus, if he had intercourse with his deceased brother's wife, and she was a menstruant and he did not know it, he is exempt from a sin offering since what he did was done permissively. But if he had intercourse with his wife while she was menstruous, he is liable to a sin offering, since he did not first ask of her and then have intercourse; whereas with his deceased brother's wife he was not so familiar with her as to ask this of her.

So, too, if a man had two children of whom the one was to be circumcised on the Sabbath and the other was to be circumcised on the day before the Sabbath or on the first day of the week, and he forgot and circumcised them both on the Sabbath, he is exempt from a sin offering, since he had the right to circumcise one of them on the Sabbath, and he was faced with a Sabbath that could be overridden and with the fulfillment of a positive commandment; although they were two separate objects, inasmuch as he was anxious to fulfill the commandment in its due time, he did not pay sufficient attention. But if neither of them was eligible to be circumcised on the Sabbath and he forgot and circumcised on the Sabbath one that was not eligible, he is liable to a sin offering.

9. If the surgeon came to circumcise a child toward eventide on the Sabbath day and it was told him, "There is no time during the day for thee to circumcise, and if thou begin the circumcision thou canst not complete it until after the Sabbath is ended and thou wilt thus inflict a wound on the Sabbath without fulfilling a commandment"; and if he said, "I am well practiced and speedy, and I will circumcise quickly," and he did not complete his task until after the Sabbath was ended, he is liable to a sin offering, since he had been forewarned.

10. If a man brought forth a *lulab* on the first festival day of the Feast which fell on a Sabbath in order to take it out with him,

and he conveyed it as far as four cubits in public domain, acting through error, he is not liable to a sin offering since he brought it forth permissively. So, too, if a man slaughtered the Passover offering on the fourteenth day of Nisan which fell on a Sabbath, and it was afterward known to him that its owners had withdrawn from their share in it or had died or had become unclean before the slaughtering, or if it was found to be tĕrefah in some hidden part—if, for example, it was pierced in the bowels or the lungs—he is exempt from a sin offering, since he slaughtered it permissively. But if it was found to have a blemish or was manifestly tĕrefah, he is liable to a sin offering since it was his duty to examine it and then slaughter it. And the same applies in every like case.

11. If a man slaughtered a Passover offering on the Sabbath but under some other name by mistake, he is exempt from a sin offering because the animal offering itself was valid, since eradication of its proper name by mistake is not accounted eradication, as we have explained in Laws Concerning Hallowed Things Which Become Invalid.

12. If he slaughtered some other animal offering under the name of a Passover offering by mistake, and it was suitable for a Passover offering, he is exempt from a sin offering since he had slaughtered it permissively. If it was not suitable—if, for example, it was a female or two years old—he is liable to a sin offering since it was not suitable for a Passover offering.

So, too, if he erred and slaughtered it on the Sabbath for other than those who should eat of it or for other than those who were enrolled for it or for such as were uncircumcised or unclean, he is liable to a sin offering. If he slaughtered it both for those who should and for those who should not eat of it, or for those who were enrolled and for those who were not enrolled for it, or for some who were circumcised and for some who were not circumcised, or for some who were unclean and for some who were clean, he is exempt from a sin offering, since the Passover offering was valid. And the same applies in every like case.

13. If a man slaughtered a public offering on the Sabbath under some other name, he is liable to a sin offering, and he must burn the sacrificial portions at eventide. So, too, if he slaughtered more than the day's obligation, he is liable to a sin offering on account of the excess.

14. If a man, through error, slaughtered on the Sabbath offerings of a single person, which do not override the Sabbath, he is liable to a sin offering; and the flesh of those offerings is permissible for gainful use and their blood may not be tossed. But if he transgressed and tossed the blood under the name of such offerings whether through error or wantonly, they count to their owner's credit in fulfillment of an obligation, and the sacrificial portions must be burned at eventide and the flesh may be eaten; but he who slaughtered them must bring a sin offering for his error.

15. If a man had before him two beasts, to be offered for the community, the one lean and the other fat, and the day's obligation was that but one should be offered, whether as a sin offering or as a whole offering, and he erred and slaughtered them both—if he first slaughtered the lean beast and afterward slaughtered the fat beast, he is exempt from a sin offering; indeed, one may even say to him directly, "Bring the fat beast and slaughter it." But if he first slaughtered the fat beast and afterward the lean beast, he is liable to a sin offering on account of the excess.

If the first, the fat beast, was found to be ṭerefah in the small entrails, even though he did not know that it was ṭerefah at the time when he slaughtered the lean beast, and this had not been in his mind, inasmuch as the later beast was slaughtered in rightful manner, he is exempt from a sin offering.

So, too, if through error a man spread out a net to bring up fish from the sea and he brought up a child together with the fish, whether or not he had heard that a child was drowned, inasmuch as he brought up a child he is exempt from a sin offering even though his intention had been only to catch fish, since he had committed the act of spreading the net through error. And the same applies in every like case.

16. If on the night of Passover there lay before a man roasted flesh from the Passover offering and a remnant from Hallowed Things, and his intention was to eat of the roasted flesh—which was the fulfilling of a commandment—and he erred and ate of the remnant, he is liable to a sin offering, since by this act of eating he fulfilled no commandment. And the same applies in every like case.

CHAPTER III

1. If witnesses testified of a man that he had committed a sin for which liability to a fixed sin offering was incurred and they had not forewarned him, but they said, "We saw that thou didst commit an act of work on the Sabbath" or "that thou didst eat fat," and he said, "I know of a certainty that I did not do this thing," he is not liable to a sin offering. Since, if he were to say, "I did so willfully," he would be exempt from the offering, when he said to them, "I did not eat" or "I did not do this," he is counted as one who said, "I did not eat through error but willfully"—who is exempt from the offering—and thus did not contradict the witnesses.

2. If he kept silence and did not gainsay the witnesses, even if a woman said to him, "Thou didst eat fat" or "Thou didst commit an act of work on the Sabbath," and he kept silence, he is liable to a sin offering. If one witness said to him, "That is fat," and he kept silence, and then he ate it again through error, he must bring a sin offering. But if they forewarned him he is scourged for it, even though the essential evidence depended on one witness.

3. We have already explained in Laws Concerning Hallowed Things Which Become Invalid that if a man had set apart his sin offering because of fat which he had eaten, he may not offer it because of a Sabbath which he had profaned or because of blood which he had eaten, for it is said: *then he shall bring for his offering a goat, a female without blemish, for his sin which he hath sinned* (Lev. 4: 28): it is valid only if his offering was brought ex-

pressly for the sake of his sin; he is not permitted to offer it if its purpose was changed from one sin to another sin, and if he did thus offer it, it is invalid.

Moreover the Sages have said: if a man set apart his sin offering because of fat which he ate yesterday, he may not offer it because of fat which he ate today, but if he did thus offer it, it effects atonement.

And, needless to say, if his father set it apart and then died, and the son incurred liability for that same sin, the son may not offer it for his own sin, as is there explained.

4. If a man brought one sin offering because of two sins, it must be left to pasture until a blemish befalls it when it must be sold and with one half of its price one offering must be brought because of the one sin, and with the other half of its price another offering must be brought for the other sin. So, too, if two men brought one sin offering for their two sins: it must be left to pasture until a blemish befalls it when it must be sold, and the one brings his sin offering with one half of its price and the other brings his sin offering with the other half of its price.

5. If a man brought two sin offerings because of one sin, he may offer which of them he pleases, and the other must be left to pasture until a blemish befalls it, and its price accrues as a freewill offering.

6. If he brought two sin offerings because of two sins, one must be slaughtered expressly for the sake of the one sin and the other expressly for the sake of the other sin.

7. We have already explained in Laws Concerning the Manner of Making Offerings that from one who is perverted to idolatry or who openly profanes the Sabbaths, no offering at all may be accepted; and from one who is perverted to any other transgression, no sin offering may be accepted from him regarding that sin. Thus, if one who was perverted to the eating of fat ate fat through error and brought his sin offering, it may not be accepted from him until he returns in penitence. Even if he had been perverted to the eating of fat to satisfy the appetite and he mistook forbidden fat

for permitted fat and he ate it and brought an offering, it may not be accepted from him; for once he has eaten fat wantonly, whether from malice or to satisfy his appetite, he counts as one who is perverted.

If he had been perverted to the eating of fat and he erred and ate blood, his offering may be accepted from him, as we have explained.

8. If a man, having transgressed through error, set apart his sin offering, but then became perverted, and he afterward returned in penitence, or if he became imbecile and then again became of sound mind, although the offering in the meantime was in abeyance, it once again becomes fit and seemly; for dedicated animals are not forever to be discarded as offerings, as we have explained in Laws Concerning Hallowed Things Which Become Invalid. Therefore he may offer the selfsame offering. And just as when, after a passing blemish had arisen in a beast and it was later healed, it again becomes valid, so if its owner was once unacceptable but later became fit and seemly, it may be offered.

9. If there were any who were liable to sin offerings and to offerings for undoubted guilt and the Day of Atonement intervened, they must offer them after the Day of Atonement; but they who were liable to suspensive guilt offerings are exempt, for it is said: *From all your sins shall ye be clean before the Lord* (Lev. 16:30). Thus is it learned from oral tradition that atonement is made for any sin that is known only to God. Therefore if a man committed any transgression which was in doubt, even toward nightfall on the Day of Atonement, he is exempt from a suspensive guilt offering, since any part of the day effects atonement.

Thus we learn that a suspensive guilt offering is brought for an unknown sin committed on the Day of Atonement only if the Day of Atonement does not effect atonement for it, as will be explained.

10. Neither the Day of Atonement nor any sin offering or guilt offering effects atonement except for those who repent and have

faith in the atonement made for them; but if a man disdains them they effect no atonement for him. Thus if a man was disdainful, yet brought his sin offering or guilt offering while saying or thinking in his heart that these did not effect atonement, even though they were offered in their rightful manner, he will be granted no atonement; and when he returns in penitence from his disdainfulness he must bring again his sin offering or his guilt offering.

So, too, if a man disdains the Day of Atonement, the Day of Atonement effects no atonement for him. Therefore if he was liable to a suspensive guilt offering and the Day of Atonement intervened and he disdained it, he will be granted no atonement. And when he returns in penitence after the Day of Atonement he is bound to bring any suspensive guilt offering to which he had been liable.

11. Any guilt offering enjoined by the Law, if it is not brought, serves as a bar to atonement, excepting the nazirite's guilt offering. All offerings prescribed by reason of a condition of doubt respecting the nazirite or those whose atonement is not complete or the suspected adulteress must be brought after the Day of Atonement.

12. If a man liable to a sin offering or a guilt offering was on his way from the court to be put to death and his offering was already sacrificed, he is held back until the blood has been tossed, and then put to death; but if the offering had not yet been slaughtered, he is not held back until it is offered for him.

CHAPTER IV

1. If a man committed many transgressions during a single spell of unawareness, he is liable to a sin offering for every one of them: even if he committed all of the forty-three transgressions which we have enumerated during a single spell of unawareness, he is liable to forty-three sin offerings.

So, too, if he committed a single act whereby he becomes liable under several categories, he is liable to a sin offering for each single category, provided that the prohibited acts all occurred at the same time or that there was an extensive prohibition or that there was a comprehensive prohibition.

Thus if a man slaughtered a dedicated beast outside the Temple Court on the Sabbath in honor of an idol, he would be liable to three sin offerings, in virtue, namely, of slaughtering outside the Temple Court, of profaning the Sabbath, and of committing idolatry, since the three forbidden acts occurred at the same time. This applies to one who intends to worship the idol by completing the act of slaughtering the animal. But if such was not his intention, so soon as he has cut through but little of its throat in honor of the idol it becomes forbidden, whereas one becomes culpable because of slaughtering outside the Temple Court only when he has cut through both the windpipe and the gullet or through the greater part of the two. In this case, when he had completed the slaughtering he would have slaughtered a beast which was not eligible as an offering, so that he would not be culpable because of slaughtering it outside the Temple Court, as we have explained.

If it was a sin offering of birds and half of the bird's windpipe was slit and he widened the slit at all on the Sabbath in honor of an idol, he would be liable to three sin offerings, since three forbidden acts occurred at the same time.

So, too, if a man did an act of work on the Day of Atonement which fell on a Sabbath, he would be liable to two sin offerings, since two forbidden acts occurred at the same time.

If a man had intercourse with the wife of his brother who was yet alive, and she was menstruous, he must bring three sin offerings, in virtue, namely, of the laws concerning another man's wife and his brother's wife—two forbidden acts which occurred at the same time—and concerning a menstruant, which counts as an extensive prohibition; for since this prohibition concerning her extends to her husband it extends also to her brother-in-law. And the same applies in every like case.

If a man had intercourse with his father, he is culpable on two counts: in virtue of the law *The nakedness of thy father . . . shalt thou not uncover* (Lev. 18:7); and of the law *Thou shalt not lie with mankind* (Lev. 18:22). So, too, he who has intercourse with his father's brother is culpable on two counts, for it is said: *Thou shalt not uncover the nakedness of thy father's brother* (Lev. 18:14).

If a man had intercourse with a male and brought upon himself a male during a single spell of unawareness, although these are two separate agents, he is liable to but one sin offering, for it is said: *Thou shalt not lie with mankind,* implying that he who commits and he who suffers the act fall within a single class. So, too, if a man had intercourse with a beast and brought a beast upon himself during a single spell of unawareness, he is liable to but one sin offering. The Sages have counted committer and sufferer, whether with a beast or with a male, guilty of one and the same act of intercourse.

2. By but a single act of intercourse a man may become liable to eight sin offerings. Thus, suppose that Jacob had a daughter by Zilpah and her name was Timna, and Laban married Timna and got by her a daughter Serah, and Laban had no other daughter but Rachel; then Serah would be Jacob's daughter's daughter and his wife's sister by the same father—hence two forbidden acts which occurred at the same time. If Serah was married to Reuben and was thus forbidden to the other sons of Jacob, respecting her a further prohibition would be added to Jacob, since she was his daughter-in-law. If Reuben died or divorced her, and this Serah was married to Jacob's brother by the same mother, inasmuch as she was forbidden to the rest of Jacob's brothers, respecting her a further prohibition would be added to Jacob, since she was his brother's wife. If Jacob's brother died or divorced her and this Serah was married to Ishmael, inasmuch as she was forbidden to the rest of Ishmael's brothers, respecting her a further prohibition would be added to Jacob, since she was the wife of his father's brother. If Ishmael died and she thus became the widow of Isaac's deceased brother, and Isaac transgressed and took her in levirate marriage—although she was akin to him within the secondary grade of forbidden degrees—inasmuch as she was forbidden to the rest of his brothers, respecting her a further prohibition would

be added to Jacob, since she was now his father's wife and also another man's wife, namely, two forbidden acts which occurred at the same time.

If Jacob transgressed through error and had intercourse with this Serah at a time when she was menstruous during the lifetime of Isaac her husband and during the lifetime of Rachel, Jacob's wife, he would thereby become liable to eight sin offerings, in virtue, namely, of the prohibitions concerning his daughter's daughter, his wife's sister, his daughter-in-law, his brother's wife, his father's brother's wife, his father's wife, another man's wife, and a menstruant.

And the same applies in every like case.

3. Wherever an extensive prohibition would be applicable respecting such a case of consanguinity, it is needful that the other persons be in existence so that she would be forbidden to them and that, being forbidden to them, an additional prohibition is extended to the man concerned. But if they were not in existence we do not say, "Whereas, if the man concerned had sons or brothers, she would have been forbidden to them, therefore let a further prohibition respecting her be added to the grandfather," since at the time there was neither son nor brother. And the same applies in every like case.

4. If a man was married to three wives and he had intercourse with the mother of one of them and she was the mother of the second wife's mother and the mother of the third wife's father, although this old woman was his mother-in-law and mother of his mother-in-law and mother of his father-in-law, thus coming within three categories of prohibited degrees, and it was a forbidden act whereby three transgressions occurred at the same time, he is liable to but a single sin offering because it is said of a woman and her daughter and her son's daughter and her daughter's daughter: *They are near kinswomen: it is lewdness* (Lev. 18:17). Scripture has treated the three as though they were one, therefore the three categories are reckoned as one category.

5. But if a man had intercourse with his sister who was his father's sister and also his mother's sister, he is liable to three sin offerings, for it is said: *He hath uncovered his sister's nakedness* (Lev. 20:7). He is culpable because of his sister as such, even though she was also his mother's sister and his father's sister. And how could such a thing happen? It could happen if, for example, a man had intercourse with his mother and got two daughters by her and then had intercourse with one of his daughters and got a son by her. If then this bastard had intercourse with the other daughter, sister of his bastard mother who was his sister by the same father and also his father's sister by the same mother, then he is liable to three sin offerings. And the same applies in every like case.

CHAPTER V

1. If a man committed many acts of intercourse with a woman who was forbidden to him during a single spell of unawareness, even though many days passed between each act, inasmuch as it remained unknown to him in the meantime and the transgression was with but one person, the whole counts as a single transgression committed through error and he is liable to but a single sin offering. But if he transgressed with her through error and it became known to him, and he again transgressed through error with the same woman and had intercourse with her and afterward it became known to him, and he then again transgressed through error with the same woman and had intercourse with her, he is liable for each act of intercourse; for the several times of knowledge keep distinct the several acts of error.

2. If a man committed many acts of intercourse during a single spell of unawareness with one who was forbidden to him, whereas she who suffered intercourse became aware of it between each act of intercourse, the acts befalling her during many spells of unawareness, he need bring but one sin offering while she must bring a sin offering for each single act. If he became aware of it

in the meantime, whereas she suffered during a single spell of unawareness, he must bring many sin offerings while she need bring
but a single sin offering.

3. If during a single spell of unawareness a man had intercourse
with many women who were forbidden to him, even though they
all came within a single category, inasmuch as they were distinct
persons, he is liable because of each one of them. Thus, if he had
intercourse during a single spell of unawareness with his five wives
who were menstruous or with his five sisters or with his five
daughters, he is liable for each one of them. Hence we learn that
whereas the Sages have said, "If a man had intercourse with a male
and brought a male upon himself during a single spell of unawareness, he is liable to but one sin offering," this applies if it was the
same male; but if it was another male, whether he had intercourse
with the two, or had intercourse with the one and brought the
other upon himself, he is liable for each one of them. And the same
rule applies to him who had intercourse with a beast and brought
a beast upon himself.

4. If a woman brought many beasts upon herself during a single
spell of unawareness, she is liable to a sin offering for each beast,
since they count as separate bodies; and she counts as one who
suffered intercourse from many men during a single spell of unawareness, who is liable to a sin offering because of each one of
them.

5. If a woman's husband went beyond the seas and she heard that
he was dead or witnesses came and testified that he was dead and
she was married again, whether by her own testimony or by permission of the court, and it became known that her husband was
yet alive, she is liable to a single offering. If she was married to
many men or played the harlot with many men, she is liable to a
sin offering for each one of them, since they are separate persons,
even if all befell through a single error.

If through error a man had intercourse with a menstruant and
she became clean from her impurity and immersed herself and then

she once again suffered a flow and he had intercourse with her a second time through the same error, he is liable for each occasion, even though they happened during a single spell of unawareness and with but a single person, since the one menstruous occasion was distinct from the other and it is as though it was with two menstruous women.

6. If a man had intercourse with his wife other than at the time of her fixed period and she suffered a flow at the moment of intercourse, they are exempt from a sin offering, since he counts as one who transgressed under constraint and not through error. For as regards one who transgresses through error, he ought to have inquired and shown care, and if he had inquired diligently and made careful questioning he would not have fallen into transgression through error; but since he had not been at pains first to search and examine and then to take action, he is in need of atonement, whereas the other man—what ought he to have done? Since she was clean and he had intercourse with her other than at the time of her fixed period, he is but under constraint. Therefore whether blood was found on her test rag or on his test rag, they are not culpable.

But if he transgressed and had intercourse with her near to the fixed period and supposed that he would have intercourse and withdraw before she suffered a flow and she suffered it at the moment of intercourse, they are liable to an offering, since this was a transgression committed through error. Therefore if blood was found on his test rag, they are both unclean and they are liable to an offering. If it was found on her test rag and she wiped herself forthwith when her husband withdrew and she did not delay, they both are unclean and they are liable to an offering. But if she delayed long enough to stretch her hand beneath the pillow or cushion and take a test rag to test therewith and afterward wiped herself, they both are unclean only by reason of doubt and are not liable to an offering. But if she delayed long enough to alight from the bed and rinse her nakedness and then wiped herself and blood was found, her husband is deemed to be clean.

7. If a man transgressed and had intercourse with his wife near to the fixed period, supposing that he would do so before she suffered a flow, and at the moment of intercourse she felt that she had become unclean and said to him, "I am become unclean," he may not withdraw while the member is rigid, as we have explained in Laws Concerning Forbidden Intercourse. If he did not know that it was forbidden to withdraw forthwith and he withdrew while the member was rigid, he is liable to two sin offerings: one for the ingress, since he had intercourse with a menstruant; and one for the egress, since he derived pleasure from the egress as from the ingress.

This applies if he knew that it was forbidden to have intercourse at the time of the fixed period but supposed that he could do so before she suffered a flow, and did not know that it was forbidden to withdraw forthwith; for thus there befell him two spells of un-awareness during two acts of intercourse.

But if he did not know that it was forbidden to have intercourse at the time of the fixed period and did not know that it was forbidden to withdraw forthwith from the uncleanness, even if he withdrew forthwith and the member was rigid, he is liable to but one sin offering, because his ingress and his egress which count as two acts of intercourse happened during the single act of error and he committed them both during a single spell of unawareness.

And the same rule applies to other forbidden acts of intercourse, so that if a man transgressed through error and had intercourse with one who was forbidden to him, supposing that she was not forbidden, and during the intercourse it became known to him that she was forbidden to him, he may not withdraw forthwith since he derives pleasure from the egress as from the ingress. And if he did not know that it was forbidden to withdraw forthwith and he withdrew while the member was rigid, he is liable to but one sin offering, since both were but a single act of error.

CHAPTER VI

1. The rule about transgressions committed through error against the prohibitions concerning foodstuffs is in accordance with the rule about transgressions committed through error against the prohibitions concerning acts of intercourse. Therefore if, during a single spell of unawareness, a man committed many acts of eating such as come within a single category of transgression, even if many days intervened between them, he is liable to but one sin offering. Thus if he ate fat today and ate fat tomorrow and ate fat the day after, during a single spell of unawareness, even though they were three separate dishes, he is liable to but one sin offering. But if he ate an olive's bulk of fat and it became known to him, and he ate again an olive's bulk of fat and it became known to him, he is liable for each act of eating, for the several times of knowledge keep distinct the several acts of error.

If he ate a half olive's bulk of fat and again ate a half olive's bulk of fat during a single spell of unawareness, although they were two separate dishes and although he made a break between them, they are to be included together and he must bring a sin offering, since the dishes do not keep distinct the two pieces of a half olive's bulk, provided that he did not delay between them longer than would suffice for the eating of three eggs, as we have explained in Laws Concerning Forbidden Foods. For just as smaller portions can be included together to make up the prescribed quantity in the case of one who acts wantonly so that he becomes liable to scourging, so smaller portions can be included together to make up the prescribed quantity in the case of one who acts through error so that he becomes liable to an offering.

2. If during a single spell of unawareness a man ate remnant from five animal offerings, an olive's bulk from each, even if he ate them from five dishes, he is liable to but one sin offering, since they all fall within a single category; and the dishes do not avail to keep each act distinct, nor do the separate bodies of the animal

offerings, for it is all one whether he ate flesh from many animal offerings or from one.

So, too, if a man slaughtered five animal offerings outside the Temple Court during a single spell of unawareness, he is liable to but one sin offering. To what is this like? To one who worships five images during a single spell of unawareness.

3. If a man bled his beast and received the blood in two bowls and drank them during a single spell of unawareness, he need bring but one sin offering.

4. If a man ate many foodstuffs belonging to many categories during a single spell of unawareness, he becomes liable because of each category. Thus, if he ate an olive's bulk each of fat and blood and remnant and refuse during a single spell of unawareness, he must bring four sin offerings. And the same applies in every like case.

If during a single spell of unawareness a man ate an olive's bulk wherein several categories of transgression were accumulated, whether they were accumulated in virtue of an extensive prohibition or a comprehensive prohibition or of prohibited acts occurring at the same time, he becomes liable because of each category. Therefore if one who was unclean ate an olive's bulk of fat and remnant of Hallowed Things on the Day of Atonement, he must bring four sin offerings and a guilt offering: one sin offering because, being an unclean person, he ate of Hallowed Things, one because he ate fat, one because he ate remnant, and one because of the Day of Atonement, provided that other food was included together with this olive's bulk to bring it up to a date's bulk; and he must bring an offering for undoubted guilt on account of sacrilege because, through error, he made gainful use of what had been dedicated.

5. If a man ate and drank on the Day of Atonement during a single spell of unawareness, he is liable to but one sin offering: eating and drinking fall within a single category.

6. If a man performed an act of work on the Day of Atonement which fell on a Sabbath, he is liable to two sin offerings, since this constitutes two forbidden acts which occur at the same time.

7. If a man ate a half olive's bulk of fat and a half olive's bulk of blood during a single spell of unawareness, he is not liable to an offering: just as forbidden acts cannot be included together to render a man liable to scourging, as we have explained in Laws Concerning Forbidden Foods, so they cannot be included together to render him liable to an offering.

8. If he ate a half olive's bulk and he became aware of it, and again he forgot and ate another half olive's bulk during a second spell of unawareness, he is not liable, since he had become aware of his act in the meantime and he had knowledge only respecting a half of the prescribed measure.

So, too, if through error a man wrote a single letter on the Sabbath and he became aware of it, and again he forgot and wrote a second letter near to it during a second spell of unawareness, he is not liable to a sin offering. And the same applies in every like case.

So, too, if a man took out a burden on the Sabbath for a distance of two cubits through error and two cubits willfully and two cubits through error, if he did so by throwing it, he becomes liable to a sin offering, not because awareness respecting half the prescribed measure is negligible but because it was not in his power to fetch it back; therefore the awareness in the meantime does not profit him. But if he did so by carrying it, he is not liable; the knowledge respecting half of the prescribed measure counts as awareness as we have explained.

9. If a man ate an olive's bulk of fat during a single spell of unawareness and he became aware of this first act, and he ate again and he became aware of this second act, he must bring two sin offerings, since the several spells of awareness keep the several acts distinct, even though he had not yet set apart an offering. But if

he became aware of them both at the same time, he need bring but one sin offering.

And the same rule, it seems to me, also applies in the case of acts of intercourse.

10. If a man ate an olive's bulk and a half during a single spell of unawareness and he became aware of his act respecting the one olive's bulk, and again he ate a half olive's bulk during the same spell of unawareness in which he ate the other half olive's bulk, he is liable to but one sin offering, since the latter half olive's bulk cannot be included together with the former, even though he remained in his state of unawareness, because he had become aware of part of what he ate during the first spell of unawareness.

11. If he ate two olive's bulk of fat during a single spell of unawareness and he became aware of one of them, and he again ate another olive's bulk during the same spell of unawareness in which he ate the second, and he brought a sin offering for the first, atonement is effected for the first and the second, but not for the third; but when he becomes aware of that he must bring another sin offering.

If he brought a sin offering for the third, atonement is effected for the third and the second, because they both were eaten during the one spell of unawareness; but atonement is not effected for the first by this sin offering. If he brought a sin offering for the second of the three, atonement is effected for all the three, since the first and third were eaten during the same spell of unawareness as the second. And when he becomes aware of the first and the third, he does not need to bring another sin offering.

12. If a man ate one of two pieces (of fat) and he was in doubt whether he had eaten forbidden fat or permitted fat, and then he ate another of two pieces and he was in doubt whether he had eaten forbidden fat or permitted fat, and afterward he became aware of a certainty that it was forbidden fat which he had eaten the first time and the second time, he is liable to but one sin offering; for although awareness of doubt which came to him in the meantime avails to

keep the several acts distinct in the case of guilt offerings, it does not avail to keep the several acts distinct in the case of sin offerings.

CHAPTER VII

1. If a man bowed down to an idol, poured out a libation, burned incense, and sacrificed to it during a single spell of unawareness, he is liable to four sin offerings. So, too, if he exposed himself to Peor and cast a stone at a *Merḳolis* during a single spell of unawareness, he is liable to two sin offerings. And the same applies in every like case: he is liable for each act of worship.

This applies if he acted wantonly respecting the idol, but through error respecting these acts of worship; but if he acted wantonly respecting these acts of worship and through error respecting the idol, he is liable to but one sin offering. Thus, if he knew that this was an idol and that it was forbidden to worship it, but did not know that to bow down and to pour out a libation was a transgression, and he bowed down and poured out a libation, he is liable to two sin offerings. If he knew that these were acts of worship and that it was forbidden thus to worship another god, but did not know that this was an idol since it was not made of silver or gold, and he had supposed that that alone was called an idol which was made of silver or gold, and he worshiped it with every act of worship, he is liable to but one sin offering.

2. Concerning the Sabbath the Sages have laid down a main general rule: if a man forgot the principle of the Sabbath and forgot that commandments concerning the Sabbath were imposed upon Israelites, or if he was held captive among Gentiles while yet a child, or if as a child he had been made a proselyte while yet among Gentiles, even if he performed many acts of work on many Sabbaths, he is liable to but one sin offering, since they all count as a single transgression committed through error. So, too, he is liable to but one sin offering for all pieces of fat which he ate, and to but one sin offering for blood which he ate. And the same applies in every like case respecting these acts.

If a man knew the principle of the Sabbath, but forgot that the day was a Sabbath and thought that it was a common day, even if he performed therein many acts of work, he is liable to but one sin offering for the whole of the day and, likewise, one sin offering for each Sabbath wherein he transgressed through error.

3. If any man knew that the day was a Sabbath and performed acts of work through error, not knowing that these acts of work were forbidden, or if he knew that they were forbidden, but did not know that thereby he incurred extirpation, and performed many acts of work, he is liable to a sin offering for each primary act of work; even if he performed the thirty-nine classes of work during a single spell of unawareness, he must bring thirty-nine sin offerings.

4. If he forgot that the day was a Sabbath and also acted in error respecting acts of work, not knowing that these acts of work were forbidden, he is liable to but one sin offering.

5. If a man performed a primary act of work together with acts of work subsidiary to it during a single spell of unawareness, he is liable to but one sin offering; and, needless to say, if he performed many acts subsidiary to a single primary act of work, he is liable to but one sin offering.

6. If a man performed acts subsidiary to one primary act of work and an act subsidiary to another primary act of work during a single spell of unawareness, it seems to me that he is liable to two sin offerings.

7. If a man performed many acts falling within the same class of work—if, for example, he sowed and sank a vine shoot and engrafted—during a single spell of unawareness, he is liable to but one sin offering.

It has been explained already in Laws Concerning the Sabbath what are primary and what are subsidiary acts of work and what acts come within the class of primary acts of work.

8. If a man performed many acts falling within a single class of work, on many Sabbaths, whether wantonly as to the Sabbath and

through error as to the acts of work, or whether through error as to the Sabbath and wantonly as to the acts of work, he is liable for each act. Thus, if he had known that the day was a Sabbath and he sowed during it because he did not know that sowing was an act of work; and, on a second Sabbath, he knew that it was a Sabbath and planted during it because he did not know that planting was forbidden as an act of work; and, on the third Sabbath, he sank a vine shoot because he did not know that sinking a vine shoot counted as an act of work, he is liable for each act, although they belonged to the same class of work, since the Sabbaths count as separate objects.

9. If he acted through error, not knowing that the day was a Sabbath, and sowed during it, knowing that sowing counted as an act of work; and, on the second Sabbath, he forgot that it was a Sabbath and planted during it, knowing that planting counted as an act of work; and, on the third, he forgot that it was a Sabbath and sank a vine shoot, knowing that to sink a vine shoot counted as an act of work, he is liable for each act of work, since the days between each Sabbath count as a time of awareness to keep distinct the several acts of work.

10. If a man reaped and milled a dried fig's bulk of grain through error as to the Sabbath but wantonly as to the acts of work, thereby becoming liable to a single sin offering, and he then reaped again and milled a dried fig's bulk wantonly as to the Sabbath but through error as to the acts of work, thereby becoming liable to a sin offering for each act of work, and he then became aware of the reaping committed through error as to the Sabbath but wantonly as to the acts of work; then atonement for the first reaping carries with it atonement also for the second reaping, and atonement for the first milling carries with it atonement also for the second milling, and it is as though he performed all the four acts in but one spell of error as to the Sabbath and of wantonness as to the acts of work, for which he is liable to but one sin offering; and when he has offered this sin offering, atonement is effected for him

for them all. And even when he was afterward made aware of them he does not need to bring another sin offering.

But if he became aware first of the reaping committed wantonly as to the Sabbath but through error as to the acts of work, and he brought a sin offering, atonement is effected for him for that reaping of which he became aware and for the reaping and milling committed through error as to the Sabbath and wantonly as to the acts of work, because both are as but a single act of work; and atonement for the reaping and the milling carries with it atonement for the reaping, but there remains the milling committed wantonly as to the Sabbath until he becomes aware concerning it, when he must bring a second sin offering.

If he reaped only half a dried fig's bulk through error as to the Sabbath but wantonly as to acts of work, and again reaped half a dried fig's bulk wantonly as to the Sabbath but through error as to the acts of work, they are to be included together; atonement for the first reaping carries with it atonement for the second reaping. And the same applies in every like case with the other acts of work.

11. If a man intended to cut what was already plucked but he cut what was still attached to the ground, although the act of cutting was intentional, inasmuch as he did not carry out his intention he is not liable to a sin offering, for he counts as one who missed his purpose. And the Law has forbidden only a purposeful act of work, as we have explained many times.

12. If during the Sabbath a man scooped up burning embers, quenching those above and enkindling those below, and his intention was to quench and to enkindle, he is liable to two sin offerings. If he scooped up embers with which to warm himself and they enkindled of themselves, he is liable to two sin offerings, since a man becomes liable for any resultant act of work even though it was not needful on its own account, as we have explained in Laws Concerning the Sabbath; and as punishment by extirpation is incurred if such an act was committed wantonly, so he is liable to a sin offering if he committed it through error.

CHAPTER VIII

1. Wherever liability to a fixed sin offering would be incurred for a transgression committed through error, if it was committed without knowledge, liability to a suspensive guilt offering is incurred. What is meant by "without knowledge"? If a man remained in doubt whether in such a matter he had or had not transgressed through error, it is his duty to offer a guilt offering, for it is said: *And if any one sin . . . though he know it not, yet is he guilty, and shall bear his iniquity. And he shall bring a ram without blemish out of the flock, according to thy valuation, for a guilt offering* (Lev. 5: 17–18); and it is this which is called a suspensive guilt offering because it makes atonement for what is in doubt and holds it "in suspense" for him until it is known to him of a certainty that he had sinned through error, when he must bring his sin offering.

2. A man becomes liable to a suspensive guilt offering only if some prohibition is definitely involved. Thus, if a man ate forbidden fat and it is in doubt whether it was an olive's bulk or less than an olive's bulk, or if there lay before him a piece of forbidden fat and a piece of permitted fat and he ate one of them and it is not known which of them he ate, or if his wife and his sister were with him in the room and he had intercourse with one of them and he does not know with which of them he had intercourse, or if there was a Sabbath and a common day and he performed acts of work on one of them and he does not know on which day he did so, or if he performed an act of work on the Sabbath and he does not know what was the class of work which he performed—such a one must bring a suspensive guilt offering. And the same applies in every like case.

But if there lay before him one piece and it is in doubt whether it was forbidden fat or permitted fat and he ate it, he is not liable to a suspensive guilt offering since no prohibition was definitely involved. And if any man ate the fat of a *koy* he is not liable to a suspensive guilt offering since no prohibition was definitely involved. So, too, if a man had intercourse with a woman of whom it was in doubt whether she was menstruous, or of whom it was in doubt whether she was forbidden through near kinship, he is not liable to a suspensive guilt offering.

Therefore in the case of a woman on whose test rag blood was found some time after her intercourse, or of any man who married his deceased brother's widow within three months and it is not known whether what was born was a nine-month child of the former husband or a seven-month child of the latter husband, none is liable to an offering. And the same applies in every like case, since no prohibition was definitely involved.

3. If a man ate a certain piece and one witness said to him, "What thou didst eat was forbidden fat," and another witness said, "Thou didst not eat the forbidden fat," or if one woman said, "He did eat," and another woman said, "He did not eat," inasmuch as the forbidden food was definitely there, and he did not know whether he had or had not sinned, he must bring a suspensive guilt offering.

So, too, if a man had intercourse with another man's wife of whom one witness says, "Her husband is dead," and another says, "He is not dead," he is liable to a suspensive guilt offering.

The same rule applies in case of doubt as to whether the woman was divorced or not, since the prohibition as such was definitely in force. But in a case of doubt as to whether the woman was betrothed or not, the prohibition itself is not definite.

4. If before a man there lay two pieces, one forbidden fat and one permitted fat, and he ate one of them and a Gentile or a dog came and ate the other, or if a Gentile or a dog ate the first and an Israelite came and ate the second, or if he ate the first wantonly and the second through error, or if he ate the first through error and the second wantonly, he is liable to a suspensive guilt offering since forbidden food was definitely there. If he ate them both wantonly he is not liable to an offering. If he ate them both through error he must bring a sin offering. If he ate the first through error and another came and ate the second through error, they are both

liable to a suspensive guilt offering. And the same applies in every like case.

5. If fat and remnant lay before him and he ate one of them and it is not known which of them he ate, or if his menstruant wife and his sister were with him in the room and he transgressed through error with one of them and it is not known with which of them he had intercourse, or if a Sabbath was followed by the Day of Atonement and he performed an act of work during the twilight between them, he is not liable to an offering: he brings no sin offering, since he does not know what was the actual sin, as we have explained, and he brings no suspensive guilt offering, since he knows of a certainty that he has sinned.

6. Wherever liability to a single fixed sin offering is incurred for a transgression which is beyond doubt, liability to a suspensive guilt offering is incurred if it was committed without knowledge; and wherever liability to many sin offerings is incurred for a transgression which is beyond doubt, liability to many suspensive guilt offerings is incurred if it was committed without knowledge, corresponding to the number of sin offerings.

Thus, just as when a man who eats fat and blood and remnant and refuse during a single spell of unawareness is liable to four sin offerings, so, if he was in doubt whether he ate them or ate only pieces of permitted flesh which were among them, he must bring four suspensive guilt offerings.

So, too, if he was in doubt whether she with whom he had intercourse was his wife or some woman forbidden to him on whose account he would be liable to eight sin offerings, he must bring eight suspensive guilt offerings.

7. If a man ate one of two pieces and he is in doubt whether what he ate was one of forbidden fat or one of permitted fat and, after the doubt arose in him, he ate one of two other pieces and he was in doubt whether what he ate was one of forbidden fat or one of permitted fat, he must bring two suspensive guilt offerings.

8. Just as certain knowledge in the meantime avails to keep distinct the several acts when sin offerings are in question, so

knowledge in the meantime promoting doubt avails to keep distinct the several acts when guilt offerings are in question. Therefore if a man ate five olives' bulk of fat during a single spell of awareness and knowledge came to him promoting doubt respecting one of them, and again knowledge came to him promoting doubt respecting another, and so, also, respecting each one of them, he is liable to a suspensive guilt offering for each one of them.

9. If there was a piece of permitted fat and a piece of forbidden fat, and he ate one of them but it is not known which, and he brought a suspensive guilt offering, and he then returned and ate the second, he must bring a sin offering. So, too, if another man ate the second the other must bring a suspensive guilt offering, as we have explained.

10. If there was a piece of fat and another piece of fat which was remnant of Hallowed Things, and he ate one of them but it is not known which, he must bring a sin offering for the fat and a suspensive guilt offering because of the remnant. If he ate the second during a second spell of unawareness, he must bring three sin offerings. And if it had the value of a *pĕruṭah* he must bring an offering for undoubted guilt because of the sacrilege.

If one man ate one of the two pieces and another man came and ate the second, they must each bring a sin offering and a suspensive guilt offering. And the same applies in every like case.

CHAPTER IX

1. There are five transgressions for which a guilt offering must be brought, and it is this which is called "an offering for undoubted guilt" since it is not brought by reason of doubt. Such are the guilt offerings brought because of the betrothed handmaid, because of what is wrongfully gotten, because of sacrilege, because of uncleanness incurred by a nazirite, and because of leprosy brought when the leper is cleansed.

"Because of the betrothed handmaid": thus, if a man had intercourse with a betrothed handmaid, whether wantonly or through error, he must bring a guilt offering, provided that she was of age and acted wantonly and by her consent, and that she suffered congress in such manner as to render herself liable to scourging, for it is said: *There shall be inquisition* (Lev. 19:20) and *He shall bring his guilt offering* (Lev. 19:21): she is punished by scourging and he must bring an offering.

2. From oral tradition it is learned that when she becomes liable to scourging, he is liable to an offering; but when she is not liable to scourging, he is not liable to an offering.

3. If one who was nine years old and a day had intercourse with a betrothed handmaid she incurs punishment by scourging and he must bring an offering. And it seems to me that he should bring it only when he is of age and possessed of understanding.

4. We have already explained in Laws Concerning Forbidden Intercourse what is meant by the betrothed handmaid spoken of in the Law, and that none becomes liable unless he has intercourse with her after her customary manner and with completion of congress. Therefore if two said to a man, "Thou didst have intercourse with a betrothed handmaid," and he said, "I did not have intercourse with her," he is to be believed, and he need not bring an offering on their evidence, since he alone knows whether or not he completed the intercourse; and in that he said, "I did not have intercourse," it is as though he said, "I did not complete it."

5. If a man had intercourse with the handmaid many times, he is liable to but one guilt offering. Thus if he had intercourse with the handmaid many times wantonly, or if he had intercourse with her through error and he became aware of it and he again had intercourse with her through error and he became aware of it—even a hundred times during a hundred spells of unawareness—he need bring but one guilt offering and be granted atonement for them all, both the acts committed wantonly and the acts committed through error. This applies with a single handmaid; but if he had intercourse with many handmaids during even a single

spell of unawareness, he is liable to a guilt offering for each one of them.

6. If he had intercourse with a handmaid and set apart his guilt offering, and he again had intercourse with her after he had set apart his guilt offering, he is liable for each act, since the setting apart of the offering keeps the acts distinct and he thus counts as one who had brought his offering and afterward had intercourse with her. So, too, if he five times had intercourse during a single spell of unawareness with one handmaid and he became aware of one of these times and set apart his guilt offering, and he afterward became aware of the second time, he must set apart another guilt offering, even if this all happened during a single spell of unawareness. Inasmuch as he became aware only after he had set apart his offering, he counts as one who had intercourse after he had set apart his offering, since in the case of the handmaid the same rule applies both to him who transgresses through error and to him who transgresses wantonly.

7. "Because of what is wrongfully gotten": thus, if a man had a pĕruṭah's worth or more of an Israelite's property, whether he acquired it by robbery, whether he stole it, or whether it was deposited with him or lent to him or he held it in joint ownership or in any other way, and he denied that he had it and swore falsely, whether through error or wantonly, he must bring a guilt offering for his sin. And it is this which is called "the guilt offering for what is gotten wrongfully." It is expressly taught in the Law that no one is granted atonement by the guilt offering unless he gives back to its owner the property which is in his hand. But neglect of the added fifth does not hinder the atonement.

We have already explained in Laws Concerning Oaths when it is that a man becomes liable through this oath so that he must bring this guilt offering, and when he is exempt from it, and how he becomes liable to many guilt offerings according to the number of oaths imposed on him, and how he becomes liable to but one guilt offering.

8. "Because of sacrilege": thus, if through error a man derived profit to the value of one pĕruṭah from anything that is hallowed, he must make restitution of his profit and add a fifth of the value and bring a guilt offering, and so will he be granted atonement. And we have already explained in Laws Concerning Sacrilege that neglect of the offering or of restoring the value of the profit hinders atonement, but neglect of the added fifth does not hinder it.

9. If during a single spell of unawareness a man ate anything from five dishes whereby sacrilege is committed, even if it was from but a single animal offering, and he consumed a pĕruṭah's worth at each meal, he is liable to a guilt offering for each of them, since the separate dishes avail to mark distinction when sacrilege is in question and they count as many kinds, although they are not kept distinct when liability to extirpation is in question.

Especial stringency applies to sacrilege in that he who suffers another to profit is equally culpable with him who profits, and anything needed to make up the forbidden quantity can be included after a long time, and the agent who fulfills his errand renders liable him who had sent him—rules which do not apply to other forbidden acts.

10. Wherever a man is made liable to an offering for undoubted guilt, his sin must first have become known to him and then he must bring his guilt offering; but if he brought it before his sin became known to him and it became known to him only after he had offered it, it does not effect atonement for him.

As for any sin whereby liability to an offering for undoubted guilt is incurred, it is all one whether it be a king or an anointed priest or any of the common people—in this all are alike.

11. As for any sin whereby liability to an offering for undoubted guilt is incurred, if a man was in doubt whether he did or did not commit it, he is in no wise liable. Therefore if a man brought to pass what was but doubtfully sacrilege, he incurs no liability, as we have explained in Laws Concerning Sacrilege.

12. If there lay before a man a piece of ordinary flesh and a piece of consecrated flesh, and he ate one of them and it is not known which, he is not liable. If he returned and ate the other, he must bring a guilt offering for his sacrilege. If another ate the second piece, neither of them is liable.

13. If there was a piece of forbidden fat and a piece of consecrated flesh, and a man ate one of them, he must bring a suspensive guilt offering because of the fat; if he ate the other, he must bring a sin offering because of the fat and an offering for undoubted guilt because of sacrilege against the consecrated flesh. If another came and ate the second piece, the other, too, must bring a suspensive guilt offering.

If there was a piece of fat and a piece of consecrated fat, and he ate one of them, he must bring a sin offering. If he ate the second after he had become aware concerning the first, he must bring two sin offerings and an offering for undoubted guilt because of his sacrilege. If another came and ate the second, each need bring only one sin offering.

We have already explained in Laws Concerning Forbidden Foods why the prohibition respecting consecrated things is applied in addition to the prohibition respecting fat. And the same applies also in every like case of forbidden acts.

CHAPTER X

1. There are six whose duty it is to bring a rising and falling offering and these are they: a leper; a woman after childbirth; he who swears an oath of testimony, wantonly or through error; he who swears a useless oath falsely through error; an unclean person who through error eats what is hallowed; and an unclean person who through error enters the Temple.

2. As for the offering of a woman after childbirth, if she is rich she brings a year-old lamb for a whole offering and a young pigeon or a turtledove for a sin offering; and if her means do not suffice, her offering "falls" and she brings two turtledoves or two young

pigeons, one for a whole offering and one for a sin offering; even though her means suffice for a lamb, yet not for its drink offerings, she may bring the poor person's offering.

3. The leper when he is "cleansed" brings three beasts: two male lambs, one for a whole offering and one for a guilt offering, and a female lamb for a sin offering. If his means do not suffice he brings two turtledoves or two young pigeons, one for a whole offering and one for a sin offering, and a male lamb for a guilt offering.

4. Because of the oath of testimony, and because of a useless oath sworn falsely through error, and because of error whereby uncleanness befalls the Temple or its Hallowed Things, a man brings a female sheep or goat, as for other prescribed sin offerings. But if his means do not suffice, he brings two turtledoves or two young pigeons, one for a whole offering and one for a sin offering; and if his means do not suffice for birds, he brings the tenth of an ephah of fine flour. And it is this which is called "the sinner's meal offering," the manner whereof has been expounded in Laws Concerning the Manner of Making Offerings.

5. These offerings are all plainly prescribed in the Law, and it is plainly prescribed who is liable to bring them, excepting only him who while unclean enters the Temple through error or eats what is hallowed. For thus is it there written: *If anyone sin in that he heareth the voice of adjuration . . . or if anyone touch any unclean thing . . . or if anyone swear clearly with his lips . . . And it shall be, when he shall be guilty in one of these things . . . he shall bring his guilt offering unto the Lord* (Lev. 5:1 ff.).

From oral tradition it is learned that he who is here made liable to an offering is the unclean person who, having become unclean, entered into the Temple or ate unwittingly of what was hallowed. Although this rests on tradition it is, as it were, plainly prescribed, for the Law has plainly condemned to extirpation the unclean person who eats what is hallowed and the unclean person who enters the Temple. Of him who eats it is said: *But the soul that eateth of the flesh of the sacrifice of peace offerings that pertain unto the Lord, having his uncleanness upon him, that soul shall be cut off* (Lev. 7:20); and of him who enters the Temple it is said: *That soul shall be cut off from the midst of the assembly, because he hath defiled the sanctuary of the Lord* (Num. 19:20). Since the Law has condemned them to extirpation for defiling the Temple and its Hallowed Things it has fixed the offering which they must bring if they transgress through error.

6. Offerings to which a woman is liable may be offered on her behalf by her husband: if he is poor he brings a poor man's offering, and if he is rich he brings a rich man's offering on her behalf. But on behalf of his son or his daughter or his bondman or his bond-woman he need bring but a poor man's offering and thereby enable them to eat of animal offerings.

7. The king and the anointed priest bring the same offering as do ordinary people because of the oath of testimony or the useless oath or uncleanness brought upon the Temple and its Hallowed Things, for Scripture has not distinguished the offering of the king from the offering of an ordinary person or from the offering of the anointed priest except in respect of the commandments for which, if they transgress them in error, they are liable to a pre-scribed sin offering, as we have explained. But in what concerns the rising and falling offering, all are equal.

We have already explained in Laws Concerning Oaths when it is that a man becomes liable because of an oath of testimony and because of a useless oath sworn in error, and when he is not liable because of them, and how he becomes liable to many offerings cor-responding to the number of the oaths, and how he becomes liable to but a single offering. And in Laws Concerning Those Whose Atonement Is Not Complete I will explain how a woman after childbirth and a leper become liable to many offerings and how each of them becomes liable to but a single offering.

8. As for any one of those who must bring an offering alike whether they transgressed wantonly or in error, if he transgressed

under constraint, he is not liable to an offering; and, needless to say, with respect to other transgressions for which he is liable to a sin offering only if he committed them through error, he is not liable if he acted under constraint.

9. If a man set apart money to buy a female lamb for his sin offering and he became in need of the money, he may bring a female goat and exchange that money for the female goat and have the benefit of the money. So, too, if he set apart money for a female goat but took a female lamb, he may have the use of that money.

10. If he set apart money for a beast and then became poor, he may take two turtledoves or two young pigeons and exchange that money for them and have the use of the money. If he set apart money for young pigeons or turtledoves and then became poor, he may bring the tenth of an ephah and exchange that money for it and have the use of the money.

So, too, if he was poor and set apart money for the tenth of an ephah and then became rich, he may add to the money and bring birds. If he set money apart for birds and became richer, he may add to the money and bring a female lamb or a female goat.

Even if he from whom he would inherit was at the point of death, he still counts as a poor man until he from whom he would inherit dies and he inherits from him.

11. If a rich man set apart a female lamb or a female goat and it suffered a blemish, if he pleases he may bring birds with its price; but if he set apart birds and they became invalid, he may not bring a tenth of an ephah with their price, since birds can never be redeemed.

12. If a man set apart the tenth of an ephah and he grew rich before it was consecrated in the vessel, it counts as any other meal offering and may be redeemed and eaten; but if he grew rich after it was consecrated in the vessel, it must be left until its appearance spoils and it must go forth to the place of burning.

13. If a rich man set apart a pair of birds to sell them and with their price buy a female lamb or a female goat and he then grew poor, he may bring this pair even though theirs was a consecration of price which (their owner being a rich man) was unacceptable as an offering. And why do they not remain unacceptable? Because early nonacceptance does not effect permanent nonacceptance, and this pair are now become fit and seemly for him.

If a poor man offered a rich man's offering he fulfills his obligation; but if a rich man offered a poor man's offering he does not fulfill his obligation.

CHAPTER XI

1. In the case of uncleanness which is brought upon the Temple or its Hallowed Things through error there is a feature which does not apply to other transgressions involving extirpation; for with all other transgressions involving extirpation, if a man transgressed through error and became aware in the end that he had sinned, even if he was not aware in the beginning, he is liable to a sin offering, but if uncleanness is brought upon the Temple or its Hallowed Things, he need bring a rising and falling offering only if he was aware in the beginning of the uncleanness and aware also of the Hallowed Thing or of the Temple, and was aware in the end of the uncleanness and aware also of the Hallowed Thing or of the Temple, but was unaware in the meantime.

Thus, if he became unclean and entered the Temple or ate of some Hallowed Thing, and he afterward became aware that he had become unclean and that he was unclean when he ate or when he entered and that it was a Hallowed Thing which he ate or that it was the Temple which he entered, he is liable to an offering only if he knew before he had entered or before he had eaten that he had become unclean and that this was the Temple or that this was some Hallowed Thing.

Thus, if he became unclean and knew that he had become unclean and knew that this was the Temple or that this was a Hallowed Thing, and he afterward grew unaware of the uncleanness and forgot that he had become unclean and entered the Temple or ate of some Hallowed Thing while aware that this was the Temple or that this was some Hallowed Thing; or if he acted through error and forgot that this was the Temple or that this was flesh of some Hallowed Thing while aware that he was unclean, and he entered in or ate; or if he acted through error or forgot that he had become unclean and forgot that this was flesh of some Hallowed Thing or that this was the Temple, and he entered in or ate, and he afterward became aware of the things of which he had been unaware—then he must bring a rising and falling offering for any among these six classes of transgression.

And whence do we know that such is the rule in case of error respecting the Temple and its Hallowed Things? Since it is said of other transgressions committed through error: *in doing any of the things which the Lord hath commanded not to be done, and he be guilty . . . if his sin which he hath sinned be known to him* (Lev. 4: 27)—if, namely, he became aware in the end, even though he did not know in the beginning—whereas of uncleanness brought upon the Temple and its Hallowed Things it is said: *And it be hid from him; and when he knoweth of it, he be guilty* (Lev. 5: 3); since it is said *And it be hid from him,* this implies that there was awareness in the beginning. And it is said: *And when he knoweth of it* (Lev. 5: 3); thus we learn that he must needs have awareness at the beginning and awareness at the end and unawareness in the meantime.

2. If he became unclean and knew that he had become unclean but did not know from which primary uncleanness he had become unclean and he forgot that he had become unclean and he afterward entered the Temple or ate of some Hallowed Thing, and, after entering in or after eating he became aware of the primary uncleanness from which he had become unclean, even though he did not know in the beginning from which primary uncleanness he had become unclean, inasmuch as he knew that he was unclean, there was awareness of uncleanness in the beginning.

But if he was not aware of the rules concerning uncleanness—if, for example, he became unclean from a lentil's bulk of a creeping thing, and although he knew that the creeping thing conveyed uncleanness he did not know the prescribed quantity of it which conveys uncleanness, and he forgot altogether that he had touched a creeping thing and entered the Temple or ate of some Hallowed Thing, and afterward he became aware that he had touched a lentil's bulk of the creeping thing—then with such a one it remains in doubt whether or not he is liable to an offering.

So, too, if a man had never seen the Temple nor discerned where it was, and he became unclean and knew that he had become unclean, and he entered the Temple but knew not in the beginning that this was where it was, since he had never before seen it, and he afterward remembered the uncleanness and knew that this was the Temple—then with him it remains in doubt whether or not knowledge that there was a Temple in existence counts as knowledge unless he knew where it was in the beginning.

It seems to me that these who are liable to an offering by reason of doubt should not bring an offering, lest they bring what is unhallowed into the Temple Court. And if thou sayest, "But is not the sin offering of birds brought by reason of doubt, and not consumed?"—this is because he who brings it, whose atonement is not complete, is forbidden to eat of Hallowed Things until he brings his atonement; but he who is not of those whose atonement is not complete does not bring an offering by reason of doubt.

3. If a man became unclean in the Temple Court, it is needful that he know in the beginning that he had become unclean and that this was the Temple, and if afterward he became unaware that he had become unclean yet remained mindful that this was the Temple, or if he became unaware that this was the Temple but did not forget that he had become unclean, or if he became unaware of both the one and the other, when it becomes known to him he must bring a rising and falling offering, provided that he had tarried as long as the time prescribed, as we have explained in Laws Concerning Entering into the Temple.

4. If a man wantonly rendered himself unclean and he did not tarry as long as the time prescribed, with him it remains in doubt whether the time limit of (tarrying, namely, that of) a prostration applies to one who acted under constraint only or to one who acted wantonly; therefore if he became unaware of his uncleanness and went out without tarrying more than the time prescribed, he need not bring an offering.

So, too, if he suspended himself in the air above the Temple Court it remains in doubt whether the air above the Temple Court does or does not count as the Temple Court.

5. If a man was in doubt whether or not he entered the Temple or ate of any Hallowed Thing while he was unclean, he need not bring a suspensive guilt offering, since the offering in case of doubt is brought only for a transgression involving extirpation, for which, if it is committed through error, a fixed sin offering is incurred.

6. If there were two paths before a man, the one unclean and the other clean, and he went along the first and then returned and went along the second, and at the time that he went along the second he forgot that he had gone along the first, and this uncleanness was forgotten by him and he entered the Temple or ate of any Hallowed Thing, he is liable to an offering, even though in the beginning he had not complete awareness of the uncleanness but only partial awareness, since he did not know that he had gone along both paths, so that by going along them both he would of a certainty become unclean. Nevertheless he is liable to a sin offering since partial awareness counts as complete awareness.

If he went along the first path and then entered the Temple or ate of any Hallowed Thing, he is not liable because his uncleanness remains in doubt.

7. If he was sprinkled the third day and the seventh day and he immersed himself and, after he had entered the Temple, he went along the second path and again entered the Temple, he is liable to an offering, since he had entered the Temple while he

was unclean of a certainty, either at the first time or at the second time; and although knowledge at either time was knowledge which was in doubt, since there was doubt about either path, here, respecting uncleanness brought upon the Temple and its Hallowed Things, the Sages have made knowledge which was in doubt count as certain knowledge.

8. If a person was unclean and two said to him, "Thou didst enter the Temple," and he said to them, "I did not enter," he is to be believed, and he need not bring an offering, for if he wished he could say, "I did so wantonly." If two said to him, "Thou wast unclean when thou didst enter the Temple and in our presence thou becamest unclean and thou knewest that thou wast unclean," even though there were days enough between this uncleanness of which they testified and his entering the Temple to enable him to say, "I had since then immersed myself," inasmuch as he gainsaid the witnesses and said, "I never became unclean," they are believed, and he must bring an offering on their evidence. If two could have brought upon him the graver penalty of death, still more can they bring upon him the lesser penalty of an offering, since he had gainsaid them.

9. For uncleanness which is brought upon the Temple and its Hallowed Things where there was knowledge in the beginning but no knowledge in the end, the he-goat of the Day of Atonement, which is prepared within the Holy of Holies, and the Day of Atonement hold a man's guilt in suspense until he becomes aware of it and brings a rising and falling offering.

And where there was no knowledge in the beginning but knowledge in the end, the he-goat which is prepared outside on the Day of Atonement and the Day of Atonement effect atonement.

And where there was knowledge neither in the beginning nor in the end, the he-goats of the feasts and the he-goats of the New Moons effect atonement.

And for wanton defilement of the Temple and its Hallowed Things, the bullock of the High Priest offered on the Day of Atonement effects atonement if he who transgressed wantonly

was one of the priests; and if he was a (lay) Israelite, the blood of
the he-goat, which is prepared within the Holy of Holies, and the
Day of Atonement effect atonement, for it is said: *And he shall
make atonement for what is holy because of the uncleannesses of the
children of Israel* (Lev. 16:16).

CHAPTER XII

1. Wherever liability to a fixed sin offering is incurred for a
transgression committed through error, if the Supreme Court erred
in their ruling and so ruled as to declare that transgression permissible, and, owing to their ruling, the people erred and committed the transgression, relying on their ruling, if the court afterward became aware that they had erred, the court must bring a
sin offering because of the error in their ruling, even though they
themselves had committed no act; for we are not concerned
whether the court themselves did or did not act according to their
ruling, but only with their ruling as such. But the rest of the people
are not liable to an offering, even though it was they who committed the act, since they relied upon the court.

And what is the offering which the court must bring for such an
error? If they had erred in giving a ruling about idolatry, they
must bring from every tribe a bullock for a whole offering and a
he-goat for a sin offering. And this is the offering which is spoken
of in the Book of Numbers where it is said: *And it shall be if it be
done in error, it being hid from the eyes of the congregation*
(Num. 15:24). From oral tradition it is learned that this speaks
of an error respecting idolatry.

And if the court had erred in giving a ruling about any other
matters involving extirpation whereby, if the transgression was
committed in error, liability to a prescribed sin offering is incurred,
each tribe must bring a bullock for a sin offering. And this it is
which is spoken of in the Book of Leviticus where it is said: *And
if the whole congregation of Israel shall err* (Lev. 4:13).

Thus we learn that if the Supreme Court erred in their ruling
about idolatry the whole congregation must bring twelve bullocks

for whole offerings and twelve he-goats for sin offerings which must be burned since their blood enters within the Holy of Holies, and it is they which are called "the he-goats of idolatry." And if the court erred about any other of the commandments, they must bring twelve bullocks for sin offerings which must be burned since their blood enters within the Holy of Holies; and each of these bullocks is called "the bullock offered for the unconscious transgression of the congregation," since it is said: *Then the congregation (kahal) shall offer a young bullock* (Lev. 4:14). Every separate community and every tribe is called *congregation,* for it is said: *And Jehoshaphat stood in the congregation of Judah* (II Chron. 20:5). It is all one whether it was all Israel in all the Land of Israel who committed an act on the authority of the court which gave the ruling, or whether it was a majority of Israel, even though they were a minority among the number of the tribes, or whether it was a majority of the tribes who committed the act, even though they were a minority among all Israel. They must offer bullocks according to the number of all the tribes, a bullock for every tribe or, if it was a matter of idolatry, a bullock and a he-goat for every tribe. Even those who did not sin must offer them on behalf of those who sinned, even though the act was committed by one tribe alone; it being a majority of the congregation, the whole congregation must bring twelve bullocks or, in a matter of idolatry, twelve bullocks and twelve he-goats.

2. If the court were in doubt whether they had erred or had not erred in their ruling, they are not liable to a suspensive guilt offering, for it is said: *When the sin wherein they have sinned is known* (Lev. 4:14)—when it becomes known then only do they become liable to an offering, as will be explained. When does this apply, that the court are liable to an offering while they who committed the act on their authority are not liable? If they who gave the ruling were the Supreme Court of one and seventy, and the chief of the session was with them in giving the ruling, and they were all capable of giving a ruling, and they all or the greater part of them erred in this matter wherein they gave a ruling, and they taught

expressly and said to the people, "Ye are permitted to do such and such," or if they who heard it from the mouth of the court said to others, "Ye are permitted to do such and such," and all the congregation or the greater part of them acted according to their word, and they who thus acted transgressed through error on their authority, supposing that in the matter wherein the court gave the ruling they had given a ruling in accordance with the Law; and if they gave a ruling such as would in part annul and in part sustain but not uproot a commandment, and when the court became aware of it, they were aware of the essential question respecting which they had erred in giving a ruling—it is when all these things coincide that the court are liable to an offering, while he who acts on their authority is not liable. But if any one of all these conditions is lacking, the court are not liable to an offering, and if any man transgressed through error and committed some act, he must bring a fixed sin offering because of his error.

CHAPTER XIII

1. How are we to understand that, if any one of all these conditions, which we have stated, is lacking the court are not liable, but they who commit the act are liable?

Suppose that the court of a single tribe gave it a ruling that the fat of the maw was permissible, and the people of that place ate it on their authority; the court are not liable, and everyone who ate must bring the fixed sin offering because of his error.

So, too, if the Supreme Court taught that the blood of the heart was permissible, but the chief of the session was not with them or one of them was not eligible for appointment to the Sanhedrin —if, for example, he was a proselyte or a bastard or too old or had never begotten children or was disqualified on any other such ground—and the people acted on their authority and ate the blood of the heart, the court are not liable; and everyone who ate of it must bring the fixed sin offering because of his error.

And whence do we know that Scripture speaks only of the Supreme Court? Because it is said: *And if the whole congregation of Israel shall err* (Lev. 4:13). And whence do we know that this applies only when all the members are capable of giving a ruling? Because it is said: *and some thing be hid from the eyes of the congregation* (*ibid.*): it applies only when the court are like *eyes* to them. Elsewhere it says: *And the congregation shall judge . . .* (Num. 35:24): as the *congregation* here spoken of concerning cases entailing death are all of them capable of giving a ruling, so also the *congregation* spoken of concerning this matter of error must all of them be capable of giving a ruling.

So, too, if they gave a ruling and one of them was aware that they had erred and said to them, "Ye do err," but they who would permit outnumbered him and pronounced the thing permissible, the court are not liable, and everyone who acted on their authority must bring a fixed sin offering because of his error, for it is said: *And if the whole congregation of Israel shall err* (Lev. 4:13): they are liable only when the whole of the Sanhedrin err.

If one of the Sanhedrin, or a minority among them, was aware that they who would permit had erred, but kept silence, inasmuch as a ruling was given and there was none who dissented, and the ruling spread abroad among the greater part of the congregation, the court are liable to an offering, and everyone who acted on their authority is exempt. Moreover they who kept silence, if they acted on the authority of those who gave the ruling, are liable, because they were not dependent upon the court.

So, too, if they discussed any matter and said, "This thing is permitted," yet gave no ruling to the people nor said to them, "Ye are permitted to act thus," and someone had heard from them at the time when they determined that the thing was permissible and went and acted according to what he had heard, everyone who acts thus is liable to a sin offering, and the court are exempt, since they had not expressly given a ruling to them to act thus. So, too, if they gave a ruling and only a minority of the congregation acted on their authority, and the error became known, the court are exempt, and the minority which so acted are liable and each one must bring his sin offering.

2. If the Sanhedrin themselves acted in accordance with their own ruling they may not be included together to make up a majority of the congregation; but a majority is accounted a majority only if they who acted in error were a majority apart from the Sanhedrin.

If the majority of the people of the Land of Israel acted on the authority of the court, even if they who so acted were but a single tribe, or if the majority of the tribes so acted, even if they were a minority of the congregation, the court are liable, and they who acted on their authority are exempt. Thus, if the inhabitants of the Land of Israel were 600,001 and they who acted in accordance with the ruling of the court were 300,001, and they were all members of the tribe of Judah only; or if they who acted so were all of them members from among seven tribes, even though they were but 100,000 men, the court are liable, and all who acted on their authority are exempt.

No regard is paid to those who dwell outside the Land, since only inhabitants of the Land of Israel are called a *congregation*. The tribes of Manasseh and Ephraim are not reckoned as two tribes in this matter, but the two of them count as a single tribe.

3. If they who committed the act were a majority at the time of the sin but a minority at the time when the error became known, or if they were a minority at the time of the sin but a majority at the time when the error became known, all is determined by their number at the time of the act.

4. If the court ruled that a certain kind of fat was permissible and a minority of the congregation ate it on their authority, and they became aware that they had sinned and retracted, and afterward the court ruled that such and such an idol was permissible and another minority worshiped it on their authority, and when they who worshiped and they who ate were included together they made a majority, these can be included together even though they were aware of their error in the meantime. This applies if they who gave the ruling were the same court. But if the court was

dissolved which in the beginning gave the first ruling and another arose and gave the second ruling, the minorities may not be included the one with the other.

5. And the same applies even if two successive courts gave a ruling about a single matter, for example, if each gave a ruling about fat or about blood.

So, too, if they who committed the act erred, but not on the authority of the ruling, the court are exempt and all who committed the act are liable. Thus, if a court gave a ruling that it was permissible to eat all of the fat of the maw, and one of the congregation knew that the court had erred and that the fat of the maw was forbidden, yet he ate it because of their ruling, thinking that it was a duty to obey the court even though they had erred, he who eats it is liable to a fixed sin offering because of what he ate, and he may not be included in the number of those who erred on the authority of the court. This applies if he who knew that they had erred was a scholar or a disciple who was competent to render decisions; but if he was an unlearned person, he is not liable, since his knowledge about forbidden things was not certain knowledge, and he must be included among the total of those who erred on the authority of the court.

So, too, if he did not know that the court had erred, and his intention was to eat of permitted fat and forbidden fat, and he ate the fat of the maw, which they had pronounced permissible, and he did not know that it was the fat of the maw, he is liable to a sin offering since his eating was because of his own error and not because of the ruling; and he may not be included in the number of those who erred on the authority of the court, for it is said: *For in respect of all the people it was done in error* (Num. 15:26): it applies only when there was a single error respecting all of them.

So, too, if he depended upon his own opinion and ate the fat of the maw, which the court had ruled to be permissible, and he ate it not because of their ruling but because in his opinion it was permissible, he is liable to a fixed sin offering on his own account.

This is the general rule: if a man depended on the court he is exempt, provided that there lacked none of all the conditions which we have stated; but if a man depended upon his own opinion he may not be included to make up a majority of those who acted in error.

6. If the court willfully gave a ruling permitting what was forbidden, and the congregation acted in error on their authority, the court are not liable to the offering, because they acted willfully, and each one of those who acted on their authority is liable to an offering on his own account, because he acted in error. If the court gave a ruling through error and the congregation knew that they had erred, and that it was improper to accept the ruling from them, yet nevertheless the congregation acted on their authority, both alike are exempt from the offering: the court are exempt because it was not as a result of their ruling that the congregation transgressed; and all who committed the act are exempt from the offering because they had acted willfully, since they knew that the court erred and that it was improper thus to act.

CHAPTER XIV

1. If the court erred and gave a ruling such as would uproot some main principle of the Law, and all the people acted on their authority, the court are exempt and everyone who so acted is liable to a fixed sin offering, for it is said: *and some thing be hid* (Lev. 4:13)—but not a whole main principle.

2. The court never become liable unless they so rule as partly to annul and partly to sustain matters not explicit and plainly stated in the Law, whereupon the court become liable to the offering and they who act on their authority are not liable. Thus, if the court erred and ruled that it was permissible to prostrate oneself before an idol, or that it was permissible to carry a burden on the Sabbath from one domain to another, or that it was permissible to have intercourse with a woman who awaits day against day, it is as though they had said, "There is nothing in the Law about the Sabbath," or "There is nothing in the Law about idols," or "There is

nothing in the Law about the menstruant," for they would have uprooted a whole main principle. And this or the like of it is not an error of ruling but forgetfulness. Therefore the court are not liable to the offering, and one who acts on their authority is liable to a sin offering on his own account.

But if the court erred and gave a ruling saying that he is culpable who carries a burden from one domain to another since it is said: *Let no man go out of his place on the seventh day* (Exod. 16:29), but that it is permissible if he throws it out or hands it out, or if the court uprooted one of the primary acts of work and ruled that it was not an act of work, they are liable.

So, too, if the court erred and said that he is culpable who prostrates himself before an idol by stretching out arms and legs, since it is said of it: *Thou shalt not prostrate thyself before any other god* (Exod. 34:14), but that it is permissible if he kneels on the ground and does not stretch out his arms and his legs, they are liable.

So, too, if the court erred and said that he is culpable who has intercourse with a woman who awaits day against day and who suffers a flow during the day, since it is said: *All the days of the issue of her uncleanness* (Lev. 15:25), but that he is permitted to have intercourse with her if she suffered it by night; or if the court gave a ruling saying that if a man's wife perceived herself to be menstruous at the moment of congress, it is permissible for him to withdraw from her while the member is rigid, they are liable.

So, too, if the court erred and said that he is culpable who eats the blood that issues at the moment of slaughtering but that he is permitted to eat the blood of the heart, they are liable.

And the same applies with every like error: if the court gave such rulings and the greater part of the congregation acted on their authority, the congregation are not liable, and the court must bring an offering because of their error.

3. If the court ruled that the Sabbath was ended because the sun was covered up and they thought that the sun had set, and it afterward shone, this is not a ruling but an error; and anyone

who did an act of work is liable, but the court are not liable. So, too, if the court gave permission to a man's wife to be married because it had been testified in their presence that her husband was dead, and afterward her husband came forward, this is not a ruling but an error, and the woman and her second husband are liable to a sin offering on account of their error. And the same applies in every like case.

4. If the court gave a ruling through error, forgetting the very sin about which they had given their ruling, even though they knew of a certainty that they had sinned through error, and even though the people made it known to them and said to them, "In such and such a matter did ye give us a ruling," they are exempt, and they who acted on the authority of the court are liable on their own account, for it is said: *When the sin wherein they have sinned is known* (Lev. 4:14), and not that they who sin shall make it known.

Thus, if the court had erred and pronounced permissible the fat which is on the maw, and the greater part of the people ate of it, and after the court knew that they had erred in the ruling and had pronounced permissible an act for which, if done wantonly, extirpation was incurred, and if through error, a fixed sin offering —if the court were in doubt whether they had pronounced permissible only some of the fats or only some of the blood, they are not liable, and if anyone ate of the fat or the blood he must bring a fixed sin offering.

5. If the court gave a ruling through error and their error became known to them, whether they had brought their atonement offering or whether they had not brought it, and anyone acted in accordance with their ruling, which had spread abroad throughout the greater part of the congregation after the court had become aware of their error, such a one must bring a suspensive guilt offering: inasmuch as he should have inquired at all times concerning the things which were newly enacted in the court, but had not inquired, he counts as one who was in doubt whether he had sinned or had not sinned. This applies to one who was in the same region

as the court; but if a man had seen the ruling and gone to some other region, even though he committed the act after the court had become aware of their error, he is not liable since he had relied upon the court and it was not possible for him to inquire. Moreover, if a man was in haste to go, even though he had not yet gone on the journey, and he committed an act on the authority of the court after they had become aware of their error, he is not liable.

CHAPTER XV

1. We have already explained that if the *Naśi* committed any error for which a common person must bring a female lamb or a female goat as his fixed sin offering, he must bring a he-goat, and that if the anointed priest so erred, he must bring a bullock.

When does this apply, namely, that the anointed priest must bring a bullock because of his error? When he has erred in giving a ruling of his own and committed an act through the error of his own ruling alone, provided that he was an outstanding scholar, for it is said: *If the anointed priest shall sin so as to bring guilt on the people* (Lev. 4:3); thus the anointed one counts as the community: just as the community that constitutes the court is liable to an offering only if the members were scholars qualified to render a ruling and erred in their ruling—while those who committed the act acted on their authority—and only if they so ruled as partly to annul and partly to sustain a principle of the Law, so is it with the anointed one in all these respects.

2. Thus, if the anointed priest erred in giving a ruling on his own authority and thought that it was permissible to throw anything from one domain to another on the Sabbath, and he threw something from one domain to another, relying on his own ruling, when he becomes aware of his sin he must bring a bullock for a sin offering; but if he did not rely on his own ruling but merely erred and threw something because of his error, or if he relied on his own ruling but was not an outstanding scholar, or if he uprooted an entire principle of the Law by his own ruling, or if he erred

in his ruling in such wise as partly to annul a main principle yet committed no act while relying on his own ruling, but acted out of some other error, or if he acted willfully in giving the ruling but committed the act through error—he is not liable to any offering at all, for his position in relation to his own ruling is in all respects like the position of the congregation in relation to the court's ruling.

If he gave a ruling of his own but forgot for what reason he gave the ruling, and at the moment of committing the act he said, "I am acting on the strength of my ruling," he must bring a bullock as a sin offering.

3. If he gave a ruling of his own such as partly to annul and partly to sustain the law against idolatry and he committed an act in accordance with his ruling, he must bring a female goat, as does a common person, provided that he gave the ruling by error, as we have explained; for the anointed priest is liable to an offering only if *some thing be hid* (Lev. 4: 13) in his ruling and, at the same time, the act be committed in unawareness, as in the case of the congregation. But if he erred only in committing some act without giving any ruling, whether concerning idolatry or any other of the commandments, he need bring no offering at all.

4. If the anointed priest together with the court gave a ruling, and both he and the court erred in their ruling, even though they committed an act in accordance with this ruling wherein they had erred, inasmuch as he did not rely at the time of action on his own ruling alone but on his ruling together with the ruling of the court, he is exempt and need not bring an atonement offering on his own account; but if the court brought an offering, atonement is effected for him within the whole body of the congregation. And if it was they who committed the act (and not the court) who brought the offering, he need bring no offering, since he does not need atonement on his own account.

5. If he gave a ruling through error together with the court, and they erred in a question of blood and he in one of fat, atonement is not effected for him together with the congregation, but he must bring a bullock on his own account.

6. If the anointed priest was in doubt whether he had or had not committed such an error—namely, an error in ruling as well as in the commission of the act—he need not bring a suspensive guilt offering since he is therein like the congregation, which does not bring a suspensive guilt offering for doubtfulness in case of a decision given in error.

But the Naśi, if he was in doubt whether he had sinned or had not sinned, must bring a suspensive guilt offering, as do the common people, because his error does not depend on his own ruling. Who is the Naśi spoken of in the Law? He is the king, over whom no man in Israel has authority and above whom in his kingdom there is none save the Lord his God, whether he is of the house of David or of any other tribe of Israel. And if there are many kings, none of them subject to the other, each one of them *shall bring for his offering a goat* (Lev. 4: 23) because of his error.

And who is the "anointed priest"? He is the High Priest who is anointed with the oil of unction, not he who is dedicated by the many garments.

7. If a High Priest who had been anointed with the oil of unction retired from his ministry because of a blemish or old age or the like, and he sinned through such an error, he must bring a bullock because of his error, since there is no difference between a ministering anointed priest and a retired anointed priest except the bullock of the Day of Atonement and the daily tenth of an ephah, which none offers save the priest who fulfills the duties of the High Priesthood. But in respect of the bullock which is brought because of transgression of any of the commandments, they are equal.

8. If the Naśi committed some act together with the congregation because of a decision given by the court, atonement is effected for him within the whole body of the people, for if it was the court who brought an offering because of their error, all the people and the king would be exempt from an offering, as we have explained. And if it was the people who had committed some act on the authority of the court who were liable to an offering, and the king was among those who committed the act, then he must bring

a he-goat, for the he-goat of the Naśi stands in the stead of the female goat of a common person.

9. A Naśi who suffered leprosy is withdrawn from his rulership; and a Naśi who is withdrawn from his rulership counts as a common person. If he sinned while he was yet Naśi and then retired from his dignity, he must bring a he-goat, for it is said: *For his sin, wherein he hath sinned* (Lev. 4:23)—in accordance with his rank at the time of his sin must he bring it.

10. If an anointed priest or a king had sinned before he was appointed, even though he was not aware of his sin until after he was appointed, he counts as a common person, for it is said: *When a ruler sinneth* (Lev. 4:22), *If the anointed priest shall sin* (Lev. 4:3): they count as common persons unless the one sins while he is the ruler or the other while he is the anointed priest.

Therefore if he ate what was doubtfully fat while he was a common person, and he became aware of his condition of doubt after he was appointed High Priest, he must bring a suspensive guilt offering.

If a man ate a half olive's bulk of fat while he was a common person and a half olive's bulk while he was Naśi, during a single spell of unawareness, or if he ate a half olive's bulk while he was Naśi and a half olive's bulk after he withdrew from office, these are not to be included together and he is not liable to an offering.

If he ate a half olive's bulk while he was a common person and he was appointed Naśi and then withdrew from office and he then ate a half olive's bulk while he was again a common person, it is in doubt whether the two are to be included together or whether the period of rulership keeps them apart.

TREATISE V

LAWS CONCERNING
THOSE WHOSE
ATONEMENT
IS NOT COMPLETE

Involving Four Positive Commandments

To Wit

1. That a woman with flux, when she becomes clean, shall bring an offering;
2. That a woman after childbirth, when she becomes clean, shall bring an offering;
3. That a man with flux, when he becomes clean, shall bring an offering;
4. That the leper, when he becomes clean, shall bring an offering.
   And after they have brought their offerings their cleanness becomes complete.

An exposition of these commandments
is contained in the following chapters.

NOTE

In the list of the 613 commandments prefixed to the Code, those which deal with the subject of this Treatise are cited in the following form.

Positive commandments:

[3] 74. That a man with flux shall bring an offering after he is become clean from his flux, as it is said: *And when he that hath an issue is cleansed of his issue . . . he shall take to him two turtledoves, or two young pigeons . . . And the priest shall offer them, the one for a sin offering, and the other for a burnt offering* (Lev. 15: 13-15);

[1] 75. That a woman with flux shall bring an offering after she is become clean, as it is said: *But if she be cleansed of her issue . . . she shall take unto her two turtledoves, or two young pigeons . . . And the priest shall offer the one for a sin offering, and the other for a burnt offering* (Lev. 15: 28-30);

[4] 76. That the leper shall bring an offering after he is become clean, as it is said: *And on the eighth day he shall take two he-lambs without blemish . . .* (Lev. 14: 10 ff.);

[2] 77. That a woman after childbirth shall bring an offering after she is become clean, as it is said: *And when the days of her purification are fulfilled . . . she shall bring a lamb of the first year for a burnt offering, and a young pigeon, or a turtledove, for a sin offering* (Lev. 12: 6).

CHAPTER I

1. There are four who are described as "those whose atonement is not complete": a woman with flux, a woman after childbirth, a man with flux, and a leper. And why are they described as those whose atonement is not complete? Because even though they had become free of their uncleanness and had immersed themselves and awaited sunset, they each lack somewhat and their cleanness does not become complete, so that they may eat of Hallowed Things, until they bring their offering; and until they bring their atonement offering they are forbidden to eat of Hallowed Things, as we have explained in Laws Concerning Hallowed Things Which Become Invalid.

2. If a proselyte had been circumcised and had immersed himself but had not yet brought his offering, although he is forbidden to eat of Hallowed Things until he brings his offering, he is not reckoned among those whose atonement is not complete, since failure to bring his offering bars him from becoming a complete proselyte and becoming like any authentic member of Israel; and it is because of this that he cannot eat of Hallowed Things, inasmuch as he has not yet become one who is deemed an authentic Israelite. But so soon as he brings his offering and becomes an authentic Israelite he may eat of Hallowed Things.

If he brought one of a pair of birds in the morning, he may eat of Hallowed Things at eventide and afterward bring the second of the pair, since the proselyte's offering is a whole offering of a beast or two young pigeons or two turtledoves, both of which are offered as a whole offering, as we have explained in Laws Concerning the Manner of Making Offerings.

3. For the man or the woman with flux the offering prescribed for each is two turtledoves or two young pigeons, the one a whole offering and the other a sin offering. For a woman after childbirth the offering prescribed is a lamb as a whole offering and a young pigeon or a turtledove as a sin offering; and if her means do not

suffice, she may bring two turtledoves or two young pigeons, the one a whole offering and the other a sin offering. And for the leper the offering prescribed is three lambs: one a whole offering and one a guilt offering and a female lamb as a sin offering; and if his means do not suffice, he may bring a pair of birds, the one a whole offering and the other a sin offering, and a lamb as a guilt offering.

4. The man with flux and the woman with flux and the leper—all three must bring their atonement offering on the eighth day of their cleansing; for they must each count seven days of cleanness and immerse themselves on the seventh day and await sunset and bring their offering on the eighth day.

5. A woman after childbirth may not bring her offering on the fortieth day after bearing a male or on the eightieth day after bearing a female, but she must await sunset and bring her offering on the morrow, namely, the forty-first day after bearing a male and the eighty-first day after bearing a female, which is the day whereof it is said: *And when the days of her purification are fulfilled, for a son, or for a daughter* . . . (Lev. 12:6); and if she brought her offering during the days of fulfilling her purification she has not fulfilled her obligation.

Even if she brought an offering for previous births during the days of fulfilling her purification for this birth, she has not fulfilled her obligation.

If these days went by and they had not brought their atonement offering, they may bring their atonement offering after this time. So long as they have not brought their sin offering they are forbidden to eat of Hallowed Things, but failure to bring the whole offering or the guilt offering is no hindrance.

We have already explained in Laws Concerning the Manner of Making Offerings that in the case of all who are bound to bring an offering, it may be offered on their behalf only with their consent, excepting those whose atonement is not complete, whose consent is not needful, because a man may bring an offering for his sons or his daughters who are under age if they are of those whose atonement is not complete and so enable them to eat of animal offerings.

6. Who is deemed to be "a woman with flux"? She whose blood has flowed on three succeeding days other than during her time of menstruation; and such a one is "a woman with flux of greater degree" who must make count of seven clean days and who is liable to an offering.

And we have already explained in treating of the menstruant when a woman is to be deemed a woman with flux, because of issues which she suffers, and when she is not to be deemed a woman with flux, but either a menstruant or one who is clean, and when she is to be deemed a woman with flux because of doubt. Wherever we have said that she is a woman with flux and that she makes count of seven clean days, she must bring an offering and her sin offering is to be eaten; and wherever we have said that she is a woman with flux because of doubt, she must bring an offering but her sin offering is not to be eaten, for we have stated already that a sin offering of birds brought because of doubt is to be burned.

And we have there explained what a woman may give birth to or with what she may miscarry and thereby count as "unclean by childbirth," and what she may give birth to or with what she may miscarry and not thereby count as unclean by childbirth. And wherever we have said that she is unclean by childbirth she is liable to an offering and her sin offering is to be eaten; and wherever we have said that she is not unclean by childbirth she is not liable to any offering.

7. If a woman who was not presumed to be pregnant cast something and knew not what she had cast, whether it was an abortion for which she was liable to an offering or something for which she was not liable to an offering, she counts as "a woman after childbirth whose condition is in doubt," and she must bring an offering, but her sin offering is not to be eaten.

So, too, if there were two women who cast two abortions, one abortion such that an offering must be brought because of it and the other abortion such that no offering is thereby incurred, and neither recognizes which is her abortion, each of the two must bring an offering because of the doubt, and neither of the two sin offerings is to be eaten, since the sin offering of birds which is brought because of doubt must be burned: perchance she was not liable, and this sin offering of hers would therefore count as a thing unhallowed slaughtered in the Temple Court, which is forbidden for gainful use, as we have explained in Laws Concerning Slaughtering.

8. No matter whether a woman gave birth or miscarried with one abortion or with many abortions, she need bring but one offering for them all provided that she bore them all during the days of fulfilling her purification. But if she miscarried after the days of fulfilling her purification, she must bring an offering for the second also. Thus, if she gave birth to a female, any abortions with which she miscarries from the day of that birth until the end of the eighty days are included together with the first birth, and it is as though she bore twins one after the other, and she need bring but a single offering. If she miscarried on the eighty-first day or from the eighty-first day onward, and it was such as to render her liable to an offering, she must bring an offering because of that miscarriage on its own account. If she gave birth to a female and after sixty or seventy days she miscarried with a second female, she is not liable to an offering because of any abortion with which she miscarries during the eighty days assigned for this second female.

So, too, if she miscarried with a third female after sixty or seventy days during the fulfilling of her purification for the second female: because of any abortion with which she miscarries during the eighty days of her purification for the third female, she does not become liable to an offering, since it is included together with the third abortion; and the third abortion is included together with the second, since it came within the days assigned for the fulfillment of its purification; and the second is included together with the first, and she need bring but one offering for them all.

9. If a woman gave birth to one of doubtful sex or of double sex and forty days after its birth she miscarried with an abortion, she must bring an offering for this abortion: perchance the first was a male and she had miscarried after the fulfilling of her purification. And her sin offering may not be eaten: perchance the first was a female and she had miscarried during the fulfilling of her purification, for which miscarriage she was not liable to a second offering.

10. If a woman suffered five births which were in doubt or five issues which were in doubt, she need bring but one offering and may then eat of animal offerings; and she is not liable because of the others. If she suffered five births which were not in doubt or five issues which were not in doubt, she need bring but one offering and she may then eat of animal offerings; but she is still liable because of the others. And the same rule also applies to a man who suffers a flux.

If she suffered five births which were not in doubt and five births which were in doubt, or five births which were not in doubt and five issues which were in doubt, she must bring two offerings: one for what was not in doubt, which is to be eaten (and she is still liable because of the rest of the cases not in doubt); and one for what was in doubt, which is not to be eaten (and she is not liable because of the others); and she may then eat of animal offerings.

11. If a woman became a proselyte and it was not known whether she gave birth before she became a proselyte or whether she gave birth after she became a proselyte, she must bring an offering because of doubt, and her sin offering may not be eaten.

We have already explained in Laws Concerning Offerings for Transgressions Committed through Error that in a case of doubt respecting any whose atonement is not complete, if the Day of Atonement intervened, they are bound to bring their offering after the Day of Atonement, for it is this offering which renders them fit to eat of Hallowed Things.

12. If a woman suffered a birth or an issue she may bring the money for the pair of birds and put it in the shofar chest and she

may then eat of Hallowed Things at eventide. The presumption is that the court of the priests would not rise thence until they had expended all the money in the shofar chest and offered a corresponding number of pairs of birds, as we have explained in Laws Concerning Shekel Dues and in Laws Concerning the Vessels of the Temple and Those Who Minister Therein.

13. If a woman had brought her sin offering and then died, her heirs must bring her whole offering: even though she had not set it apart while she lived the offering is a lien on her property, and this lien rests on the authority of Scripture.

CHAPTER II

1. The flux spoken of in the Law is semen which comes from the privy parts wherein it had collected; and when the flux comes forth it comes forth not when the member is rigid as does (other) semen, nor is there lust or pleasure when it comes forth, but it comes forth dribbling like barley dough, dull in tinge like the white of a bad egg; but white semen is glutinous like the white of an egg which is not bad.

2. A man is not deemed to be a *zab* if it was by reason of sickness or constraint or the like that he suffered issues of flux which would have (normally) caused him to be deemed a zab, for it is said: *When any man hath an issue from his flesh* (Lev. 15:2). It is by reason of his flesh that he becomes unclean and not by reason of anything else. Hence the Sages have said: Along seven lines should he who suffers a flux be examined: concerning what he had eaten, what he had drunk, what he had carried, whether he had jumped, whether he had been sick, what he had seen, and whether he had had erotic thoughts. Thus, if he had eaten a heavy meal or had drunk much or had eaten or drunken foodstuffs or liquids which induce a flow of semen; or if he had lifted a heavy burden or had jumped from one place to another; or if he had been struck on his back or had been sick; or if he had seen a woman and lusted after her or had harbored thoughts of congress, even though he had not

harbored thoughts of congress with a woman whom he knew—if any one of these preceded an issue of flux, it is attributed to one of these and he does not convey uncleanness.

3. If a man suffered a pollution he is not deemed unclean by flux throughout twenty-four hours, since this issue of flux was by reason of a flow of semen. So, too, concerning what he may have seen or concerning erotic thoughts: these may be relied upon as sufficient cause for twenty-four hours. But concerning what he ate or drank, or if he had jumped or had borne a burden—these may be relied upon as sufficient cause throughout such time as he feels any pain.

4. If a man was circumcised and he afterward suffered a flux, whether he was a Gentile or an Israelite, the circumcision may be relied upon as sufficient cause during such time as he feels any pain.

A Gentile who suffered a pollution and then became a proselyte is forthwith deemed unclean by a flux, and nothing else may be relied upon throughout twenty-four hours.

In case of a minor, neither what he had seen nor erotic thoughts may be relied upon, for with one who is yet a child what he sees or erotic thoughts are not inducive of flux. Therefore he needs to be examined along only five lines.

5. Just as we may, in case of a minor, rely upon his sickness as sufficient cause, so we may also rely upon the sickness of his mother, if he had received suck from her or had been in need of his mother.

When does it apply that one who suffers a flux is examined along these lines? To his second issue of flux, whereby he would become a zab, as will be explained. But if he suffered a first issue, even through constraint, and a second *from his flesh,* he is accounted unclean by a flux. Nevertheless he is examined respecting the first, so as to count it among the three issues which will render him liable to an offering. Concerning the third issue he is not examined, even if he suffered it through constraint, inasmuch as he was already within the bonds of uncleanness; for the issues whereby he had become a zab were *from his flesh,* and he is therefore liable to an offering.

6. If a man suffered a single issue of flux he counts only as one who suffers a pollution. If he suffered two issues, such is deemed to be flux and he must needs count seven clean days and bathe in running water; but he is not liable to an offering. If he suffered three issues he becomes an assured zab and he is liable to an offering. And there is no difference between the zab who suffers two issues and him who suffers three, except that the latter is liable to an offering.

And these are all matters which have come down by tradition, from the mouth of Moses our Master, from Sinai.

7. No matter whether a man suffered two issues or three within a single hour one after the other, or whether he suffered one issue each succeeding day, he is to be deemed a zab: whereas Scripture has made the status of the *zabah* dependent on days—in that it is said: *If a woman have an issue of her blood many days* (Lev. 15:25)—the status of the zab it has not made dependent on days.

8. If a zab enjoyed respite for a complete day between one issue and the next, the two issues may not be reckoned together. Thus, if he suffered an issue on the Sabbath and a second issue on the second day of the week, they may not be reckoned together and he is not deemed to be a zab. So, too, if he suffered a second issue on the first day of the week and suffered a third issue on the third day of the week, he is not liable to an offering, for this is not to be reckoned together with the other two, since one day intervened between them. But if he suffered one issue during the day and one during the following night, these are to be reckoned together. And, needless to say, if he suffered one during the night and a second during the next day, they are to be reckoned together. So, too, if he suffered three issues during three nights, one night after the other, these are to be reckoned together.

9. The issue of a zab has no prescribed quantity, but however little of it he may suffer he is to be deemed unclean, for it is said:

If his flesh be stopped from his issue (Lev. 15:3): whatsoever is perceptible in his flesh conveys uncleanness.

10. If the issue came forth dribbling without intermission and there was time enough from its beginning to its end for an immersion and a drying, or even more, such counts as two issues, inasmuch as it was as prolonged as two. If it was not prolonged so much as this, even though the issue was intermittent, it counts as a single issue only. So, too, if one issue was as prolonged as three issues, so that there was time enough from its beginning to its end for two immersions and two dryings, it counts as three issues and he must bring an offering.

11. If he suffered one issue in the day and it stopped time enough for an immersion and a drying and afterward he suffered two issues, or one as prolonged as two, or if he suffered two or one as profuse as two and it stopped time enough for an immersion and a drying and afterward he suffered one issue, then such a one is an assured zab.

12. If he suffered an issue, part of it at the end of the day and part of it at the beginning of the night, even though it was not so prolonged as two, it is deemed to be two issues, since the days effect a division in the issue. Therefore if a man suffered one issue at twilight, which is neither day nor night, he remains in a condition of doubt respecting uncleanness.

13. If a man suffered one issue during the day and one at twilight, his uncleanness is beyond doubt, but his liability to an offering is in doubt, and he must bring an offering, but it is not to be eaten.

14. If he suffered one issue at twilight before a Sabbath and a second issue at twilight at the close of Sabbath, his uncleanness is in doubt and his liability to an offering is in doubt. His uncleanness is in doubt—peradventure the first issue befell during the day before the Sabbath and the second after the close of the Sabbath, when the Sabbath would have intervened between them, and thus

they would not count as issues at all. And his liability to an offering is in doubt—peradventure part of one of them befell during the day and part during the night, when it would count as two, and thus he would have suffered three issues and so be liable to an offering; therefore he must bring an offering, but it is not to be eaten.

CHAPTER III

1. A zab is accounted unclean all the days wherein he suffers an issue, and when the issues cease he must count, as does a zabah, seven clean days and immerse himself on the seventh day and await sunset, and, if he had suffered three issues, he may bring his offering on the eighth day. But if he suffered any issue of flux even at the close of the seventh day after he had immersed himself, this renders void all the seven clean days, and he must begin again and count seven clean days beginning after the day of this last issue.

2. If a zab suffered a pollution during one of the seven days of counting, this renders void that day only and he may complete the number of seven days and then bring his offering. Thus, if he suffered a pollution on the fifth day, he may count three more days after it and immerse himself on the third day, and on the fourth he may bring his offering.

3. If a zab examined the member on the first day of the days of counting and found it clean and did not examine it during the other seven, and on the seventh day he examined and found it clean, he is presumed to be clean. Even if he examined it on the day of uncleanness itself and found it clean and the flux ceased and he did not examine it on the morrow at the beginning of the days of counting, and he examined it on the seventh day or on the eighth and found it clean, the days of counting are credited to him and he is presumed to be clean.

4. No issue which renders void the preceding clean days renders him liable to an offering. Thus, if he suffered two issues and one

day or two days intervened and he began counting the seven clean days and, during the seven, he suffered an issue of flux, this is not included together with the two, but it makes void the preceding clean days and he must begin to count anew, as we have explained. Even if, during the days of counting, he suffered three issues, one after the other, even if he suffered them in the one day, and even if he suffered three issues at the end of the seventh of the seven clean days, he need not bring an offering, for these issues serve only to render void the preceding clean days.

If he suffered three issues during the eighth night he should bring the offering since these issues do not render void the preceding clean days. This applies to a zab who had suffered two issues; but with a zab who had suffered three issues and then suffered three other issues during the eighth night after seven clean days, he need not bring a second offering because of these three issues, but one offering for the first three; for although the last three do not render void the preceding clean days, he had not yet reached the time when he was fit to bring the offering, seeing that the night does not enter into the count of time for anyone—except a woman after childbirth who miscarries on the night of the eighty-first day, who must bring a second offering, as we have explained. And this is a matter which has come down by tradition.

5. If a man suffered one issue on the eve of the eighth and two issues on the eighth day, these are to be included together, and he must bring a second offering for the later issues, since the first issue of any zab counts only as a flow of semen; but if after it he suffered two issues, it is included together with them to render him liable to the offering. But if he suffered two during the eve of the eighth and one on the eighth day, this is not included and he need not bring an offering on account of this later issue.

6. All are susceptible to uncleanness by flux, even a day-old child, proselytes, slaves, a deaf-mute, and an imbecile. And it seems to me that the atonement offering must be brought on their behalf to enable them to eat of Hallowed Things. And their sin offering may be eaten since they are like a minor who is not accountable.

And a man-made eunuch or a eunuch by nature is susceptible to uncleanness by flux like any other man.

7. To those of doubtful sex or of double sex must be applied the more stringent rules affecting a man and the more stringent rules affecting a woman. They suffer uncleanness through blood, like women, and through white issue, like men. Their uncleanness remains in doubt; therefore if one of them suffered three issues or was a zaḇah who suffered a blood flow on three succeeding days, that one must bring an offering but it may not be eaten. If such a one was making count of seven clean days by reason of white issue and suffered a red issue, or by reason of red issue and suffered a white issue, this does not render void the preceding clean days.

CHAPTER IV

1. When the leper is healed of his leprosy and after he has been cleansed by cedar wood, hyssop, scarlet wool, and the two birds, and his whole body has been shaven and he has been immersed— after all this he may enter into Jerusalem. And he must make count of seven days, and on the seventh day his hair must be shaven off a second time in the manner of the first shaving and he must immerse himself, and so he counts as one "who was immersed that day," and he must await sunset; and, on the morrow, on the eighth day, he must immerse himself a second time, and after that he brings his offerings.

And why must he immerse himself on the eighth day after having been immersed the day before? Because uncleanness had been habitual to him such time as he was a confirmed leper and he was not at pains to avoid uncleanness and he may perchance have become unclean after immersing himself. Therefore he must immerse himself on the eighth day in the Court of Women, in the Chamber of the Lepers which is there, even if his attention had not been distracted.

2. If he was dilatory and did not shave off his hair on the seventh day but shaved on the eighth or several days later, on the day

whereon he shaves he must immerse himself, and he must await sunset and, on the morrow, he may bring his offerings after immersing himself the second time, as we have stated.

After what manner is he treated? The leper stands outside the Court of the Israelites opposite the Eastern Door at the threshold of the Gate of Nicanor with his face turned to the west. There, too, all those whose atonement is not complete are made to stand such time as they are being rendered clean; and there, again, women suspected of adultery are made to drink of the bitter water. The priest takes the leper's guilt offering while it is yet alive and he waves it to the eastern side of the altar, together with the *log* of oil, in the manner of all wave offerings. And if he waves each of them by itself, that suffices. Afterward he brings the leper's guilt offering to the door and the leper thrusts his two hands into the Court and lays them upon the guilt offering, and it is forthwith slaughtered. Two priests receive its blood: one receives some of it in a vessel and tosses it against the altar, and the other receives some of it in his right hand and empties it into his left hand and sprinkles it with his right forefinger. But if he changed the order and received it first in his left hand, he renders it invalid.

The priest who received some of the blood in a vessel first takes it and tosses it against the altar; then the priest who received the blood into his hand comes beside the leper, the priest standing inside and the leper outside; and the leper thrusts in his head and the priest smears some of the blood in his hand on the ridge of the leper's right ear; and then he thrusts in his right hand and the priest smears some on his thumb; then he thrusts in his right foot and the priest smears some on his great toe. If he smeared it on the left thumb or the left great toe, he has not fulfilled his obligation.

Then he offers his sin offering and his whole offering, and after the priest has smeared the blood on the thumb and the great toe, he takes some of the *log* of oil and pours it on his fellow's left palm; but if he poured it on his own palm that suffices. And he dips his right finger into the oil on his palm and sprinkles it seven times in the direction of the Holy of Holies, at each sprinkling dipping his finger into the oil. If he sprinkled but did not direct it toward the Holy of Holies the sprinklings are valid.

He then comes beside the leper and smears some of the oil on the same place as the blood of the guilt offering—the ridge of the ear and the thumb and the great toe. What is left of the oil in his hand he smears on the head of him who is being cleansed. If he does not smear it, he does not effect atonement.

What is left of the log of oil is divided among the priests.

3. The remains of the log of oil may be consumed only in the Temple Court and by males of the priestly families, in the manner of the Most Holy Things, since it is analogous to the guilt offering. It is forbidden to consume any of the log of oil until the priest has performed the sevenfold sprinkling and the smearing of the thumb and the great toe; and if the priest thus consumed it, he is to be scourged in the manner of one who eats of Hallowed Things before the blood has been tossed.

CHAPTER V

1. What is the *tĕnuk* ("the ridge") of the ear? It is the middle wall.

If the priest smeared the blood on the sides of the thumb or the great toe it is valid. If he smeared it on the sides of their sides, it is not valid. Whether he smeared the oil above the very blood of the guilt offering or whether he smeared it at the side of the blood, even if the blood was wiped off before he smeared the oil on the thumb or the great toe, that suffices, for it is said: *Upon the place of the blood of the guilt offering* (Lev. 14: 17). If he had no right thumb or right great toe or if he had no right ear, he can never be rendered clean.

2. If the leper's guilt offering was slaughtered not with its proper intention or if none of its blood was smeared on the thumb and the great toe, it is nevertheless offered on the altar, and it requires drink offerings, like the drink offerings of a leper's guilt offering;

but the leper must needs bring another guilt offering to render him fit to eat of Hallowed Things.

3. If his sin offering was brought before his guilt offering, none should keep on stirring its blood, but it is left until its appearance is spoiled and then it goes to the place of burning.

4. A man may bring his guilt offering on one day and his log of oil ten days later. If the priest wishes to use the log for some other leper's guilt offering he may do so, even though it was already dedicated in the vessel. If the log lacked anything before he poured it out, he may fill up its measure. If it lacked anything after he poured it out, other oil must be brought anew.

5. If the priest poured out some of the oil into his hand and began the sprinkling and the log was spilled, if the log was spilled before he had finished the sevenfold sprinkling, other oil must be brought and he must begin again the sevenfold sprinkling. If he had finished the sevenfold sprinkling and the log was spilled, other oil must be brought and he must begin anew with the thumb and the great toe.

If he had begun with the thumb and the great toe and the log was spilled before he could finish, other oil must be brought and he must begin anew with the thumb and the great toe. If he had finished the thumb and the great toe and the log was afterward spilled before he could smear the rest of the oil which was in his hand on the head of him who was being cleansed, he need not bring another log, since the smearing of the head does not hinder the cleansing, for it is said: *And the rest of the oil that is in the priest's hand he shall put upon the head of him that is to be cleansed* (Lev. 14: 18), *And of the rest of the oil that is in his hand* (Lev. 14: 17).

6. If he smeared the oil before smearing the blood, he must refill the log of oil and smear the oil again after the blood. If he smeared the oil on the thumb and the great toe before the sevenfold sprinkling, he must refill the log and smear the thumb and the

great toe again after the sevenfold sprinkling, for it is said: *This shall be the law of the leper* (Lev. 14:2), namely, that the entire law prescribed for him shall be fulfilled in due order.

7. If the priest performed the sevenfold sprinkling not with its proper intention, no atonement is effected for the leper, nor is he rendered fit to eat of Hallowed Things.

8. If a leper became afflicted with leprosy again after bringing his guilt offering, he must bring another guilt offering for the second leprosy. So, too, if he brought his guilt offering and was yet again afflicted, he must bring an offering for each single affliction. But if he had been afflicted and been healed and had brought his birds and he again became afflicted and was healed and brought his birds, one offering suffices for them all.

9. If a leper brought his offering as a poor man and he became rich, or if he was rich and became poor, before he could bring his other offerings, all must be in accordance with what was the guilt offering: if he was rich when the guilt offering was slaughtered he must supplement it with the offering of one who is rich; and if he was poor, he may supplement it with the offering of one who is poor.

10. If the offerings of two lepers were confused and the blood of one of their two sin offerings was tossed and then one of the lepers died, what should the living leper do? He may not bring another beast as his sin offering: peradventure it was the blood of his own sin offering which was tossed, and a beast may not be brought as a sin offering in a case of doubt; and he may not bring birds as a sin offering, for if one who is rich brings the offering of one who is poor, he does not fulfill his obligation. What should he do? He should assign all his property to another, so that he will become poor, and then he may bring birds as a sin offering because of the case of doubt; but it may not be eaten, as we have explained. And thus he is enabled to eat of Hallowed Things.

11. If one who was rich said, "I take upon myself the offerings of this leper," and the leper was poor, he must bring on his behalf the offerings of one who is rich, since the means of him who vows suffice for this. And if one who was poor said, "I take upon myself the offerings of this leper," and the leper was rich, he must bring on his behalf the offerings of one who is rich, since he who vowed was liable for the offerings of one who was rich.

TREATISE VI

LAWS CONCERNING
SUBSTITUTED OFFERINGS

Involving Three Commandments
One Positive and Two Negative

To Wit

1. That one beast may not be changed for another;
2. That if a beast is changed, what is substituted also becomes holy;
3. That beasts may not be changed from one class of sanctity to another.

An exposition of these commandments
is contained in the following chapters.

NOTE

In the list of the 613 commandments prefixed to the Code, those which deal with the subject of this Treatise are cited in the following form.

Positive commandment:

[2] 87. That the substituted offering shall become hallowed, as it is said: *Then both it and that for which it is changed shall be holy* (Lev. 27: 10).

Negative commandments:

[1] 106. That none may change what has been dedicated, as it is said: *He shall not alter it nor change it* (Lev. 27: 10);

[3] 107. That none may change what has been dedicated from the one kind of offering to another kind, as it is said: *Howbeit the firstling among beasts which is born as a firstling to the Lord, no man shall sanctify it* (Lev. 27: 26); that is to say, that none shall sanctify it so that it shall become some other kind of offering.

CHAPTER I

1. If a man substituted other beasts in place of beasts which he assigned as offerings, he is to be scourged because of each beast which he substitutes, for it is said: *He shall not alter it nor change it* (Lev. 27: 10). And although he committed no act it is learned by oral tradition that for breach of any negative commandment involving no act of commission, punishment by scourging is incurred only in the case of false swearing, substitution, and cursing another by the Divine Name. With these three negative commandments it is not possible that there be any act of commission, yet scourging is incurred.

And why is scourging incurred for substitution, seeing that the negative commandment therein is transformed into a positive commandment, for it is said: *and if he shall at all change it . . . then both it and that for which it is changed shall be holy (ibid.)*? Because one positive commandment and two negative commandments are here involved. Moreover the negative commandment therein is not equivalent to the positive commandment; for if a congregation or joint owners substituted another for a dedicated beast, it is not deemed to be a substituted offering, even though they are forbidden to substitute another.

Thus we may say that if a private person substituted another beast, what is substituted is deemed to be holy, and even if he substituted it on the Sabbath, he must suffer the forty stripes; but if it was one among joint owners who substituted it, or if a man brought a substitute for any of the public offerings, inasmuch as he was a part owner thereof he is to be scourged, but what was substituted is not deemed to be holy.

2. No matter whether he substituted a beast willfully or substituted it through error, he has effected a substitution and therefore he is to be scourged.

Thus, if he intended to say, "This is a substitute for my whole offering," but said, "This is a substitute for my peace offering," it is a valid substitute and he is to be scourged. But if he had sup-posed that it was a permissible act to substitute another beast and he substituted it, or if he said, "I will go into this house and substi-tute another beast, knowingly," and he went in and he forgot and substituted another beast unknowingly, it is a valid substitute; but he is not scourged because of it.

3. A man cannot substitute some other beast for an offering which does not belong to him; but if the owner of an offering said, "Whosoever wishes to substitute his beast for my beast, let him come and substitute it," he can substitute his beast for it. If a man changed his offering for a beast which was not his, it is not a valid substitute, since none can dedicate what does not belong to him.

4. It is he who seeks atonement and not he who dedicated a beast who may make a valid substitute. Thus, if a man dedicated a beast wherewith his fellow might seek atonement—if, for ex-ample, he dedicated his beasts to be a nazirite's offerings wherewith a certain nazirite might seek atonement, it is that nazirite who may substitute other beasts for them and not he who dedicated them, since they are then no longer his.

5. If a man inherited a dedicated beast he can substitute another for it. But if a man died and left a beast to his two sons, this beast itself must be brought and they cannot substitute another for it, since they are joint owners of it, and joint owners cannot effect a substitute, as we have explained.

6. A substitute may not be brought in place of offerings dedicated by Gentiles, on the authority of Scripture; but on the authority of the Scribes, if it was the Gentile who made the change, it is a valid substitute.

If a Gentile dedicated a beast wherewith an Israelite might seek atonement and the Gentile changed it for another, it is in doubt whether it is a valid substitute.

7. No matter whether it be men or women, if they substituted another for a dedicated beast, it is a valid substitute.

8. If a minor, who had reached the age of vows, substituted another for a dedicated beast, although he is not to be scourged, it remains in doubt whether or not this is a valid substitute.

9. Priests may not substitute another beast for a sin offering or for a guilt offering, for although these belong to them, they acquire no rights thereto while they are yet alive, for the flesh does not become theirs until the blood has been tossed. And priests may not substitute another beast for a firstling, for although a priest acquires rights thereto while it is yet alive, he does not acquire rights thereto from the beginning, since its beginning was in the home of a (lay) Israelite. But if the owner substituted another beast for a firstling any time while it was yet in his home, it is a valid substitute. So, too, if a priest substituted another beast for a firstling which was born to his own flock, and not for a firstling which he took from a (lay) Israelite, it is a valid substitute.

10. A substitute can be effected for the ram of the High Priest but not for his bullock (cf. Lev. 16:3), even though it had been given from his own property; inasmuch as his brethren the priests gain atonement thereby, they are, as it were, joint owners thereof.

11. No substitute is valid for bird offerings and meal offerings, since only a beast is spoken of in Scripture.

12. No substitute is valid for offerings made to the Temple treasury; for it is said of tithe of cattle: *He shall not inquire whether it be good or bad, neither shall he change it* (Lev. 27:33). Now does not tithe of cattle come within the general scope of Hallowed Things? Why, then, was it mentioned in particular? To instruct us respecting the entire class: just as tithe of cattle is an offering of a private person, therefore offerings of the congregation and likewise of joint owners are excluded; just as tithe of cattle is an offering pertaining to the altar, therefore things dedicated to the Temple treasury are excluded; and just as tithe of cattle is analogous to tithe of corn, to which Israelites alone are liable and not Gentiles, therefore the offerings of Gentiles are

excluded, and thus no substitute is valid for them, as we have explained.

13. If a man dedicated a beast having an abiding blemish, a substitute for it is not valid, since its body does not acquire complete sanctity and its sanctity is that of its value alone; but if he dedicated a beast having but a passing blemish, or if he dedicated an unblemished beast and an abiding blemish afterward arose in it, a substitute for it is valid.

14. No matter whether a man substituted unblemished for blemished or blemished for unblemished, or whether he substituted oxen for small cattle or small cattle for oxen, or sheep for goats or goats for sheep, or females for males or males for females, or whether he substituted one for a hundred or a hundred for one, whether all at once or one after the other—such counts as a valid substitute, and he is scourged in accordance with the number of beasts which he substituted.

15. A substitute cannot effect a valid substitute, nor can there be a valid substitute for the offspring of dedicated beasts, for it is said: *Then both it and that for which it is changed* (Lev. 27: 10); i.e., *it* but not its offspring, and *that for which it is changed* but not the substitute of that for which it is changed. Yet if a man gave a substitute for a beast, and again gave a substitute for it, and still again gave a substitute for it, even a thousand, every one is valid as a substitute; and he is to be scourged because of each one of them, as we have explained.

16. None may substitute members of a beast or unborn young for whole beasts, or whole beasts for them. Thus, if a man said, "The hindleg of this beast, or its foreleg, shall take the place of this whole offering," or if he said, "The unborn young of this beast shall take the place of this whole offering," it is not a valid substitute. So, too, if he said, "This beast shall take the place of the foreleg or the hindleg of this whole offering," or if he said, "This beast shall take the place of the unborn young of this sin offering," it is not a valid substitute.

17. If a man gave as a substitute a beast which was crossbred or ṭĕrefah or born from the side of its dam or of doubtful or double sex, no sanctity befalls it, and he is as one who gives a camel or an ass as a substitute, because no offering can be brought of their kind, and therefore he is not to be scourged. How do these differ from a blemished beast? The blemished beast belongs to a kind which can be a valid offering, but of those other kinds there can be no valid offering.

18. Beasts which commit or suffer unnatural crime count as beasts that have incurred a (passing) blemish and a substitute for them is valid. And the same applies in every like case.

19. If one half of a beast was dedicated and the other half was not dedicated, no substitute for it is valid, nor may it be given as a substitute.

20. No substitute is valid for any sin offering whose lot it is to be left to die; but a substitute is valid for a sin offering whose lot it is to pasture until a blemish befalls it and then to be sold.

21. If a man set apart a female beast as his Passover offering or his whole offering or his guilt offering, a substitute for it is valid. Although these are not eligible to be offered, yet inasmuch as they acquire sanctity as regards their value and they were unblemished, they acquire an intrinsic sanctity of body. But if a man set apart a he-goat as his sin offering, or if a Naśi set apart a female goat as his sin offering, or if a High Priest set apart a heifer as his sin offering, no substitute for them is valid, for if a beast of the wrong sex is brought as a sin offering it acquires no sanctity at all, not even a sanctity of value, as we have explained in Laws Concerning Hallowed Things Which Become Invalid.

CHAPTER II

1. A substituted offering is deemed to be such when he who owns the offering says of some undedicated beast which belongs to him, "This shall be in place of that," or "This shall be an exchange

for that." And, needless to say, if he said, "This shall be instead of this sin offering" or "instead of this whole offering," it counts as a valid substituted offering.

So, too, if he said, "This shall be instead of a sin offering which I have within the house," or "instead of a whole offering which I have in such a place," it counts as a valid substituted offering, provided that he owns such an offering. But if he said of an undedicated beast, "This shall be in place of a sin offering," he has said nothing at all. So, too, if he said, "This shall become free for profane use in exchange for that," it does not count as a valid substituted offering.

2. If before him were two beasts, the one undedicated and the other dedicated but suffering a blemish, and he laid his hand on the undedicated beast and said, "This shall be in place of that," it is deemed a valid substitute and he is to be scourged. If he laid his hand on the dedicated beast and said, "This shall be in place of that," he renders it free for profane use by exchanging it for the undedicated beast; and this beast does not count as a substituted offering, but it is as though with this beast he redeemed the beast which was blemished.

3. If before him were three beasts dedicated to the altar, one being blemished and awaiting redemption, and three undedicated and unblemished beasts, and he said, "These shall be in place of these," then as regards the substitution of two of the undedicated beasts for the two unblemished beasts, they count as valid substitutes, and he is to be scourged twice because of them. And the third beast takes the place of the blemished beast which, by exchange with the other, was thus rendered free for profane use; and it was his intention to render it free for profane use and not to substitute another for it, for since he had before him a forbidden course, to wit, substitution, and a permissible course, to wit, to redeem it, the presumption is that he would not leave what was permissible and practice what was forbidden. Therefore he does not incur a threefold penalty of stripes.

So, too, if a man said, "These ten beasts shall be instead of these ten beasts," and one of them was blemished, he incurs the penalty of stripes nine times only, since his intention had been to redeem the tenth beast and not to substitute another for it; for although he was to be presumed liable to many scourgings, yet inasmuch as there was open to him a permissible course, he would not leave what was permissible and practice what was forbidden.

If there were two dedicated beasts, of which one was blemished, and two undedicated beasts, of which one was blemished, and he said, "These shall be instead of these," the unblemished beast counts as a valid substitute for the other unblemished beast and he incurs a single scourging; and the blemished beast is rendered free for profane use by exchange with the other blemished beast, since he would not leave what was permissible and practice what was forbidden.

4. If a man said, "This shall be a substitute for a whole offering and a peace offering," his words hold good; and it must be sold and with half of its price he must bring a substitute for the whole offering and with half of its price, a substitute for the peace offering.

If he said, "This shall be a substitute for a whole offering and *a substitute* for a peace offering," and such had been his intention from the outset, his words hold good; but if at the beginning he had intended it only as a substitute for the whole offering and had then changed his mind and said "a substitute for a peace offering," even though he changed his mind while he was still speaking, we hold only to the first statement and it counts as a substitute for the whole offering alone.

CHAPTER III

1. What is the rule as to the offering of a substitute? The substitute for a whole offering must be offered as a whole offering; but if the substitute was a female or blemished, the female beast must be left to pasture until a blemish befalls it, when it must be sold and a whole offering brought with its price.

The substitute for a sin offering is left to die, as we have explained in Laws Concerning Hallowed Things Which Become Invalid.

The substitute for a guilt offering is left to pasture until a blemish befalls it, when its price accrues as a freewill offering.

The substitute for a peace offering is treated as a peace offering in every respect; it requires the laying on of hands and drink offerings and the waving of breast and shoulder.

The substitute for a thank offering is treated as a thank offering, except that it requires no bread offering, as we have explained in Laws Concerning Hallowed Things Which Become Invalid.

The substitute for a Passover offering: if a beast was substituted for it before midday of the fourteenth of Nisan, its substitute cannot be offered, but it must be left to pasture until a blemish befalls it and with its price a peace offering must be brought; but if a beast was substituted for it after midday, the substitute itself must be brought as a peace offering.

No substitute for a firstling or for tithe of cattle may ever be offered, for it is said of the firstling: It *shall be the Lord's* (Exod. 13:12). From oral tradition it is learned that it, itself, must be offered and no substitute for it may be offered. And the rule for tithe of cattle is like that for the firstling: what is substituted for them must be left to pasture until a blemish befalls it, when it may be eaten.

2. The substitute for a firstling falls to the priests, and the substitute for tithe of cattle to the owner. As a firstling or tithe of cattle which have incurred a blemish cannot be redeemed, as we have explained in Laws Concerning Things Forbidden for the Altar, so what is substituted for them cannot be redeemed.

3. If one half of a beast had been dedicated as a whole offering and one half as a peace offering, the same dedication will apply to its substitute.

Similarly, any dedicated beast that could not be offered because of a condition that prevailed at the time of its dedication conveys the same condition to its substitute.

If a man said, "One half of this beast shall be a substitute and the other half shall be a whole offering," it must be offered as a whole offering. And if he said, "One half of it shall be a whole offering and the other half tithe of cattle," it must be offered as a whole offering. If he said, "One half of it shall be a substitute and the other half tithe of cattle," its condition remains in doubt and it may not be offered.

4. If a man dedicated a beast which had a passing blemish—or, needless to say, one which was unblemished—and there afterward arose in it an abiding blemish and it was redeemed and he substituted another for it after it was redeemed, the substitution itself holds good, yet it may not be offered and it may not be redeemed, but must be left until it dies. It may not be offered since it derives its status from a sanctity that had been abandoned; and it may not be redeemed since its sanctity is not strong enough to make its redemption take effect.

5. If any substitutes suffered abiding blemishes from the outset, they must be redeemed; but they do not in all respects become free for profane use in such wise that they may be shorn or used for labor after they have been redeemed, since sanctity as a substitute befalls a beast which suffers an abiding blemish, for it is said: *Or a bad for a good* (Lev. 27: 10); and the *bad* which is here spoken of is one having a blemish or the like, which is not fit to be an offering. Yet even so, it is written concerning it: *It shall be holy* (*ibid.*).

6. If a whole offering was confused with (one of) other animal offerings and a man brought a substitute for one of those which were confused together, he must bring another (a fourth) beast and say, "If that (the third) was a substitute for the whole offering, let this beast be a peace offering; and if that (the third) was a substitute for the peace offering, let this beast be a whole offering." Thus the beast which he brought together with the substitute correspond to the whole offering and the peace offering which were confused together.

If again he substituted (a fifth beast) for one of the two (the third and the fourth), and it is not known for which of them he brought the substitute, he must bring another (a sixth) animal offering from his own household and say over the second substitute, "If this was a substitute for the substitute, let this which I have brought be free of any sanctity; and if it was a substitute for the whole offering or for the peace offering, let this which I have brought be a whole offering or a peace offering." Thus this which he brought together with the second substitute correspond to the animal offering and the substitute which were confused together.

And we have already stated the rule about confused offerings in Laws Concerning Hallowed Things Which Become Invalid.

7. If a peace offering was confused with a firstling or tithe of cattle and a man brought a substitute for one of them, this may not be offered, but it must be left to pasture until a blemish befalls it when it may be redeemed and eaten in the manner of a firstling or tithe of cattle, as we have explained.

CHAPTER IV

1. What is the rule as to the offspring of dedicated beasts? The offspring of a peace offering and the offspring of a substitute for a peace offering are offered as a peace offering and they themselves count as a peace offering in every respect. So, too, the offspring of a thank offering and the offspring of a substitute must be offered as a thank offering, but they require no bread offering, for the bread offering is brought only with the thank offering itself, for it is said: *He shall offer with the sacrifice of thanksgiving unleavened cakes* (Lev. 7: 12); namely, with it, but not with its offspring and not with its substitute, as we have explained.

This applies to the offspring themselves; but the offspring's offspring are not offered, since it is evident from his behavior that the owner holds them back to rear from them many flocks; therefore a fine is imposed on him and he does not offer them.

2. The offspring of a sin offering is left to die and, needless to say, the offspring also of its substitute.

3. If a sin offering was slaughtered and there was found in it a four-month living offspring, it may be consumed like the flesh of the sin offering, for offspring of dedicated beasts are deemed holy while yet in their mothers' bowels.

4. The offspring of the substitute for a guilt offering and its offspring's offspring, and so on to the end of time, must be left to pasture until a blemish befalls them, when they should be sold and their price falls (to the Temple) as a freewill offering. And if it bore a male after its owner had offered his guilt offering, the offspring itself is to be offered as a whole offering. If he had set apart a female as his guilt offering and it bore offspring, it and its young must be left to pasture until a blemish befalls them, when they should be sold and with the price of them both he must bring his guilt offering. And if he had already offered his guilt offering, their price falls (to the Temple) as a freewill offering.

5. The offspring of the substitute for a whole offering and its offspring's offspring, and so on to the end of time, count as a whole offering, and they themselves must be offered as a whole offering. If a man set apart a female as his whole offering and it bore young, even though it bore a male, this must be left to pasture until a blemish befalls it and a whole offering must be brought with its price.

We have already explained in Laws Concerning the Manner of Making Offerings that wherever we say, "It falls as a freewill offering," it means that the money must be put in the shofar chests that are in the Temple, the number whereof we have stated in Laws Concerning Shekel Dues, and with that money the court brings freewill whole offerings and their drink offerings are at the charges of the congregation; and they do not require the laying on of hands. But where it is said, "It, itself, must be offered," or "He must bring a whole offering with its price," this requires the laying on of hands and its drink offerings are at his own charges.

6. The offspring of tithe of cattle, the offspring of a substitute for tithe of cattle, the offspring of a substitute for a firstling, the off-

spring of their offspring, and so on to the end of time—these may not be offered but must be left to pasture until a blemish befalls them when they should be eaten like a firstling or like tithe of cattle which have incurred a blemish.

Offspring of a substitute for a firstling fall to the priest; offspring of tithe of cattle and of its substitute fall to the owner.

7. The offspring of a substitute for a Passover offering is treated like the substitute for a Passover offering. If its dam was offered as a peace offering, its offspring must be offered as a peace offering; and if its case was that it should be sold and a peace offering brought with its price, the offspring also must be sold and a peace offering brought with its price.

If a man set aside a female beast as his Passover offering and it bore young, or if he had set it aside while it was with young, it and its offspring must be left to pasture until a blemish befalls them and a Passover offering must be brought with their price. And if this female beast remained until after the Passover, or if it bore young after the Passover, it and its offspring must be left to pasture until a blemish befalls them and a peace offering must be brought with their price.

8. If the offspring of dedicated beasts were born from the side of the dam, or if dedicated beasts bore offspring which were of doubtful sex or of double sex or crossbred or ṭĕrefah, they must be redeemed, and with their price an offering must be brought such as is proper to be brought with the price of the young of such a beast.

9. The offspring of a blemished beast counts as the young of an unblemished beast in all respects and must be offered in the manner proper to it.

10. If dedicated beasts cast an abortion or an afterbirth, these must be buried and it is forbidden to make gainful use of them.

11. If a man changed anything consecrated from one class of sanctity to another, he transgresses a negative commandment, for

it is said concerning the firstling: *No man shall sanctify it* (Lev. 27:26); he may not sacrifice it as a whole offering or as a peace offering. And the same rule applies to anything else that is dedicated—that they may not be changed from one category of sanctity to another, no matter whether they were dedicated to the altar or to the Temple treasury. Thus, if a man dedicated anything to the fund for the repair of the sanctuary, he may not change it to the fund for the repair of the altar. And the same applies in every like case. But no one incurs punishment by scourging on account of this prohibition.

12. How can the law of the firstling be evaded so that a firstling may be dedicated to the altar within some other class of sanctity? A man may dedicate it while it is yet unborn, for it is said: *That which is born as a firstling to the Lord, no man shall sanctify it* (Lev. 27:26): after it is born as a firstling we may not dedicate it, but we may dedicate it in the womb. Therefore it is possible for a man to say, "If the firstling within the womb of this beast is a male, it shall be a whole offering"; but he may not say, "it shall be sacrificed as a peace offering," since he cannot strip it of its sanctity in such wise as to derive gain thereby.

But if when the greater part of its head had emerged he said, "It shall be a whole offering," it is nevertheless a firstling and it is not a whole offering.

13. Concerning a dedicated beast, there can be no evasion such that its unborn young can be consecrated within some other class of sanctity, but the sanctity of the young is that of its dam. For the offspring of dedicated beasts are dedicated from their dams' womb, as we have explained. And thus the sanctity of every unborn young is according to the sanctity of its dam, and it cannot be changed in the womb as happened with the firstling; for it is at its issuing forth that the firstling acquires its sanctity.

Although the statutes in the Law are all of them divine edicts, as we have explained at the close of Laws Concerning Sacrilege, yet it is proper to ponder over them and to give a reason for them, so far as we are able to give them a reason. The Sages of former times said that King Solomon understood most of the reasons for all the statutes of the Law. It seems to me that in so far as Scripture has said: *Both it and that for which it is changed shall be holy* (Lev. 27: 10)—as also in that matter whereof it has said: *And if he that sanctified it will redeem his house then he shall add the fifth part of the money of thy valuation* (Lev. 27: 15)—the Law has plumbed the depths of man's mind and the extremity of his evil impulse. For it is man's nature to increase his possessions and to be sparing of his wealth. Even though a man had made a vow and dedicated something, it may be that later he drew back and repented and would now redeem it with something less than its value. But the Law has said, "If he redeems it for himself he shall add the fifth." So, too, if a man dedicated a beast to a sanctity of its body, perchance he would draw back, and since he cannot redeem it, would change it for something of less worth. And if the right was given to him to change the bad for the good he would change the good for the bad and say, "It is good." Therefore Scripture has stopped the way against him so that he should not change it, and has penalized him if he should change it and has said: *Both it and that for which it was changed shall be holy.* And both these laws serve to suppress man's natural tendency and correct his moral qualities. And the greater part of the rules in the Law are but *counsels from of old* (Isa. 25: 1), from Him who is *great in counsel* (Jer. 32: 19), to correct our moral qualities and to keep straight all our doings. And so He saith: *Have not I written unto thee excellent things of counsels and knowledge, that I might make thee know the certainty of the words of truth, that thou mightest bring back words of truth to them that sent thee* (Prov. 22: 20).

NOTES

References consisting of numbers only indicate passages found in the Code outside the present volume. The numbers refer, respectively, to the Book, the Treatise, the Chapter, and the Section.

Treatise I: The Passover Offering

Chapter I

1. "a positive commandment." See Exod. 12: 5, 6.
"men and women alike"—B. Pes 91b; cf. B. San 12b.
2. "he being neither *unclean* nor *on a journey afar off*"—Num. 9: 9–13.
"extirpation"—Num. 9: 13, *that soul shall be cut off from his people.* The term (*karet,* variously rendered "excision," "extinction," "extermination") denotes divine punishment as distinct from punishment at man's hand. Such divine punishment is incurred for certain transgressions (see Mishnah, *Kěritot* 1: 1) if committed willfully. See below, IV, i.
"he is not liable"—i.e., to extirpation; but he must bring a sin offering (Lev. 4: 27 ff.).
3. "in the Temple Court." Cf. Pes 5: 1 ff.
"like other Hallowed Things." The term is used here in its narrower sense—the various offerings brought to the Temple. They include Most Hallowed Things (e.g., whole offerings, sin offerings, and guilt offerings) and Lesser Hallowed Things (e.g., the peace offerings of individuals, the Passover offering, firstlings, and tithe of cattle). Both kinds must be slaughtered within the Temple Court, but the latter may be consumed by their owners outside the Temple Court but within the walls of Jerusalem. See VIII, v, i, 17; Zeb 5: 1–8.
"when high places were permissible"—Zeb 14: 4–9; B. Meg 9b. See VIII, i, i, 2–3.
"was scourged." See XIV, i, xviii, 1 ff. Scourging is the punishment for an act committed in breach of a negative commandment where no specific punishment is prescribed by the Written Law. See below, Sec. 7.
"From oral tradition it is learned"—B. Pes 91a; Sif Deut. 16: 5 (ed. Friedmann, 101b).
4. Pes 5: 1, 3; B. *ibid.,* 59a.
"afternoon"—literally: "between the two evenings." EVV (Exod. 26: 6) *at dusk.* According to rabbinical interpretation it is the period between the time when the sun passes the meridian and when it sets (B. Pes 58a).
"daily afternoon whole offering." This was offered (Pes 5: 1) in the afternoon between 2.30 and 3.30 on ordinary days; between 1.30 and 2.30 on the eve of Passover; and between 12.30 and 1.30 when the eve of Passover fell on the eve of Sabbath.
"the afternoon incense." See Tam 5: 2–4.
"After the lamps have been trimmed." See Tam 3: 9; 6: 1.

5. Pes 5: 4; P. *ibid.*, 5: 4.

"sacrificial portions." Those parts of a slaughtered beast specified in Lev. 3: 3–4. See VIII, v, i, 18.

"remains valid"—Tos Pes 3: 3.

6. Pes 5: 9, 10; B. *ibid.*, 89a.

"with its hide"—B. Pes 65b.

7. Mek Exod. 23: 18 (ed. Horowitz-Rabin, p. 334).

8. B. Pes 59b.

"until daybreak"—literally: "until the pillar of dawn arises," namely, the light which appears in the east about an hour before actual sunrise.

"can be offered on a festival day." This is inferred from Num. 28: 10, *The burnt offering of the Sabbath* [shall be burned] *on its sabbath.*

9. Pes 5: 5; B. *ibid.*, 64b.

10. B. Pes 64b.

11. "but if they do, it is valid"—so Bodl. MSS 568, 601, 602, ed. Venice (1524). It is omitted by Bodl. MS 603 and edd. Rome (1480 [?]), Constantinople (1509), Venice (1575).

"How is it slaughtered?"—Pes 5: 5.

"the Levites sing the Hallel"—namely, Psalms 113–118. Pes 5: 7; Tos *ibid.*, 3: 11.

12. Pes 5: 5; P. *ibid.*, 5: 5.

"a sustained, a quavering, and a sustained blast." The exact meaning of the Hebrew expressions is uncertain. See III, vi, iii, 2.

"during the libation"—as at the offering of the daily whole offering (the *tamiḏ*). See VIII, vi, vi, 6; Tam 7: 3. Drink offerings were required for whole offerings and peace offerings. See VIII, v, ii, 2.

13. Pes 5: 5.

14. Pes 5: 6, 9, 10; Tos *ibid.*, 3: 10.

"so that many might play a part"—B. *ibid.*, 64b (applying Prov. 14: 28: *In the multitude of people is the king's glory*).

"cleans out the entrails"—B. *ibid.*, 68a.

15. Pes 5: 7.

16. Pes 5: 8; B. *ibid.*, 65a.

"*šĕḇuṭ*"—Referring to the extensions of the biblical law as devised and multiplied by rabbinical interpretation. See Eruḇ 10: 15 (end).

17. Pes 5: 10.

"none removes his Passover offering." See above, i, 6.

"Rampart." A raised causeway surrounding the inner precincts of the Temple. See Mid 2: 3.

18. Pes. 6: 1; B. *ibid.*, 68b; B. Eruḇ 103a.

19. B. Pes 66a, b.

"may dedicate his festal offering." See below, ii, i, 8.

20. Cf. Pes 6: 6.

Chapter II

1. B. Pes 61a.

2. Pes 8: 7; B. *ibid.*, 93a, 95a.

3. Pes 8:7.

"not one of them." The rendering "not every one of them" is here possible. According to Rashi the meaning is "all of them." The Mishnah (Pes 5:3) pronounces it valid if it was slaughtered "both for such as can and such as cannot eat of it." See below, Sec. 5.

4. Pes 8:7; B. *ibid.*, 91a, b; B. Suk 42b.

"mourners." According to Lev. 10:19 f. one who is mourning his near of kin may not eat the flesh of offerings on the day of the death; but he may eat on the night following. See below, vi, 9.

5. Pes 5:3.

6. B. Pes 61b; 78b.

"essence of the offering." See Lev. 17:11.

7. B. Pes 78b.

8. B. Pes 88a; Tos *ibid.*, 7:4.

9. *Ibid.*

10. *Ibid.*

11. Pes 8:1; Tos *ibid.*, 7:3; P. *ibid.*, 8:1.

12. Pes 8:1; B. *ibid.*, 88a.

"steal some advantage"—i.e., by sharing his Passover offering with the bondman a joint owner increases the bondman's preference for him.

13. *Ibid.*

14. Pes 8:3; B. *ibid.*, 78b.

15. Pes 8:4; B. *ibid.*, 89b.

Chapter III

1. Pes 8:2; B. *ibid.*, 88b.

"place of burning." See VIII, v, vii, 3, 4.

"for the sake of the peace of the kingdom." It would be imprudent to inform the ruler that it was forbidden to eat of either.

2. Pes 8:2; B. *ibid.*, 88b.

3. Cf. Pes 9:9.

4. Pes 9:9.

5. *Ibid.*

6. *Ibid.*

7. Pes 9:10.

8. Pes 9:11.

9. B. Pes 88b–89a.

"a wen." This would render the offering invalid. See VIII, III, vii, 10.

"requires pouring out"—in a single action. Cf. above, i, 14. See VIII, v, v, 17; Zeb 5:8.

"requires tossing"—in two actions. See VIII, v, v, 6; Zeb 5:7.

Chapter IV

1. "Hallowed Things Which Become Invalid." See VIII, VII, XV, 11.

"If a man slaughtered." Tos. Pes 3:7.

2. Pes 7: 5, 7; Tos *ibid.*, 6: 4.

"the High Priest's Plate"—Exod. 28: 36–38. See Zeb 8: 12.

"uncleanness from the deep"—uncleanness conveyed by a corpse the presence of which had not been known.

"Entering into the Temple"—VIII, III, iv, 6.

3. Pes 7: 9; B. *ibid.*, 82b.

"This applies . . ." P. *ibid.*, 7: 13 (end).

"If the whole . . ." Pes 7: 8; B. *ibid.*, 81b, 82a.

"before the *birah*"—the actual structure of the Temple. See B. Zeb 104b; VIII, v, vii, 4.

"that none suspect them"—as might happen if a person, using his own fuel, removed what was left unused.

"so, too, with what is left over"—i.e., "remnant" (*notar*), flesh which has been left uneaten within the time prescribed for its consumption.

"sacrilege"—breach of the law laid down in Lev. 5: 15 f. See VIII, IX, i, for the rabbinical interpretation of this law.

4. Pes 9: 7; Shek 2: 5.

5. Pes 9: 7; B. *ibid.*, 98a; B. Tem 19a.

"a mourner." See below, vi, 9.

6. Pes 9: 6; B. *ibid.*, 96b.

7. B. Pes 86b.

"by reason of a Passover offering"—as in the cases cited above in Secs. 4–6.

"laying on of hands"—Lev. 3: 2.

"drink offerings"—Num. 15: 10.

"waving of breast and shoulder"—Lev. 7: 30.

8. Pes 9: 8; Tos *ibid.*, 9: 3 ff.; B. *ibid.*, 96b.

"[and be sold]"—some such phrase, required by the context, must have been omitted by an early copyist; cf. Rashi ad B. Pes 98a.

"the added cost." If he had sold one for three *zuz* and the other for five, the new offerings must both be worth five zuz, since he does not know which he had intended for which offering.

"Hallowed Things Which Become Invalid." See VIII, VII, vi.

"If it is confused with firstlings." See VIII, VII, vi, 12.

"as though they are all blemished firstlings." See below, III, i, 3.

9. P. Pes 8: 8.

"dedicated animals are not for ever to be discarded"—after dedication. B. Pes 98a states the contrary—that live animals may be rejected. The present view is that found in B. Yom 63b. See below, IV, iii, 8.

"as we have explained"—VIII, VII, vi, 1; cf. VIII, v, xv, 4.

10. B. Zeb 9a; B. Pes 89b, 90a.

"his festal offering." See below, x, 3, and II, i, 1 ff.

"it is to this end"—namely, that others would give money to secure a share of the offering and that the money would thereupon become free for profane use.

11. B. Pes 90a.

Chapter V

1. Num. 9: 9 ff. Pes. 9: 1; B. *ibid.*, 93a.
2. B. *ibid.*
   The introductory "Thus" is found in Bodl. MSS 568, 601, 602, 603, and ed. Venice (1524); it is omitted by edd. Rome (1480 [?]), Constantinople (1509), Venice (1575).
3. B. Pes 92b.
   "it is not accepted." The offering, so far as he is concerned, is not valid.
4. B. Pes 69b.
5. B. Yeb 70b.
   "in respect of their bondage"—i.e., to free them from the restriction implied by Exod. 12: 44–45.
   "And this comes from tradition." See Tos Pes 8: 18.
7. B. Pes 93a.
8. B. Pes 91b.
   "And what is accounted *a journey afar off?*" Pes 9: 2; B. *ibid.*, 93b.
9. B. Pes 94a; P. *ibid.*, 9: 2.
   "If a man was imprisoned"—Pes 8: 6; B. *ibid.*, 91a.

Chapter VI

1. B. Pes 93a.
   "by reason of his uncleanness"—i.e., the fifteenth of Nisan falls within his seven-day period of uncleanness. For the five examples cited, see Lev. 12: 2; 15: 13, 19, 24, 28.
   "But any who had touched carrion"—B. Pes 90b. These suffer only "evening uncleanness." See Lev. 11: 24, 25.
2. B. Pes 90b.
   "for which a nazirite must needs cut off his hair"—Num. 6: 6–10. See VI, III, vii, 6; X, I, iii, 3.
3. Pes 8: 5; B. *ibid.*, 90a, b.
   "two issues of flux"—Lev. 15: 1–15.
   "who awaits day against day"—a woman who suffered a flow during the eleven days between one fixed period and the next. She must immerse herself on the next day and await a whole day free of a flow, after which she is deemed to be clean.
   "Laws Concerning Forbidden Intercourse." See V, I, vi.
4. B. Pes 90a.
   "whose atonement is not complete." See below, Treatise v.
5. B. Pes 92a.
   "a leper's eighth day"—Lev. 14: 9 f. See below, v, iv, 1.
   "who was immersed that day." Until he has awaited sunset he may not enter the Temple beyond the Court of the Gentiles. See Kel 1: 8.
   "Court of the Women." See Kel 1: 8. It lay to the east, outside the Temple Court. See Neg 14: 9.
   "Laws Concerning Entering into the Temple." See VIII, III, iii, 6.

6. B. Pes 92a.

"he may not be sprinkled." See X, ɪɪ, xi.

"as we have explained." See above, Sec. 2.

7. Pes 8:8; B. *ibid.*, 92a.

"severs himself from the grave." On the basis of Num. 19:11 ff., he remains unclean for seven days.

" 'I immersed myself and ate at eventide.' " He does not understand that, in the past year, he was yet a Gentile and so not susceptible to uncleanness (see X, ɪ, i, 13), whereas he is now, as an Israelite, susceptible to the several uncleannesses defined by the Law.

"on the subject of conversion." See V, ɪ, xiv, 5. For "conversion (*gērūṯ*), edd. Venice (1524, 1575) and Rotterdam (1702) read "menstruants" (*niddōṯ*), the main subject of V, ɪ.

8. B. Pes 92a, b.

"Laws Concerning Corpse Uncleanness." See X, ɪ, x, ɪ.

9. Pes 8:8; B. *ibid.*, 92a; B. Zeb 100a.

"A mourner." See above, ii, 4 n.

"If his kindred died on the thirteenth." See MḲ 3:5.

10. Pes 8:6; B. *ibid.*, 91a.

"a round heap"—i.e., not elongated and extensive. It could therefore be assumed that he had stood immediately above the buried corpse and so became unclean. See X, ɪ, ii, 15.

11. B. Pes 81b.

" 'uncleanness from the deep.' " See above, iv, 2 n.

"deemed unclean for heave offering." See VII, ɪɪɪ, xii, ɪ.

"Laws Concerning the Nazirite's Vow." See VI, ɪɪɪ, vi, 18.

12. Pes 7:7; B. *ibid.*, 80b.

13. B. Naz 64b.

Chapter VII

1. Pes 7:6; B. *ibid.*, **79a, b.**

"vessels of ministry"—namely, the slaughtering knives, basins for catching the blood, and the like.

"Laws Concerning Entering into the Temple." See VIII, ɪɪɪ, iv, 16.

2. B. Pes 79a–80a.

3. *Ibid.*

4. *Ibid.*

5. *Ibid.*

6. *Ibid.*

"as we have stated." See Sec. 4: "particular persons do not keep the Second except when the greater part of the congregation keeps the First."

"How are the numbers at Passover estimated?"—P. Pes 7:6; B. *ibid.*, 94b.

7. P. Pes 8:8 (end).

"as will be explained in its proper place." See X, v, xv.

8. Pes 7:4; 9:4; B. *ibid.*, 95b, 96a.

"they are not culpable"—i.e., not liable to extirpation.

9. B. Pes 78b (end).

"If the vessels of ministry were rendered unclean"—B. Pes 79a.
"as will be explained in its proper place." See X, v, iv.
"Hallowed Things Which Become Invalid." See VIII, VII, xviii, 13.

Chapter VIII

2. B. Pes 120a.
3. Mek Exod. 12: 8 (ed. Horowitz-Rabin, p. 20).
"a festal peace offering." See below, x, 13.
4. Pes 9: 3.
"If a man ate of it both raw and sodden." B. *ibid.*, 41a.
5. B. Pes 41b.
"a negative command"—i.e., the implied "they shall not eat it before nightfall."
6. B. Pes 41b.
7. *Ibid.*
"liquid or fruit juice"—Pes 2: 8.
8. Pes 2: 8; B. *ibid.*, 41a.
9. B. Pes 74a.
"with anything else." It must derive heat directly from the fire and not from heated iron or earthenware.
10. B. Pes 75a.
"If he cut into it"—making deep cuts into the flesh to make it roast through more readily.
"How should it be roasted?" Pes 7: 1; B. *ibid.*, 74a.
11. Pes 7: 2.
12. *Ibid.*
13. *Ibid.*
"that part must be pared off." The text of the Mishnah reads: "He must take a handful away from that place." "Paring off" is here an unsuitable expression. KM suggests that Maimonides' text is faulty.
14. Pes 7: 3.
"we have explained in its proper place." See VII, v, ii, 3.
"Two Passover offerings may not be roasted together"—B. Pes 76b.
"We have already stated"—VIII, v, x, 8.
"only until midnight"—Mek Exod. 12: 8 (ed. Horowitz-Rabin, p. 20); B. Ber 9a; Zeb 57b.
"until daybreak." B. Ber 9a.
"Laws Concerning Leaven and Unleavened Bread." See III, v, viii.
"the Hallel must be recited"—Pes 7: 3.
"after they had fallen asleep"—Pes 10: 8.

Chapter IX

1. Pes 7: 13; B. *ibid.*, 85a, 86b.
"as it is written also of the Sabbath"—cf. Exod. 16: 29.
"both taking up and laying down"—i.e., it must be removed out of one domain and deposited in another. See B. Shab 2a.

"And there can be none who transgresses"—P. Pes 7: 13.

"From the doorjamb"—Pes 7: 12.

2. "are accounted ṭĕrefah." Exod. 22: 30 applies to it: *and flesh in the field is ṭĕrefah: ye shall not eat it.* (EVV render less literally: *Ye shall not eat any flesh that is torn of beasts in the field.*) The text of Maimonides adopted in the translation is that of Bodl. MSS 601, 602, 603, and ed. Amsterdam 1702. The reading "must be burned" is found in Bodl. MS 568 and edd. Rome (1480 [?]), Constantinople (1509), Venice (1524 and 1575).

"Laws Concerning the Manner of Making Offerings." See VIII, v, xi, 6.

"If part of a limb"—Pes 7: 12; B. *ibid.*, 85a.

"one of the other Hallowed Things." See Zeb. 5: 6 ff. They must not project beyond the walls of Jerusalem.

3. Pes 7: 13; B. *ibid.*, 85b.

4. Pes 7: 13.

5. B. *ibid.*, 86b.

6. B. Pes 86b (end). The Talmud's text is obscure and, according to Rashi and RABD, does not deal especially with the Passover meal. It reads:

"R. Huna said: The members of a company come in three at a time and they leave even one at a time. Rabba said: Provided that they come in at the time when it is usual to come in and provided that the waiter noticed them. Rabina said: And they must make payment [a variant here adds: And the last must give more]. And the rule is not according to him."

7. Cf. B. Pes 96a.

"resident alien"—a Gentile allowed to live among Jews on condition of abstaining from idolatry, blasphemy, murder, theft, incest, and from eating flesh with the blood in it, and on condition that he submitted to the Jewish courts.

"with the beating of contumacy" (*makkaṭ marduṭ*). Not the biblical punishment of "forty stripes save one," but a lesser punishment imposed at the discretion of the court. See Naz 4: 3, and Code, XIV, I, xvi, 3.

8. B. Pes 96a.

9. B. Yeb 70b.

"if, for example, his fever subsided." See II, vi, i, 16; B. Shab 137a.

CHAPTER X

1. Pes 7: 11; B. *ibid.*, 84a.

2. B. *ibid.*, 83a.

3. B. *ibid.*, 85a.

"If there was an olive's bulk of flesh on it"—B. *ibid.*, 84b.

4. P. *ibid.*, 7, 11.

"after another had broken it." An addition, "namely, the one bone," is found in Bodl. MSS 568, 601, 602, 603, and edd. Rome (1480 [?]), Constantinople (1509). It is not in ed. Venice (1575). It is bracketed in ed. Amsterdam (1702).

5. B. Pes 84b.

6. *Ibid.*

" 'refuse' "—literally: "abomination" (*piggul*); see Lev. 7: 18. The flesh of an offering which it is proposed to eat at a time or place other than is prescribed for it.

7. B. Pes 84b.

8. Pes 7:11.

9. B. Pes 84a.

"This is the general rule." Pes 7:11.

"the shoulder blades"—literally: "wings." See E. Baneth, *Traktat Pesachim* (ed. Itzkowski, Berlin, 1927), p. 217, n. 61.

10. B. Pes 84a, b.

11. B. *ibid.*, 84a.

"not to be scourged." Cf. B. Mak 14b.

12. Pes 6:3, 4.

13. Pes 6:4; B. *ibid.*, 70a.

"like any other peace offering." See Zeb 5:7.

"And he who leaves anything remaining"—Pes 7:11.

14. P. Pes 6:4.

"to avoid confusion." The flesh of the Passover offering might otherwise be left uneaten at daybreak by being confused with flesh of the festal offering. The latter could legitimately be left unconsumed until daybreak of the second day.

15. Pes 9:3, 5; Tos *ibid.*, 8:7; B. *ibid.*, 95a, 96a.

"outside its company." This is the reading of ed. Amsterdam (1702) and is based on the suggestion of KM that this is the proper reading instead of "outside the place where it is eaten." The latter is the reading found in MSS and early editions.

"ordained in Egypt." See Exod. 12:3.

Treatise II: The Festal Offering

Chapter I

1. B. Ḥag 6b.

"pilgrimage seasons" (Passover, Pentecost and Tabernacles). The Hebrew term is *rĕḡalim*, Exod. 23:14. EVV "times." Its literal meaning is "feet."

"the duty to appear." Hebrew *rĕ'iyyah*—literally: "appearance." The word is also used of the offering brought on this occasion and is rendered (see below, Sec. 2) "pilgrimage offering."

"only from cattle." See VIII, v, i, 11.

"not incumbent upon women." See Exod. 23:17.

"this commandment is incumbent upon women"—B. Ḳid 34b; B. Pes 109a.

2. Pe 1:1; Ḥag 1:2, 5; B. *ibid.*, 7a.

"pilgrimage offering" (rĕ'iyyah)—literally: "appearance," i.e., the offering brought when fulfilling the duty 'to appear.'

"festal offering" (*ḥăḡiḡah*), brought in fulfillment of the duty to "keep the feast."

"two pieces of silver"—namely, two *ma'ah*.

3. "If at the time when he would go up"—B. Beḳ 51a.

4. Ḥag 1:6; B. *ibid.*, 9a.

5. "*I will gather them*"—i.e., remove, destroy them. This paragraph and proof text are not in Mishnah or Gemara.

6. Ḥag 1:6.

7. *Ibid.;* B. *ibid.,* 17a; B. MK 24b.
8. Pes 6: 2.
"they override the laws of a festival day"—B. Beṣ 19a; B. Ḥag 17a. See III, iv.
9. B. Ḥag 16b.
"is no hindrance"—i.e., it is not essential to the validity of the offering.
"Laws Concerning the Manner of Making Offerings"—VIII, v, iii, 12.
"rules respecting šĕḇuṭ." See above, i, i, 16 n. Cf. Beṣ 5: 2.
10. P. Ḥag 1: 1; B. *ibid.,* 7b.
"It is permissible to offer vow offerings"—B. Tem 14b.
"leper's whole offering"—Lev. 14: 10.
"a woman after childbirth"—Lev. 12: 6.
"the sinner's meal offering"—Lev. 5: 11.
"the meal offering of jealousy"—Num. 5: 15.
"the nazirite's meal offering"—Num. 6: 15.
11. Ḥag 1: 5.

Chapter II

1. Ḥag 1: 1; B. *ibid.,* 2a–4a.
"on their own feet." See i, 1 n. This is derived from the literal meaning of rĕḡalim ("feet"), otherwise to be understood in the sense of "pilgrimage seasons," "foot-going times."
"Laws Concerning Entering into the Temple." See VIII, iii, iii.
2. B. Ḥag 4a.
3. Ḥag 1: 1; B. *ibid.,* 4a, 6a.
4. Cf. B. Ḥag 6a.
"Laws Concerning Entering into the Temple." See VIII, iii, iii.
"Laws Concerning the Manner of Making Offerings." See VIII, v, iii, 8.
5. B. Ḥag 9a.
6. *Ibid.,* 7a.
7. *Ibid.,* 8b.
"as a remainder"—deliberately.
8. Ḥag 1: 3; B. *ibid.,* 7b, 8a; B. Pes 70b, 71a.
"the prescribed measure for the first meal"—i.e., the first festal offering.
9. Ḥag 1: 4.
"tithe of cattle on a festival day." Tithing cattle (see Bek 9: 7) involved making a red mark on each tenth beast, constituting a forbidden act of work.
10. Ḥag 1: 4; B. *ibid.,* 8b.
"not flesh which promotes rejoicing"—because there is no fat in them.
"Laws Concerning Passover Offerings." See above, i, x, 13.
"not an obligatory offering"—i.e., such as must be brought after the onset of the feast on the fifteenth day.
11. B. Pes 71b.
12. *Ibid.*
13. B. Peṣ 19b.
"may not be so treated as to render them invalid." The thank offering was offered with ten loaves of leavened bread, and if these were not consumed by the

fifth hour of the fourteenth (see Pes 1: 4), they would be rendered "forbidden remnant" (*noṭar*). See Lev. 7: 13; 22: 30.

14. B. Beṣ 19b, 20a.
"for their appetite"—or, *"only for themselves."* Sec. III, IV, vi, 18.

Chapter III

1. Deut. 31: 10–13. B. Ḥag 3a.
"year of release"—Deut. 15: 1 ff.
2. B. Ḥag 3a.
"unfit to *come*"—i.e., into the Temple.
3. Soṭ 7: 8.
"Where does he read?" There is some discrepancy between the text of Maimonides and the Mishnah. According to the present paragraph the king reads without a break from Deut. 14: 22 to 28: 69; according to the Mishnah he reads only Deut. 14: 22–27; 26: 12–15; "the paragraph of the king," 17: 14–20; and 28: 2–68.
4. Soṭ 7: 8.
"Trumpets are blown"—Tos Soṭ 7: 15.
"through the service of many men." Cf. above, i, i, 14 n.
"He adds seven benedictions"—Soṭ 7: 8. According to the Mishnah, "With the same blessings with which the High Priest blesses them the king blesses them, save that he pronounces the blessing for the feasts instead of the blessing for the forgiveness of sins." The High Priest's benedictions were "for the Temple-service, the Thanksgiving, for the forgiveness of sin, and for the Temple and for the Israelites, and for the priests and for Jerusalem."
"Look favorably . . ." and "We give thanks . . ." These correspond to the Seventeenth and Eighteenth benedictions in the present form of the 'Āmiḏah (S. Singer, *Authorised Daily Prayer Book,* [8th Ed., London, 1908], pp. 50, 51).
"Thou hast chosen us . . ." Now found in the Festival 'Āmiḏah (cf. Singer, *op. cit.,* p. 240). The four benedictions which follow are not represented in the synagogue liturgy.
"in accordance with their established form"—i.e., as stereotyped by liturgical use (see II, v, i, 5), whereas the four which follow do not conform to any set formulae.
5. Soṭ 7: 2.
6. "mouth of the Lord"—literally: "mouth of Might."
7. Meg 1: 3; P. *ibid.,* 1: 4.

Treatise III: Firstlings

Chapter I

1. Other biblical proof texts are Exod. 13: 12, 13, 15; 22: 29, 30; Lev. 27: 26; Num. 3: 13; 8: 16, 17; 18: 15.
2. Ḥal 4: 9; Zeb 5: 8.
"Lesser Hallowed Things." See Zeb 5: 6–8.

"sacrificial portions." The parts specified in Lev. 3: 3–4.
"Laws Concerning the Manner of Making Offerings." See VIII, v, xviii.
3. B. Zeb 57a.
"or sell it." MSh 1: 2.
"It is the property of the priest"—Bik 2: 1. This assumes that "firstlings" (*bĕḳoroṭ*) fall within the category of "first fruits" (*bikkurim*); cf. Bik 3: 12.
4. B. Ar 59a (end).
5. Cf. B. Tem 21a; B. Ḥul 44b.
"binding both within the Land and outside the Land"—so Bodl. MSS 601, 603, edd. Rome (1480 [?]), Constantinople (1509), Venice (1575), conforming to the above-cited Gemaras of Ḥullin and Tĕmurah. Bodl. MSS 568, 602, and ed. Venice (1524) read "The commandment . . . is not binding except within the Land (of Israel)."
6. "This commandment is binding"—B. Sheḳ 11a; B. Beḳ 53a.
"but it is not binding . . ."—Ḥul 10: 2; Beḳ 2: 2, 3. See below, v, 8.
"Temple treasury." See below, vi, iv, 5; literally: "repair of the Temple" (*beḍeḳ habbayiṭ*). Cf. II Kings 12: 6.
7. Beḳ 1: 1; 2: 1.
"Law Concerning Priestly Dues." See VII, vi, xii, 14.
8. Beḳ 4: 1.
"From what time . . ."—B. RSh 6b, 7a.
"from the eighth day." See Lev. 22: 27.
9. Beḳ 4: 2; B. *ibid.*, 28a.
10. B. *ibid.*
11. *Ibid.*
"a sage"—who would decide whether the animal had acquired a blemish for which it may be slaughtered. See Tosafaṭ ad Beḳ 28a.
12. B. RSh 6b.
"from day to day"—i.e., 354 days, an exact lunar year.
"If two lambs were born"—B. Ar 31b.
13. B. RSh 5b.
"as tithe does not become invalid." Cf. Deut. 14: 28, which speaks of tithe brought *at the end of every three years.*
14. Beḳ 4: 1; B. *ibid.*, 26b.
"Laws Concerning Heave Offerings." See VII, iii, xii, 18.
"who give help"—so putting the owner under an obligation to them.
15. Beḳ 4: 1; B. *ibid.*, 26b.
16. B. Mak 17a.
17. B. Beḳ 31b; B. Tem 5b.
"So, too, it may not be sold"—B. Tem 8a, b.
18. B. Beḳ 31a; B. Tem 5a.
"And when he sells the flesh." Cf. Beḳ 5: 1.
"Things Forbidden for the Altar." See VIII, iv, i, 12.
"portion for portion"—in order to share it out equally. So Maimonides; but Rashi and later commentators interpret it as meaning that a portion of the flesh of a firstling may be exchanged against an equal weight of common flesh. See MSh 1: 2.
19. B. Tem 24a.

NOTES

201

Chapter II

1. Bek 6: 1–8.
"Concerning Things Forbidden for the Altar." See VIII, ɪv, ii.
2. "which we have there enumerated." See VIII, ɪv, ii, 6 ff.
3. Bek 6: 12; Zeb 8: 1.
"Things Forbidden for the Altar." See VIII, ɪv, ii, 9.
4. Bek 2: 9; B. *ibid.*, 19a.
"was born after it"—in normal fashion.
5. Bek 6: 12; B. *ibid.*, 42a, b.
6. Bek 2: 5.
"which suffers an abiding blemish"—B. Bek 3b.
"Even if a heifer bore the like of an ass"—Bek 1: 2; B. *ibid.*, 6a.
7. Bek 5: 3; B. *ibid.*, 34a, b.
8. B. Bek, 34a.
"if he bid a Gentile." Cf. Bek 5: 3.
9. *Ibid.*
10. B. Bek 36a.
"an 'associate' "—one who has pledged himself to be scrupulous about the
rules of cleanness and uncleanness, and about tithing. See X, ɪv, xi.
11. Bek 5: 4; B. *ibid.*, 35a.
12. Bek 5: 3.
13. *Ibid.*, 5: 2; B. *ibid.*, 33b.
14. B. Bek 3b; B. Tem 24b.
15. B. Bek 36a.
16. Bek 5: 4; B. *ibid.*, 35a.
"a (lay) Israelite"—i.e., not a priest.
17. *Ibid.*
"outside"—i.e., of Jerusalem. Deut. 12: 17–18, forbids unblemished firstlings
to be consumed *within thy gates* instead of *before the Lord thy God*.
18. Bek 5: 5.
"as we have explained." See VIII, v, xviii, 2.
19. B. Bek 36b.
"[no] scruple." This reading, *wĕ'en laḥuš*, is required by the context in place
of the *kĕde laḥuš* of the text—apparently an early scribal error.

Chapter III

1. B. San 5a.
"any firstlings except his own firstlings"—Neg 2: 5.
2. Bek 5: 5; B. *ibid.*, 36b.
3. B. *ibid.*
4. *Ibid.*, 4: 3.
5. *Ibid.*, 6: 6.
6. *Ibid.*, 4: 4; B. *ibid.*, 28b.
"will not hold it back." It should be given to the priest and slaughtered in the
Temple when still unblemished.

"or rear small cattle." See Dem 2: 3; BK 7: 7. For small cattle the penalty is relatively heavier than for large.

7. Bek 4: 5; B. *ibid.*, 29a.
8. *Ibid.*, 4: 7; B. *ibid.*, 29b.
9. *Ibid.*, 5: 6.
"Laws Concerning Buying and Selling." See XII, I, xvi, 12.
10. Zeb 12: 4; B. *ibid.*, 103b, 104a.
"Hallowed Things Which Become Invalid." See VIII, vii, xix, 9.
11. Bek 3: 4.
"Laws Concerning Sacrilege"—VIII, ix, i, 10.
"we have already stated." See above, i, 8.
12. Bek 3: 4; B. *ibid.*, 26b.
13. B. Bek 25b; Orl 3: 3.
"half-span"—Hebrew *siṭ*. Maimonides defines it as the distance between the outstretched index and middle fingers; others, as the distance between the outstretched thumb and index finger.

Chapter IV

1. B. Ḥul 135a, b; B. Bek 3a.
2. Bek 2: 1. Cf. *ibid.*, 1: 1; B. *ibid.*, 2a.
3. Bek 2: 1; B. *ibid.*, 2b.
4. Bek 2: 4; B. *ibid.*, 16b.
"and stipulated with him." This is the contract known as *ṣon barzel*, "sheep of iron," where A sells a flock to B on condition that B shares the profits with A until B has made payment in full, while B is alone responsible for all losses sustained.
5. B. Bek 13a.
"even though he did not draw it." On the significance of a purchaser's "drawing" a movable object to himself as clinching a sale, see XII, I, iii, 1. Cf. Shebi 10: 9: "All movable goods are acquired by the act of drawing them into the purchaser's possession." See also Ḳid 1: 4, 5.
6. Ḥul 134a.
7. Bek 3: 1.
8. *Ibid.*, 3: 2; B. *ibid.*, 24a.
"a beast which was in milk"—B. *ibid.*, 20b.
9. *Ibid.*, 21b.
10. Bek 3: 1; B. *ibid.*, 19b, 20a, b; Ḥul 4: 7.
"sheep or a goat"—literally: "small cattle."
"we have already explained." See above, ii, 6.
11. Ḥul 4: 7; B. *ibid.*, 77a.
12. Bek 3: 1; B. *ibid.*, 21b.
"in treating of the menstruant." See V, I, x, 1.
13. B. Nid 29a.
"unless the head was already rounded"—B. Bek 22a. See Oh 7: 4.
14. Ḥul 4: 2; B. *ibid.*, 69b.
"retroactively"—i.e., the portions which emerged earlier, though not to be deemed hallowed at the time they were cut off, now become so. All the portions must therefore be buried and may not be thrown to the dogs.

15. B. Ḥul 69b.
16. *Ibid.*, 70a.
17. *Ibid.*
18. *Ibid.*
19. *Ibid.*
20. *Ibid.*
   The translation follows the text found in Bodl. MS 568 and ed. Venice (1524), which is nearer to that of B. Ḥul 70a (Mar b. R. Ashi). Bodl. MSS 601, 602, 603, edd. Rome (1480 [?]) and Constantinople (1509), omit "and hung."
21. *Ibid.*

Chapter V

1. Beḵ 2:6.
2. *Ibid.*, 2:7, 8.
   In these cases it is assumed that no one witnessed which births were from which beasts.
3. Beḵ 2:8. See above, ii, 6.
4. Beḵ 3:2.
5. B. *ibid.*, 18b.
6. *Ibid.*
7. B. *ibid.*, 36b.
8. Beḵ 2:2, 3.
   "Laws Concerning Sacrilege." See VIII, ix, i.
9. P. MSh 1:2.
   "if he bought a beast with seventh-year produce"—B. Beḵ 12b.
   "he could derive advantage." A firstling would not be subject to the law of "removal," to be eaten or discarded forthwith (see Shebi 7:1; 9:2), but could be given to a priest who, if it is blemished, may sell it. See above, i, 3, 18.
   "Laws Concerning Forbidden Foods." See V, i, viii, 16.
   "about heave offerings." See VII, iii, xii, 21.
   "it is forbidden to traffic with firstlings"—Shebi 7:3.
   "in the manner which we have described." See above, i, 18.
10. Shebi 7:4.
   "for his son's wedding feast." The firstling is assumed to be blemished and permissible as food for nonpriests.
11. Tos Beḵ 3:20.
   "assessment"—for purposes of barter.

Chapter VI

2. Beḵ 9:1; B. *ibid.*, 53a.
   "and tithed his cattle." This follows the reading in Bodl. MSS 568, 601, 602. Ed. Rome (1480 [?]), gives an ambiguous abbreviation which later editions wrongly resolved into "and did so" ('aśah for 'iśśer).
4. Zeb 5:8; B. *ibid.*, 56b, 57a.

5. MSh 1:2. Cf. B. Tem 5b; B. Bek 31b.
"explained in its proper place." See XIV, v, viii, 6.
6. Cf. B. Bek 31a.
"flesh of a firstling may be weighed out." See above, i, 18.
7. B. Bek 31b.
"guard the orphan against loss"—literally: "to give back an orphan's lost property." Since the orphan cannot eat all of it he is permitted to sell it.
8. B. Bek 31b.
9. B. Bek 36b.
10. Bek 9:3; B. ibid., 56b.
"as something 'sold' "—i.e., in exchange for a share in the partnership.
11. Ibid.
12. Ibid.
13. B. BK 110b.
"robbery committed against a proselyte." In such a case he must make restitution (giving it to a priest) of the value plus one fifth. BK 9:11.
"what is given as a gift is exempt from tithe." See above, vi, 10.
14. Bek 9:4; B. ibid., 57a.
"too young"—i.e., not eight days old. See Lev. 22:27.
15. Ibid.
"who had bought unborn young." See above, vi, 12.
16. B. Bek 58b. Cf. Bek 9:7; Tos ibid., 7:12.

Chapter VII

1. Bek 9:7; B. ibid., 58b; Tos ibid., 7:10.
2. B. Bek 54b.
3. Ibid.
4. Bek 9:1.
5. Ibid.; B. ibid., 54b.
6. Bek 9:6.
"If two generations were born." Cf. Tos Bek 7:9.
7. "explained in its proper place." See VII, iv, ii ff.
8. Bek 9:5; B. ibid., 57b, 58a.
"counting of the 'omer." See Lev. 23:15, 16.
9. B. Bek 59b.

Chapter VIII

1. Naz 5:3; B. Bek 60b.
"But if the ninth or the eleventh he called the tenth"—Bek 9:8.
2. Bek 9:8.
"and it requires drink offerings"—B. ibid., 60a.
"and it may not be replaced by a substitute." See below, vi, i, 15.
"This applies if he who counted"—B. ibid., 61a.
"was the owner of the beasts." See below, vi, i, 15.
3. Bek 9:8.
4. Ibid.; B. ibid., 60b.

"Hallowed Things Which Become Invalid." See VIII, vii, vi, 14.
5. Beḵ 9: 8; B. *ibid.*, 60a.
6. Beḵ 9: 8.
7. B. *ibid.*, 60a.
8. B. *ibid.*, 59b.
9. *Ibid.*
10. *Ibid.*
"proper numbering." Cf. Rashi ad B. Beḵ 59b.
11. B. Beḵ 59b, 60a.
12. Cf. B. Beḵ 60a.
13. Tos Beḵ 7: 11.
14. Beḵ 9: 7.
15. *Ibid.*

Treatise IV: Offerings for Transgressions
Committed Through Error

Chapter I

1. Ker 1: 2.
2. *Ibid.*
"who neglects circumcision or the Passover offering"—B. Ker 3a.
"Therefore if a man accepted an idol"—B. San 62a.
3. Ker 1: 2.
"as will be explained." See below, xi, 1 ff.
4. "as will be explained." See below, x, 1 ff.
"twenty-six all told." For these see Lev. 18: 6 ff. The biblical references for
the other seventeen are:

1) Exod. 20: 5	2) Lev. 18: 21	3) Lev. 20: 27
4) Lev. 20: 27	5) Num. 15: 32 ff.	6) Lev. 23: 30
7) Lev. 23: 29	8) Lev. 19: 8	9) Exod. 12: 15
10) Lev. 7: 25	11) Lev. 7: 26 f.	12) Lev. 7: 18
13) Lev. 17: 4	14) Lev. 17: 9	15) Exod. 39: 33
16) Exod. 39: 38	17) Exod. 30: 33, 38	

"anointed for battle." See Deut. 20: 2 ff.
5. Hor 2: 3.
"two sin offerings"—for the two forbidden acts, eating and doing work.

Chapter II

1. Shab 11: 6.
2. B. *ibid.*, 69a.
3. Ker 4: 2.
"remnant"—Lev. 19: 8.
4. Tos Ker 2: 3.
"sin offerings which are to be eaten." See VIII, v, vii, 1.
5. Ker 4: 3.
6. B. Shab 68b.

7. B. Ker 19a, b.
"but he severed"—on the Sabbath.
"as we have stated in its proper place." See III, 1, i.
8. B. Pes 72b.
"deceased brother's wife"—so fulfilling the law of Deut. 25: 5–10.
"if a man had two children"—B. Shab 137a.
"two separate objects." See above, Sec. 5.
9. B. Shab 133b.
10. Suk 3: 14; Pes 6: 6; B. *ibid.*, 71a, b.
"*lulaḇ*"—literally: "palm branch." The branches of palm, myrtle, and willow are bound together and carried at the Feast of Tabernacles in fulfillment of Lev. 23: 40.
"first festival day of the Feast"—i.e., of Tabernacles.
11. Pes 6: 5; B. *ibid.*, 72a.
"Hallowed Things Which Become Invalid." See VIII, vii, xv, 1.
12. Pes 6: 5.
"since the Passover offering was valid." See above, 1, ii, 5.
13. Tos Pes 5: 7.
"if he slaughtered more"—Pes 6: 5.
14. Tos Pes 5: 7; cf. B. Beṣ 20b.
15. B. Men 64a.
"spread out a net"—i.e., on the Sabbath when fishing is forbidden.
16. B. Pes 72b.

Chapter III

1. Ker 3: 1.
2. B. *ibid.*, 11b.
"gainsay the witnesses." Edd. Rome (1480 [?]), Constantinople (1509), Venice (1575) add "but"; omitted by Bodl. MSS 568, 601, 602, 603 and ed. Venice (1524).
3. "Hallowed Things Which Become Invalid." See VIII, vii, xv, 6.
"Moreover the Sages have said"—Ker 6: 7.
4. Tos Ker 2: 4.
5. *Ibid.*
"its price accrues"—to the Temple treasury. See below, vi, iv, 5.
6. Tos Ker 2: 4.
7. "Manner of Making Offerings." See VIII, v, iii, 4.
"permitted fat." On the distinction between forbidden fats and permitted fats, see V, ii, vii, 9.
8. Cf. B. Ker 7a; B. Zeb 12b; B. San 47a.
"are not forever to be discarded." See above, 1, iv, 9.
"Hallowed Things Which Become Invalid." VIII, vii, vi, 1.
9. Ker 6: 4.
10. B. *ibid.*, 7a.
11. B. *ibid.*, 8b; B. Naz 18b, 19a.
"by reason of a condition of doubt"—B. Ker 26a.
12. B. Ar 7a.

NOTES

Chapter IV

1. B. Ker 2b; cf. Shab 7: 1.
   "So, too, if he committed a single act"—Ker 3: 10.
   "provided that the prohibited acts." For the three classes of composite transgression, see also below, vi, 4.
   "Thus if a man slaughtered a dedicated beast"—B. Ḥul 40a.
   "widened the slit"—cf. Rashi ad B. Ḥul 40b.
   "on the Day of Atonement which fell on a Sabbath"—B. Ḥul 101b.
   "with the wife of his brother." Cf. Yeb 3: 10.
   "with his father"—B. San 54a.
   "with a male"—B. San 54a; B. Ker 3a.
2. Ker 3: 5.
   "which occurred at the same time"—i.e., if Jacob married Serah.
   "secondary grade"—B. Yeb 21a. See IV, 1, i, 6.
3. B. Ker 14b.
   "respecting such a case of consanguinity"—Serah.
   "the man concerned"—her grandfather Jacob.
4. Ker 3: 6.
5. Ker 3: 7; B. *ibid.*, 2b.

Chapter V

1. B. Ker 15a; B. Shab 71b.
2. B. Ker 15a.
3. Ker 3: 7.
   "the Sages have said"—Ker 3a. See above, iv, 1.
5. Yeb 10: 1; B. *ibid.*, 87b, 92a.
   "If through error a man had intercourse"—B. Ker 17a.
6. B. Shebu 17b, 18a.
   "Therefore whether blood was found"—Nid 2: 2.
   "But if she delayed"—B. *ibid.*, 15a.
7. Shebu 2: 4.
   "Laws Concerning Forbidden Intercourse." See V, 1, iv, 11. B. Shebu 18a.

Chapter VI

1. Ker 3: 2; 4: 2.
   "Laws Concerning Forbidden Foods." V, 11, xiv, 8.
2. Ker 3: 2.
   "remnant." See Glossary.
3. Ker 5: 1; B. *ibid.*, 22a.
4. Ker 3: 2.
   "several categories of transgression." See above, iv, 1. On these three types of combination see V, 1, xvii, 8 and 11, xiv, 18. Cf. B. Ḳid 77b; B. Shebu 24a, b.
   "provided that other food was included"—B. Ker 14a. On the Day of Atonement it is not an olive's bulk but a date's bulk which is prohibited. See Yom 8: 2.

5. Yom 8: 3.
6. B. Ḥul 101b.
7. Ker 3: 2.
"Laws Concerning Forbidden Foods." See V, 11, xiv, 8.
8. B. Shab 71a.
"if through error a man wrote a single letter"—Shab 12: 6; B. *ibid.*, 102a.
"a distance of two cubits." The forbidden distance is four cubits. See Shab 11: 3, 4, 6.
9. B. Shab 71b.
10. *Ibid.*
11. *Ibid.*
12. B. Ker 18a.
"permitted fat." See above, iii, 7 n.

Chapter VII

1. B. San 62b, 63a.
"Peor." See San 7: 6. "If a man excretes to Baal Peor, this is how it is worshiped."
"*Merḳolis*"—*ibid.* "He who throws a stone at a Merḳolis, this is how it is worshiped." On Baal Peor, see Num. 25: 3, 5. "Merḳolis" is Mercurius, the Greek Hermes. See AZ 4: 1. The Merḳolis was a pillar surmounted by the head of Hermes. In this guise he was the patron deity of wayfarers.
2. Shab 7: 1.
"if he was held captive"—B. Shab 68b. See above, ii, 6.
3. Shab 7: 1.
"the thirty-nine classes of work"—Shab 7: 2; III, 1, vii, 1.
4. B. Shab 70b.
5. Ker 3: 10.
6. "it seems to me." Cf. B. BḲ 2a.
7. Cf. Shab 7: 2.
"Laws Concerning the Sabbath." See III, 1, vii.
8. Shab 7: 1; Ker 3: 10.
9. *Ibid.*
10. B. Shab 70b, 71a.
"dried fig's bulk." See Shab 7: 4.
"atonement also for the second reaping . . . for the second milling"—since all were done within the one spell of unawareness.
11. B. Shab 72b.
"who missed his purpose"—as in the case cited in Ker 4: 3.
"explained many times.' 'See above, ii, 7; also III, 1, i.
12. B. Ker 20a.
"explained in Laws Concerning the Sabbath." See III, 1, i, 7.

Chapter VIII

1. Ker 6: 3. See below, xi, 5.
2. Ker 4: 1.

"if there lay before him one piece"—B. *ibid.*, 18a.

"forbidden fat or permitted fat." See V, II, vii, 9.

"the fat of a *koy*." See Bik 2: 8 ff. It is thought to have been some species of wild sheep, or a cross between a goat and some kind of gazelle. It remained in doubt whether it should be classed among cattle or among wild animals

"his deceased brother's widow." Cf. B. Yeb 35a.

3. Ker 3: 1.

"So, too, if a man had intercourse"—B. Ket 22b.

4. B. Ker 18a.

5. Ker 4: 2.

6. *Ibid.*

"eight sin offerings." See above, iv, 2.

7. B. Ker 18a.

9. Ker 4: 2.

10. *Ibid.*

"because of the sacrilege"—Meil 5: 1.

Chapter IX

1. Zeb 5: 5.

"betrothed handmaid"—Lev. 19: 20.

"what is wrongfully gotten"—Lev. 6: 1–7 [Hebrew text: Lev. 5: 20–26].

"sacrilege"—Lev. 5: 15.

"incurred by a nazirite"—Num. 6: 12.

"because of leprosy"—Lev. 14: 12.

"because of the betrothed handmaid"—Ker 2: 4–5; B. *ibid.*, 9a, 11a.

"that she suffered congress." Ed. Venice (1524), adds: "after her customary manner and with completion of congress." It is omitted in Bodl. MSS 568, 601, 602, 603, and edd. Rome (1480 [?]), Constantinople (1509), Venice (1575).

"inquisition"—from which her guilt is proved.

2. B. Ker 11a.

3. Cf. Ker 2: 6.

4. "Laws Concerning Forbidden Intercourse." See V, I, iii, 14.

"Therefore if two said"—Ker 2: 4.

5. Ker 2: 4; B. *ibid.*, 9a.

6. B. Shab 72b.

7. BK 9: 5.

"the added fifth"—Lev. 6: 5 [Heb. 5: 24]. See BM 4: 8; Shebu 8: 3.

"Laws Concerning Oaths." See VI, I, vii and viii.

8. BM 4: 7.

"Laws Concerning Sacrilege." See VIII, IX, i, 4.

9. Ker 3: 9; Meil 5: 4; 6: 1.

"included after a long time"—i.e., if a half pĕruṭah's worth of benefit was gained on one occasion, if ever again another half pĕruṭah's worth of benefit is gained, after no matter how long a lapse of time, the two halves are to be included together so that the culprit must submit to the penalties.

10. B. Shab 71b; Hor 2: 7.

11. Ker 5: 2.

"Laws Concerning Sacrilege." See VIII, ix, i, 5.

12. Ker 5: 4.

13. *Ibid.*, 5: 6.

"Laws Concerning Forbidden Foods." See V, ii, xiv, 19; cf. above, iv, 1; vi, 4.

"is applied in addition"—i.e., contrary to the general rule that not more than one prohibition applies at the same time. See V, i, xvii, 8.

Chapter X

1. Ker 2: 4. The Mishnah gives the total as "five," the last two items in the present paragraph being reckoned as one.

"a leper"—Lev. 14: 21.

"a woman after childbirth"—Lev. 12: 2 ff.

"oath of testimony"—Lev. 5: 1; cf. *ibid.*, 5: 7. On this oath, see VI, i, i, 12, 13.

"a useless oath"—Lev. 5: 4 ff. Literally: "an oath of pronouncement" or "utterance." The rendering "rash oath," usual in the standard English versions of Lev. 5: 4, is not in line with rabbinic tradition. See Shebu 3: 9, 10; also VI, i, i, 2 ff. Cf. below, Sec. 5, where the translation of Lev. 5: 4 follows that in "The Holy Scriptures" (Jewish Publication Society of America, Philadelphia, 1917).

"an unclean person." Cf. Lev. 5: 2, 3.

2. "even though her means suffice for a lamb"—Sif Lev. 12: 8 (ed. Weiss, 59b).

4. "Laws Concerning the Manner of Making Offerings." See VIII, v, xii, 4.

5. "From oral tradition"—B. Shebu 6a.

6. Neg 14: 12.

"to eat of animal offerings." This they were forbidden to do until their atonement offering had been brought.

7. Cf. Hor 2: 5, 7.

"as we have explained." See above, i, 4.

"Laws Concerning Oaths." See VI, i, ix and xi.

"Those Whose Atonement Is Not Complete." See below, v, i and v.

8. Tos Ker 1: 13; cf. Ker. 2: 1, 2. The four classes are described in Ker 2: 2, namely, one who has intercourse with a bondwoman (Lev. 19: 20 f.), a nazirite who has suffered uncleanness (Num. 6: 10 ff.), he who swears an oath of testimony (Lev. 5: 1), and he who utters a false deposit oath (Lev. 6: 2).

9. Ker 6: 8.

"exchange that money"—literally: "profane" that money, set it free for common use.

10. Ker 6: 8.

"from whom he would inherit"—B. Ar 18a.

11. Ker 6: 8.

12. Tos Ker 4: 13.

"consecrated in the vessel." See Men. 1: 1–3; VIII, v, xiii, 12. Putting the handful of the meal offering in the vessel of ministry corresponds to the receiving of the blood of animal offerings.

13. Cf. B. Ker 27b, 28a; cf. KM, *ad loc.* See VIII, vii, iii, 24.

"If a poor man offered a rich man's offering"—Neg 14: 12.

Chapter XI

1. Sheḇu 1: 2; 2: 1; Tos Zeb 5: 8.
"even if he was not aware at the beginning." See above, ii, 6.
"six classes of transgression"—namely, three variations as applied to the Temple and three as applied to Hallowed Things.
"And whence do we know that such is the rule"—B. Sheḇu 4a, b.
2. Sheḇu 2: 5.
"and knew that he had become unclean." Ed. Venice (1524) adds "and knew that this was some Hallowed Thing or that this was the Temple." This is absent in Bodl. MSS 568, 601, 602, 603 and edd. Rome (1480 [?]), Constantinople (1509).
"from which primary uncleanness"—literally: "father of uncleanness"; Kel 1: 1. See X, 1, v, 7.
"even though he did not know in the beginning." This is prefixed by the clause "He is liable to an offering" in Bodl. MSS 568, 601, 602, and in edd. Rome (1480 [?]), Constantinople (1509), Venice (1524).
"not aware of the rules concerning uncleanness"—B. Sheḇu 19a.
"a creeping thing"—Lev. 11: 29 ff.
"that he had touched." These words are omitted by edd. Rome (1480 [?]), Constantinople, (1509), Venice (1575), but included in Bodl. MSS 568, 601, 602, 603, and ed. Venice (1524).
3. Sheḇu 2:3.
"Laws Concerning Entering into the Temple." See VIII, III, iii, 23.
4. B. Sheḇu 17a.
5. Cf. Ker 1: 2.
6. B. ibid., 18b, 19a.
7. Ibid.
"If he was sprinkled"—to free him from corpse uncleanness; Num. 19: 19.
8. B. Ker 11b, 12a. Cf. above, iii, 1.
"penalty of death"—if the two witnesses had charged him with an act involving capital punishment.
9. Sheḇu 1: 3–6.
"which is prepared within the Holy of Holies"—Lev. 16: 15. Cf. Yom 5: 9.
"prepared outside on the Day of Atonement." Cf. Num. 20: 11.
"the he-goats of the feasts and the he-goats of the New Moons." See Num. 28: 14, 22, 30; 29: 11, 18.
"the bullock of the High Priest"—Sheḇu 1: 7; Lev. 16: 6.

Chapter XII

1. Hor 2: 3.
"the Supreme Court"—i.e., the greater Sanhedrin of one and seventy members. See San 1: 6.
"the court must bring a sin offering"—Hor 1: 1, 2.
"And what is the offering which the court must bring"—Hor 1: 5; B. ibid., 5a.

"their blood enters within the Holy of Holies." See Lev. 4: 15.
2. Hor 1: 4; B. *ibid.,* 4b.
"a suspensive guilt offering"—such as would be required from a private person. See above, viii, 1 ff.

Chapter XIII

1. Cf. Hor 1: 5 (end).
"So, too, if the Supreme Court taught"—*ibid.,* 1: 4.
"If one of the Sanhedrin"—B. *ibid.,* 3b.
2. B. Hor 3a.
"The tribes of Manasseh and Ephraim"—B. *ibid.,* 6b.
3. B. *ibid.,* 3a.
4. *Ibid.*
5. *Ibid.*
"a disciple who was competent." See San 4: 4.
"So, too, if he depended upon his own opinion"—B. Hor 2b.
"This is the general rule"—Hor 1: 1 (end).
6. Hor 1: 4 (end).

Chapter XIV

1. Hor 1: 3; B. *ibid.,* 4a.
2. *Ibid.*
"primary acts of work." See above, vii, 7.
"*prostrate thyself before*"—usually rendered: *worship no other god* (JPS: *bow down to no other god*).
"who awaits day against day." See above, i, vi, 3, note.
"at the moment of congress"—Hor 2: 4; Shebu 2: 4.
3. B. Yeb 92a.
4. B. Hor 3b.
5. Hor 1: 2.

Chapter XV

1. Hor 2: 1, 2; B. *ibid.,* 6b, 7a.
"already explained." See above, i, 4 (end).
"*Naśi.*" See below, Sec. 6.
"the community." See above, xii, 1, on Num. 35: 24.
2. Hor 2: 1, 2; B. *ibid.,* 6b, 7a.
3. *Ibid.*
"as in the case of the congregation"—so (*kĕ-ṣibbur*), rather than "in the congregation" (*bĕ-ṣibbur*), obviously required by the context; cf. B. Hor 7a.
4. *Ibid.*
5. B. Hor 6a.
6. Hor 2: 7.
"Who is the Naśi?"—Hor 3: 3; B. *ibid.,* 11b.

"anointed priest"—Hor 3: 4.

"oil of unction"—with which the High Priests were anointed until the time of Josiah. VIII, ii, i, 8; iv, 12.

"the many garments." See Yom 7: 5.

7. Hor 3: 4.

"through such an error." See above, Sec. 5.

"since there is no difference"—Meg 1: 9.

"bullock of the Day of Atonement"—Lev. 16: 6.

"daily tenth of an ephah"—Lev. 6: 20 [Heb. 6: 13].

8. B. Hor 7a.

9. Hor 3: 2; B. *ibid.*, 10a.

10. Hor 3: 3; B. *ibid.*, 11a.

Treatise V: Those Whose Atonement Is Not
Complete

Chapter I

1. Ker 2: 1.

"a woman with flux"—Lev. 15: 25 ff.

"a woman after childbirth"—Lev. 12: 2 ff.

"a man with flux"—Lev. 15: 2 ff.

"a leper"—Lev. 14: 30 ff.

"Hallowed Things Which Become Invalid"—VIII, vii, xviii, 14.

2. Ker 2: 1; B. *ibid.*, 8b.

"Laws Concerning the Manner of Making Offerings." See VIII, v, i, 6.

5. "during the days of fulfilling." Cf. Sif Lev. 12: 5 (ed. Weiss, 59a).

"or the guilt offering." This is bracketed in ed. Amsterdam (1702). It is found in Bodl. MSS 568, 601, 602, 603, edd. Rome (1480 [?]), Constantinople (1509), Venice (1524, 1575).

"Manner of Making Offerings." See VIII, v, xiv, 10.

"may bring an offering for his sons"—Neg 14: 12; B. Ned 35b. See above, IV, x, 6.

6. Sif Lev. 15: 25 (ed. Weiss, 79a).

"in treating of the menstruant." See V, i, vi.

"is not to be eaten"—Tem 7: 6; Ker 1: 3.

"birds brought because of doubt." See above, IV, xi, 2.

"And we have there explained." Cf. V, i, v.

7. Ker 1: 4.

"Laws Concerning Slaughtering." See V, iii, ii, 2.

8. Ker 2: 4.

9. Cf. Nid 3: 5; Sif Lev. 12: 5 (ed. Weiss, 58a).

10. Ker 1: 7; B. *ibid.*, 8a.

11. B. Ḥul 134a.

"We have already explained." See above, IV, iii, 11.

12. B. Pes 90b.

"put it in the shofar chest"—referring to the tapering-shaped chests in the

Temple, put there for the reception of money for offerings and other charges. See Sheḳ 2: 1; 6: 5. One of these was labeled "For Bird Offerings."

"the court of the priests would not rise thence"—i.e., they do not leave the Temple that day.

"Laws Concerning Shekel Dues." See III, vii, ii, 2.

"Laws Concerning the Vessels of the Temple." See VIII, ii, vii, 9.

13. Ḳin 2: 5 (end); B. Ḳid 13b.

"rests on the authority of Scripture"—since the two offerings together were decreed by Scripture (Lev. 12: 8).

Chapter II

1. Tos Zab 2: 4.
"dull in tinge"—Tos (ed. Zuckermandel) reads "watery."
2. B. Ker 8a.
"zaḇ"—a male who has become unclean because of successive issues of flux. The feminine form is zaḇah.
"by reason of his flesh"—i.e., it must not have any extraneous cause.
"Hence the Sages have said"—Zab 2: 2; Naz 9: 4.
3. Zab 2: 3; Tos ibid., 2: 6.
"throughout twenty-four hours." Any issue within that period is deemed to be due to "constraint." See below, Sec. 8.
4. Tos. ibid., 2: 7.
"whether he was a Gentile"—Zab 2: 3.
"In case of a minor"—Tos ibid., 2: 6.
5. Tos ibid., 2: 6.
"When does it apply?"—Zab 2: 2 (end); B. Nid 35a.
6. Zab 1: 1.
"there is no difference"—Meg 1: 7.
7. B. BḲ 24a.
8. Cf. Zab 1: 1–2.
9. Nid 5: 2.
10. Zab 1: 5.
11. Ibid., 1: 4.
12. Ibid., 1: 3.
13. Ibid., 1: 6.
14. Cf. III, i, v.
"not count as issues at all"—i.e., such as would cause him to be deemed a zaḇ. See above, Sec. 8.

Chapter II

1. "at the close of the seventh day"—Zab 1: 2 (end).
2. Zab 1: 2.
3. Nid 7: 3; B. ibid., 68b.
4. See above, ii, 8.
"three issues, one after the other"—B. Ker 8a; B. Ḥag 9b.

NOTES

215

"had not yet reached the time"—i.e., the morning of the eighth day.
"as we have explained." See above, i, 8.
5. B. Ker 8a; B. Ḥag 9b.
6. B. Ar 3a; Zab 2: 1.
"to enable them to eat of Hallowed Things." See above, iv, x, 6.
"their sin offering may be eaten"—i.e., they are not such as can be examined
to ascertain whether their uncleanness was in doubt.
7. Zab 2: 1; Tos *ibid.*, 3: 1.

Chapter IV

1. Neg 14: 1 ff.
"as one 'who was immersed that day.'" On the relative degree of uncleanness suffered at this stage, see X, v, x, 1 ff.
"And why must he immerse himself on the eighth day?"—B. Yom 30b.
"a confirmed leper." See Lev. 13: 44–46.
"had not been distracted"—i.e., he had not, through lack of caution, exposed
himself to any uncleanness.
2. Naz 6: 6.
"After what manner is he treated?"—Sif Lev. 14: 11 (ed. Weiss, 71b); Neg
14: 7 ff.; cf. Kel 1: 8.
"There, too, all those . . . are made to stand"—Soṭ 1: 5; B. *ibid.*, 8a.
"in the manner of all wave offerings." See Men 5: 6.
"if he waves each of them by itself, that suffices"—Sif Lev. 14: 12 (ed. Weiss,
71b).
"on the ridge of his right ear." See below, v, 1.
"at each sprinkling dipping his finger into the oil"—Sif Lev. 14: 16 (ed.
Weiss, 72a).
"but did not direct it toward the Holy of Holies"—Tos Zeb 1: 9.
"is divided among the priests." Cf. Zeb 10: 8.
3. Zeb 10: 8.
"analogous to the guilt offering"—Lev. 14: 13. See VIII, v, x.
"It is forbidden to consume any of the log of oil"—B. *ibid.*, 44a.

Chapter V

1. Sif Lev. 14: 17 (ed. Weiss, 72a).
"the middle wall"—i.e., the inner cartilage. In EVV the word is usually rendered "tip" or "lobe," a meaning derived from Ḳimḥi.
"If the priest smeared the blood on the sides of the thumb"—B. Men 10a.
"If he had no right thumb"—Neg 14: 9.
2. B. Men 5a; B. Yom 61b.
"like the drink offerings of a leper's guilt offering." See VIII, v, ii, 6.
3. B. Men 5a.
"place of burning." See VIII, v, vii, 3, 4.
4. B. Men 5a.
"If the log lacked anything"—Neg 14: 10.
5. B. Yom 61a.

"for it is said." Thus what is smeared on the head is no more than the remains of a remnant.

6. B. Men 5a.

7. B. Men 27b.

8. Ker 2: 3; B. *ibid.*, 9b.

9. B. Ker 9b.

"If a leper brought his offering." See above, i, 3.

10. Neg 14: 13; B. Nid 70a.

"brought his birds"—Lev. 14: 4–7; Neg 14: 1–2.

"as we have explained." Cf. above, iv, xi, 2; v, i, 6, 7.

11. Ar 4: 2; B. *ibid.*, 17a.

Treatise VI: Substituted Offerings

Chapter I

1. Tem 1: 1; B. *ibid.*, 3a.

"although he committed no act." The procedure of substitution requires words only. See below, ii, 1.

"And why is scourging incurred for substitution?"—B. *ibid.*, 4a.

"two negative commandments are here involved"—namely, "not to alter" and "not to change."

"the negative commandment therein is not equivalent"—Tem 2: 3.

"not deemed to be a substituted offering"—i.e., they have not rendered it holy.

"even if he substituted it on the Sabbath"—Tos *ibid.*, 1: 1. On dedicating an offering on the Sabbath, see above, i, i, 19; ii, i, 8.

2. Tem 2: 3; B. *ibid.*, 17a.

3. B. *ibid.*, 9a.

4. *Ibid.*, 2b.

5. *Ibid.*, 2a; B. Zeb 5b.

6. B. Tem 2b.

7. Tem 1: 1.

8. B. *ibid.*, 2b.

"the age of vows." See VI, ii, xi, 1–4. The age was twelve years and a day for boys and eleven years and a day for girls.

9. Tem 1: 1.

"But if the owner substituted another beast"—B. *ibid.*, 8b.

10. B. Yom 50b.

11. Tem 1: 6.

12. *Ibid.*

"Temple treasury." See above, iii, i, 6; cf. below, vi, iv, 5.

"just as tithe of cattle is analogous to tithe of corn"—B. *ibid.*, 3a.

13. Ḥul 10: 2; Bek 2: 2, 3.

14. Tem 1: 2; B. *ibid.*, 9a.

15. Tem 1: 5; B. *ibid.*, 12a.

"a valid substitute"—i.e., the sanctity which passes from the original offering to its substitute does not pass to what is substituted for the substitute.

16. Tem 1:3.

17. Tem 2:3 (end).

18. Tos *ibid.*, 1:12.

19. Tos *ibid.*, 1:16.

20. "is valid"—i.e., it acquires the sanctity of a substituted beast.

21. B. Tem 19b, 20a.

"Hallowed Things Which Become Invalid." See VIII, VII, iv, 18.

Chapter II

1. Tem 5:5, 6.

2. B. Tem 27a.

3. *Ibid.*

"to redeem it"—literally: "to render it profane," i.e., unconsecrated and so free for common use.

4. Tem 5:3, 4; B. *ibid.*, 25a.

Chapter III

1. Tem 3:1 ff.

"Hallowed Things Which Become Invalid." See VIII, VII, iv, 2.

"as a freewill offering"—i.e., it falls to the Temple treasury. See below, iv, 5.

"the substitute for a thank offering." See VIII, VII, xii, 8.

"The substitute for a Passover offering"—Pes 9:6; B. *ibid.*, 96b.

"substitute for a firstling"—Tem 3:5.

2. Tem 3:5.

"Things Forbidden for the Altar"—VIII, iv, i, 12.

3. Tos *ibid.*, 3:6.

" 'one half of this beast shall be a substitute' "—B. *ibid.*, 26a.

4. Ḥul 10:2.

"substitution itself holds good"—i.e., it is not free for common use, and its owner is to be scourged.

"it may not be offered and it may not be redeemed"—B. Beḵ 16a.

5. Tem 2:3.

6. Tos *ibid.*, 3:13.

This paragraph is obscure. RABD considers it incomprehensible and doubts the correctness of the text. The present translation follows the interpretation in KM in the name of the author of *Miḡdal 'Oz* (Shem-Ṭoḇ ben Abraham Ibn Gaon, 1283-*ca.* 1330).

"Hallowed Things Which Become Invalid." VIII, VII, vi.

7. Tos Tem 3:15.

"as we have explained." See above, Treatise III.

Chapter IV

1. Tem 3: 1; B. *ibid.*, 17b, 18a.
2. Tem 4: 1.
3. B. *ibid.*, 10b.
"four-month." So Bodl. MSS 568, 601, 602, and ed. Venice (1575). The reading "eight-month" is found in edd. Rome (1480 [?]), Constantinople (1509), and Venice (1524).
4. Tem 3: 3.
5. *Ibid.*, 3: 2.
"Manner of Making Offerings." See VIII, v, iii, 7.
"Laws Concerning Shekel Dues." See III, vii, ii, 2.
"the court"—i.e., of the Priests. See above, v, i, 12.
"charges of the congregation"—Tem 3: 4.
6. Tem 3: 5.
7. Cf. Tem 3: 1.
"If a man set aside a female beast." Cf. Tem 3: 3.
9. B. Tem 10a.
10. Tem 7: 4.
11. B. Ar 29a.
"that they may not be changed from one category"—Tem 7: 3.
"the Temple treasury." See III, i, 6 n.
"sanctuary"—the *hekal*, the great hall of the Temple; Mid. 4: 7. The term is used also in a wider sense to include all three features: the porch, the *kodeš* (sanctuary) or main hall, and the *kodeš kŏdašim*, the Holy of Holies. See VIII, i, i, 5; but cf. VIII, i, vii, 22.
"no one incurs punishment by scourging." No act is involved, but only the formula of dedication. See above, i, 1.
12. Tem 5: 1; B. *ibid.*, 24a.
"to derive gain thereby"—i.e., he, and not a priest, would then consume it.
13. "Laws Concerning Sacrilege." See VIII, ix, viii, 8.
"for all the statutes of the Law." See, e.g., Eccles. R 7: 23 (§ 4).

LIST OF ABBREVIATIONS

Tractates of Mishnah, Tosefta, and Talmud

Ar—*'Arakin*
AZ—*'Ăbodah Zarah*
Bek—*Běkorot*
Ber—*Běrakot*
Beṣ—*Beṣah*
Bik—*Bikkurim*
BK—*Baba Kamma*
BM—*Baba Měṣi'a*
Dem—*Demai*
Erub—*'Erubin*
Ḥag—*Ḥăgigah*
Ḥal—*Ḥallah*
Hor—*Horayot*
Ḥul—*Ḥullin*
Kel—*Kelim*
Ker—*Kěritot*
Ket—*Kětubbot*
Kid—*Kiddušin*
Kin—*Kinnim*
Mak—*Makkot*
Meg—*Měgillah*
Meil—*Mě'ilah*
Men—*Měnahot*
Mid—*Middot*

MK—*Mo'ed Katan*
MSh—*Ma'ăśer Šeni*
Naz—*Nazir*
Neg—*Něga'im*
Ned—*Nědarim*
Nid—*Niddah*
Oh—*'Ohalot*
Or—*'Orlah*
Pe—*Pe'ah*
Pes—*Pěsahim*
RSh—*Roš haš-Šanah*
San—*Sanhedrin*
Shab—*Šabbat*
Shebi—*Šěbi'it*
Shebu—*Šěbu'ot*
Shek—*Šěkalim*
Sot—*Sotah*
Suk—*Sukkah*
Tam—*Tamid*
Tem—*Těmurah*
Yeb—*Yěbamot*
Yom—*Yoma*
Zab—*Zabim*
Zeb—*Zěbahim*

B. prefixed to the name of a tractate indicates a reference to the Babylonian Talmud; P. a reference to the Palestinian Talmud; and Tos a reference to the Tosefta. Otherwise the reference is to the Mishnah.

Other Abbreviations

EVV—standard English translations of the Old Testament
KM—*Kesef Mišneh*, the commentary on the Code by Joseph Caro (1488–1575)

THE BOOK OF OFFERINGS

220

Mek—*Mĕkilta* (ed. Horowitz-Rabin, Frankfort a. M., 1931)
R—*Midrash Rabba* (ed. Lewin-Epstein, Warsaw, 1912)
RABD—*Rabbi Abraham ben David* (1125–1198)
Sif—*Sifra* (ed. Weiss, Vienna, 1862)

GLOSSARY

Adar
    the twelfth month of the Jewish calendar, corresponding approximately to March. When the lunar year needs to be intercalated a month is inserted between Adar and Nisan (the first month of the following year), and this added month is called "Second Adar"
Elul
    the sixth month of the calendar, corresponding approximately to September
Extirpation (*karet;* literally: cutting off)
    denotes divine punishment, as opposed to punishment at man's hand; see Num. 9: 13, *That soul shall be cut off from his people.* Such punishment is incurred for the deliberate breach of certain laws (see IV, i)
Festival day (*yom tob*)
    a name given to the first and the seventh day of the Feast of Passover, the first and the eighth day of the Feast of Tabernacles, the Day of Pentecost, and New Year's Day (the first of the month Tishri). On a festival day all work is forbidden as on the Sabbath, except the preparation of necessary food; see III, IV. "Mid-festival days" are the days intervening between those festival days which mark the beginning and the end of a feast
Grave area
    a field containing a lost grave or a field in which a grave has been ploughed up
Hallel
    the group of Psalms 113–118
Hallowed Things
    a term used either generally, of anything, animate or inanimate, dedicated to the Temple or pertaining to the Temple; or, more specifically, of offerings. Such offerings are either Most Hallowed Things (e.g., whole offerings, sin offerings, and guilt offerings) or Lesser Hallowed Things (e.g., the peace offerings of individuals, the Passover offering, firstlings, and tithe of cattle)
Iyyar
    the second month of the calendar, corresponding to the latter part of April and part of May

Loḡ
  a measure of bulk or a liquid measure defined as equal to the contents of six eggs

Ma'ah
  the smallest silver coin current, equal in value to sixteen *pĕruṭah*

Naśi
  the civil head of the nation. In this book the word is used in the sense of ruler or king, as in Lev. 4: 22

Nisan
  the first month of the calendar, corresponding to the latter part of March and part of April

Pĕruṭah
  the smallest copper coin current

Refuse (*piggul;* literally: abomination)
  an offering which it is proposed to eat after its prescribed time or outside its prescribed place; see Lev. 7: 18

Remnant (*noṭar*)
  an offering which remains unconsumed after the prescribed time for eating it; see Exod. 29: 34, Lev. 7: 17

Sacrificial portions
  the parts of the beast (specified in Lev. 3: 3–4) which are to be burned on the altar when the rest of the flesh is to be eaten by the priests or by those who bring the offering

Šĕḇuṭ
  a term referring to the extensions of the law of the Sabbath as devised and multiplied by rabbinical interpretation of Scripture

Tĕfillah (literally: prayer)
  the "Eighteen Benedictions," one of the principal parts of the daily Synagogue service (Singer, *Authorised Jewish Prayer Book,* pp. 44–54)

Tĕrefah (literally: torn by beasts of prey)
  originally (cf. Lev. 22: 8) it signified clean beasts mauled or killed by beasts of prey and so unfit for food. In rabbinic writings it has the technical sense of a. a beast suffering from some defect or abnormality; b. the flesh of an animal, the ritual slaughtering of which has been declared invalid

Tishri
  the seventh month of the calendar, corresponding to the latter part of September and the first part of October

Zab
a man with flux; see Lev. 15: 1–15, *When any man hath an issue out of his flesh, his issue is unclean*

Zabah
a woman with flux; see Lev. 15: 25–30, *If a woman have an issue of her blood many days not in the time of her impurity . . . she is unclean*

Zuz
a silver coin worth six ma'ah or half a shekel; identical with a *denar*

SCRIPTURAL REFERENCES

EXODUS

12: 4, 13
12: 6, 5, 9
12: 8, 5, 35, 36
12: 9, 6, 36
12: 10, 6, 43
12: 19, 44
12: 43, 7, 40
12: 44, 26, 41
12: 45, 7
12: 46, 6, 38, 39, 40, 41
12: 47, 13
12: 48, 7, 25, 41

13: 2, 63, 75
13: 7, 44
13: 12, 182
16: 29, 146
23: 14, 48
23: 15, 48, 49
23: 17, 49, 52, 53, 54
23: 18, 6, 9
24: 34, 53
34: 14, 146
34: 25, 5, 9

LEVITICUS

4: 3, 148, 151
4: 13, 139, 141 f., 145, 149
4: 13–14, 94
4: 14, 140, 147
4: 22, 151
4: 23, 99, 150, 151
4: 27, 94, 96, 98, 135
4: 28, 104
5: 1 ff., 131
5: 3, 135
5: 7–11, 95
5: 15, 94
5: 17, 94, 123
7: 12, 184
7: 20, 132
12: 6, 154, 156
14: 2, 170
14: 10 ff., 154
14: 17, 168, 169
14: 18, 169

15: 2, 160
15: 3, 163
15: 13–15, 154
15: 25, 146, 162
15: 28–30, 154
16: 16, 139
16: 30, 106
18: 7, 108
18: 14, 109
18: 17, 110
18: 22, 108, 109
19: 20–21, 127
20: 7, 111
25: 6, 82
27: 10, 174, 175, 178, 183, 188
27: 15, 188
27: 26, 174, 187
27: 32, 62, 83, 86, 87
27: 33, 62, 83, 177

NUMBERS

9: 2, 11
9: 3, 25, 29

9: 6, 27, 32
9: 10, 8, 24, 26, 27

INDEX